THE SELECTED WORKS OF GORDON TULLOCK

VOLUME 3

The Organization of Inquiry

THE SELECTED WORKS OF GORDON TULLOCK

VOLUME 1 *Virginia Political Economy*

VOLUME 2 *The Calculus of Consent: Logical Foundations of Constitutional Democracy* (with James M. Buchanan)

VOLUME 3 *The Organization of Inquiry*

VOLUME 4 *The Economics of Politics*

VOLUME 5 *The Rent-Seeking Society*

VOLUME 6 *Bureaucracy*

VOLUME 7 *The Economics and Politics of Wealth Redistribution*

VOLUME 8 *The Social Dilemma: Of Autocracy, Revolution, Coup d'Etat, and War*

VOLUME 9 *Law and Economics*

VOLUME 10 *Economics without Frontiers* (includes a cumulative index for the series)

Gordon Tullock

THE SELECTED WORKS OF GORDON TULLOCK

VOLUME 3

The Organization of Inquiry

GORDON TULLOCK

Edited and with an Introduction by

CHARLES K. ROWLEY

Liberty Fund
Indianapolis

This book is published by Liberty Fund, Inc., a
foundation established to encourage study of the
ideal of a society of free and responsible individuals.

The cuneiform inscription that serves as our logo and
as the design motif for our endpapers is the earliest-known
written appearance of the word "freedom" (*amagi*), or "liberty."
It is taken from a clay document written about 2300 B.C.
in the Sumerian city-state of Lagash.

Printed in the United States of America

Paperback cover photo courtesy of the *American Economic Review*
Frontispiece courtesy of Center for Study of Public Choice,
George Mason University, Fairfax, Virginia

09 08 07 06 05 C 5 4 3 2 1
09 08 07 06 05 P 5 4 3 2 1

Library of Congress Cataloging-in-Publication Data
Tullock, Gordon.
The organization of inquiry / Gordon Tullock ; edited and
with an introduction by Charles K. Rowley.
p. cm.—(The selected works of Gordon Tullock ; v. 3)
Originally published: Durham, N.C. : Duke University Press,
1966.
Includes bibliographical references and index.
ISBN 0-86597-522-1 (alk. paper)—ISBN 0-86597-533-7 (pbk.)
1. Research. 2. Research—Methodology. 3. Science—
Social aspects. I. Rowley, Charles Kershaw. II. Title.
Q180.A1T78 2005
001.4′2—dc22

2003065991

LIBERTY FUND, INC.
8335 Allison Pointe Trail, Suite 300
Indianapolis, Indiana 46250-1684

CONTENTS

INTRODUCTION

Gordon Tullock wrote *The Organization of Inquiry*[1] during the mid-1960s, probably the most productive decade of his career. From a purely technical perspective, this book stands out as his best-written single-authored work. The book sets out his own views on scientific method—views that he would faithfully reflect in his subsequent scholarship.

Early Methodological Influences

Because Tullock is a largely self-taught economist, his exposure to scientific method came not from the economics classroom but from his legal training, his reading, and his direct association with two leading scholars, namely Karl Popper and James M. Buchanan. The first part of this introduction traces these intellectual influences that helped to shape the book.

Let me begin, as Tullock surely did, with his legal training at the University of Chicago. Although Chicago during the 1940s was less wedded to black-letter law than were most of its rivals, the methods of the natural and social sciences were minimal elements of the curriculum. The primary focus of Chicago legal training, at that time, was inductive rather than deductive in nature and was based on a detailed evaluation of "binding legal authority" derived from a limited number of legal precedents.

Chicago, in conformity with all other leading schools of law, trained lawyers to seek out the "universal truth" of the law through a careful selection of a number of singular statements encompassed in the written judgments of the higher courts. They were right to do so, since this is the thrust of precedent and *stare decisis* in the Anglo-Saxon legal system. However, the movement from singular to universal statements (induction) was already, following David Hume,[2] anathema to the approach endorsed by almost all economists (deduction).[3]

1. Gordon Tullock, *The Organization of Inquiry* (Durham, N.C.: Duke University Press, 1966).

2. David Hume, *An Enquiry concerning Human Understanding* (1777) (La Salle, Ill.: Open Court, 1907).

3. Mark Blaug, *Economic Theory in Retrospect* (Cambridge: Cambridge University Press, 1997), 690.

In pursuit of the inductive approach, lawyers are trained to move from the observation of facts to the formulation of theory, something that runs directly counter to the approach recommended by Karl Popper. Furthermore, because they are typically concerned with the detailed facts surrounding a particular case, lawyers are inclined to be skeptical of the model-building approach of economics, and especially of the generalizations that economists derive from such models.

Finally, because each case requires an overarching judgment derived from all relevant factual evidence and applicable law, lawyers are especially skeptical of evaluating partial relationships on *ceteris paribus* terms. Thus, any scholar trained in the law will be tempted to approach economics from a perspective that is radically different from that which is reflexively accepted by scholars trained in the natural and social sciences.[4] The degree to which such initial prejudices can be overcome by assiduous reading will become evident later when the discussion turns to Tullock's contribution to scientific method.

The three scholars of scientific method whose writings most influenced Tullock's thinking are Joseph Schumpeter, Karl Popper, and Michael Polanyi.[5] The relevant contributions of each will be reviewed in turn.

Joseph Schumpeter is one of the most highly regarded twentieth-century scholars of the history of economic thought. Schumpeter continually reminds the reader that all scientific theorizing begins with a "vision"—the preanalytic cognitive act that supplies the raw material for the analytic effort. "Analytic effort starts when we have conceived our vision of the set of phenomena that caught our interest, no matter whether this set lies in virgin soil or in land that has been cultivated before."[6] Schumpeter's interpretation of this initial phase of scientific theorizing differs from that of Popper, in the sense that it is less "pure" and potentially more open to ideological interpretation.

> Factual work and "theoretical" work, in an endless relation of give and take, naturally testing one another and setting new tasks for each other, will eventually produce *scientific models,* the provisional joint products of

4. Charles K. Rowley, "Social Sciences and Law: The Relevance of Economic Theories," *Oxford Journal of Legal Studies* 1 (winter 1981): 391–405.

5. Joseph A. Schumpeter, *History of Economic Analysis* (New York: Oxford University Press, 1954); Karl R. Popper, *The Logic of Scientific Discovery* (New York: Basic Books, 1959); and Michael Polanyi, *Personal Knowledge* (Chicago: University of Chicago Press, 1958).

6. Schumpeter, *History of Economic Analysis,* 42.

> their interaction with the surviving elements of the original vision. . . . Now it should be perfectly clear that there is a wide gate for ideology to enter into this process.[7]

Even if one accepts Schumpeter's hypothesis that science is ideological at the outset, that does not imply that the acceptance or rejection of scientific theory is also ideological.[8] If scientists are truly objective in their search for truth, they will falsify or fail to falsify their theories, however devised, by solely nonideological criteria. That is a key insight of Karl Popper.

The point of departure for Popper, in his *The Logic of Scientific Discovery* (*Logik der Forschung,* 1934), concerns the method of basing general statements on accumulated observations of specific instances. This method, known as induction, was the recognized hallmark of science prior to Popper's revolutionary contribution. It was the foundation on which Newtonian physics had long been accepted within the scientific community as the revealed truth of the law of nature.

As early as 1748, David Hume had already raised awkward questions concerning the inductive method,[9] notably by pointing out that no number of singular observational statements, no matter how large, could logically authenticate an unrestrictively general statement.[10] Troubling though this observation was, in the absence of an alternative approach, scientists continued to rely upon inductive reasoning for the better part of two centuries.

Popper's seminal achievement was to provide an acceptable solution to the problem of inductive reasoning. He starts by indicating that there is a logical asymmetry between verification and falsification. In terms of the logic of statements: no number of observations of white swans justifies the universal statement, "All swans are white"; whereas one observation of a black swan justifies the universal statement, "Not all swans are white." In this important *logical* sense, empirical generalizations are conclusively falsifiable, but not conclusively verifiable.

Methodologically, however, it is always possible, because of perceived error, for scientists to reject an observational statement that proves a theory false.

7. Ibid.

8. Bryan Magee, *Philosophy and the Real World: An Introduction to Karl Popper* (La Salle, Ill.: Open Court, 1985), 29–30.

9. David Hume, *A Treatise of Human Nature* (1748) (La Salle, Ill.: Open Court, 1907).

10. Magee, *Philosophy and the Real World,* 15.

Inevitably, scientists may abuse this escape mechanism. Popper therefore suggests, as an article of method, that scientists do not systematically evade refutation, whether by introducing ad hoc hypotheses or ad hoc definitions or by always refusing to accept the reliability of inconvenient observations. Scientists should instead formulate their theories as unambiguously as possible and should expose them as ruthlessly as possible to the test of falsification.

Popper urges that scientists not abandon their theories lightly in response to adverse observations. Instead, they should treat adverse observations as an opportunity to rigorously reexamine their theories. In this sense, Popper is a naive falsificationist in logic but a critical falsificationist in methodology.[11]

Finally, Popper provides a presumptive answer to the issue later raised by Schumpeter concerning the process by which theories are formed. Is this initial step, inductive, based on data observation? Popper's answer is as follows: because it is neither scientifically nor logically significant how a theory is formed, it follows that no method of formulating theory is illegitimate. The process of theory formulation is psychological, not logical.

Tullock spent six months working with Popper at the Center for Advanced Studies at Palo Alto during the mid-1950s. Through this association, Tullock discovered an interest in science that eventually culminated in his writing *The Organization of Inquiry*.

Tullock also acknowledges the influence of Michael Polanyi's *Personal Knowledge*.[12] In the book, Polanyi rejects the ideal of scientific detachment and replaces it with the ideal of personal knowledge, thus recognizing the importance of human behavior in scientific investigation. Polanyi regards knowing as an active comprehension of things known, an action that requires skill. Polanyi cautions, however, that personal participation of the knower in all acts of understanding does not imply that knowledge is subjective. Comprehension is neither an arbitrary act nor a passive experience. It is a responsible act claiming universal validity. Personal knowledge in this sense is an act of commitment, and as such it is inherently hazardous.

Finally, I must briefly mention the insights on scientific method obtained by Tullock through his professional association with James M. Buchanan, namely, the central importance of both microeconomic theory and the self-interest axiom in explaining economic behavior and institutional evolution.

11. Ibid., 18–19.

12. Polanyi, *Personal Knowledge*.

The Organization of Inquiry

In this book Tullock focuses attention on the social organization of science. Each of the book's eight chapters raises important questions about science and provides relevant answers. This introduction offers a brief overview of the book and identifies some of the key insights.

In chapter I, Tullock notes that a gigantic worldwide scientific enterprise exists without any conscious coordination. He poses such questions as the following: How do scientists engage in apparently cooperative contributions in the absence of central planning or hierarchic organization? and Why are scientific contributions worthy for the most part of the public's trust? The answers to these and other related questions form the basis of the remainder of the book.

In chapter II, Tullock explores the various influences that motivate scientific inquiry. Scientists, he argues, undertake investigations either because they are curious or because they hope to use the information obtained for some practical purpose. These two motives, he claims, roughly correspond, respectively, to the general fields of pure and applied research.

Tullock challenges the validity of the then strongly prevailing view, at least in the academy, that pure science is superior to applied science, explaining why the real-world interaction between the two approaches is far more complicated. By focusing only on successful examples of the subsequent practical implications of pure research, all extant studies bias the sample in favor of pure research.

Tullock also challenges the view that pure scientists in some sense are superior, presumably because they are not motivated by financial gain. He notes that most pure scientists are funded through salaries, which suggests that money can, in fact, induce curiosity. He compares the effectiveness of prize monies with the effectiveness of fixed incomes in inducing effective pure research. He also compares the relative effectiveness of journal editors with the relative effectiveness of university administrators in monitoring and ranking the quality of scientific research. In 1966 some of the answers posed by Tullock were revolutionary and deeply upsetting to many in the scientific community. With the passage of time, however, Tullock's speculations on these matters have entered into the scientific mainstream.

In chapter III, Tullock deals with the subject and methods of scientific inquiry. Tullock defines a subject of inquiry as anything that arouses curiosity or that might prove to be practically useful. He acknowledges, but rejects, the views of such skeptics as Bishop Berkeley who argued that there is no proof that the real world corresponds to the sense impressions of those who seek to understand it. Instead Tullock claims that modern scientists firmly believe that there is an objective reality that they are engaged in uncovering.

In pursuing this objective reality, scientists place only limited faith in the truth of the specific theories they promulgate. They are sensible to do so, because the history of science has been the history of disproving specific theories. In this respect, Tullock endorses the falsificationist philosophy of Karl Popper, at least within the field of pure science.

If pure scientists seek the truth, Tullock speculates, applied scientists seek useful information. Therefore, applied scientists can use theories that are known to be false if such theories provide satisfactory solutions to practical problems. This explains why applied scientists continue to use the laws of Newtonian physics to deal with a wide range of human problems long after the theory was disproved by Albert Einstein at the cosmic or quantum level.

With respect to the methods of scientific inquiry, Tullock clearly holds fast to his Popperian training. Out of the infinite universe of possible theories, those that conflict with the evidence are the first to be ruled out. Where no theory survives this test in all aspects of its predictions, the theory that is of the higher order of generality will be preferred. Simplicity is also a rule of importance.

In this process of scientific method, Tullock argues that we gain little by asking which comes first, the hypothesis or the data. The two are often inextricably intertwined. For purposes of his book, Tullock chooses to commence with data collection, which is followed by the formulation of the hypothesis, by further data collection, and finally by the testing of the hypothesis. He claims, following Popper, that the crucial problem of science is not whether the hypothesis is derived according to proper procedure but whether it survives attempts at falsification.

In chapter IV, Tullock focuses on data collection as a major activity that leads to the formulation and testing of scientific hypotheses. Following is a brief discussion of the key elements in the chapter and how they relate to Tullock's personal experience.

Tullock suggests that scientists cannot formulate hypotheses in the absence of data, even if such data are strictly limited to personal observation. As demonstrated in volume 1 of the series, Tullock is archetypical of this approach.[13] He deals in some detail in this chapter with the sources of such data, including the nature of the educational system. He discusses the likelihood that such sources will be accessed by curious pure scientists, induced-curious pure scientists, and applied scientists.

In an era before the information-technology revolution, Tullock's concern, with respect to the testing of scientific theories, focuses on problems of data collection, classification, and dissemination. He notes that the problem is not one of simply accumulating information, relevant or not, but rather one of excluding data that are highly unlikely to be relevant to future scientific work and then of focusing on the careful indexing of the data. In his own work, especially in public choice, Tullock has persistently encouraged scholars to create relevant databases to support empirical testing of important hypotheses.

In chapter V, Tullock directly confronts the problem of induction, which, even now, almost four decades later, is still before the scientific community. Given his initial training in the law, it is significant that Tullock does not even discuss the role of induction in justifying a hypothesis but rather only in establishing the initial hypothesis.

Induction, in Tullock's interpretation, involves the discovery of general principles or patterns in terms of which deductive logic can explain factual data. He illustrates his argument by reference to a number of cases in which an individual perceives patterns in the data that his sensory organs receive. Such flashes of insight, he argues, explain why sometimes an outsider will discover things that have otherwise escaped the experts. Could it be that Tullock is explaining his own behavior as an outside contributor to the scientific process?

In chapter VI, Tullock directs attention to issues concerning the verification and dissemination of scientific results. He confronts directly the possibility that scientists may lie to advance their careers and claims that the high degree of truthfulness in scientific research comes not from the superior moral probity of individual scientists but from the scientific community in which they labor. For reasons that Tullock outlines, this is especially true of the incurious pure scientist, less so of the curious pure scientist and the applied scientist.

13. Gordon Tullock, *Virginia Political Economy,* The Selected Works of Gordon Tullock, ed. Charles K. Rowley, vol. 1 (Indianapolis: Liberty Fund, 2003).

Once scientific theories are formulated and tested, scientists disseminate promising results through journals and other publications. Tullock clearly approves of this mechanism, though he identifies potential weaknesses in editing and in refereeing, and suggests a number of timely reforms, not all of which have yet been implemented.

In chapter VII, Tullock identifies reasons for the backwardness of the social sciences in research and in scholarship. He largely rejects the viewpoint, widely held even now by many social scientists, that social science is inherently more difficult than natural science because of the absence of controlled experiments. He places the blame instead squarely on differences in the social environments that exist between social scientists and natural scientists.

Tullock notes that new natural-science discoveries are always supported initially by a minority of the scientific community but eventually extend to the majority once they have withstood independent testing and are seen to be fruitful for practical applications. Acceptance by the general public follows in due course.

Social scientists, on the other hand, are often motivated to conceal the truth, for nonscientific reasons, with respect to findings that might be offensive either to themselves or to public opinion at large. The possibility of practical application is also more limited, lowering the standard to which their theories are exposed.

These checks and balances operate less effectively in the social sciences than in the natural sciences because there is less similarity of ends and, consequently, less voluntary cooperation.

In chapter VIII, Tullock concludes *The Organization of Inquiry* by outlining a number of practical proposals for improving the quality of scientific output. Two proposals are especially worthy of mention because of the particular insights they offer into Tullock's own worldview.

The first proposal underlines the classically liberal nature of Tullock's philosophy. Because most important scientific projects require only limited funding, they should be funded individually and not be included as part of a large, creativity-stifling, bureaucratic package. To avoid this outcome, and for the same reason, foundations that award research grants should also be small.

The second proposal underscores Tullock's healthy regard for the developing tenets of the public choice research program. Because of the importance of output rather than input, a much larger proportion of scientific research should be stimulated by direct prize awards. The system of prizes should be directed at two objectives, namely, specific discoveries and unspecified developments. Tullock suggests that a number of competing prize-awarding bodies, independent of the political process, would best protect science from cronyism and political lobbying.

CHARLES K. ROWLEY

Duncan Black Professor of Economics, George Mason University

Senior Fellow, James M. Buchanan Center for Political Economy, George Mason University

General Director, The Locke Institute

PREFACE AND ACKNOWLEDGMENTS

The genesis of this book was a period of about six months spent working with Karl Popper. At the time I had no intention of writing a book on science, and my studies were devoted to an entirely different problem;[1] nevertheless, Popper's approach necessarily rubbed off on me, and I became interested in the problems of science. Since I felt that I had little chance of making any significant addition to Popper's work on the philosophy of science, my inquiries were directed toward the problem of science as a social system. Philosophically, my debt to Dr. Popper is so heavy that I decided to acknowledge the debt here, instead of attempting to footnote his work in every case where it was relevant.

I have never met Michael Polanyi, but the reader will, no doubt, notice his influence also. Here, again, I have decided to omit most footnotes in the text and to handle the matter here. Although the main focus of Dr. Polanyi's work[2] is different from mine, there is clearly a close relationship.

I owe a further, rather diffuse, debt to the large number of scholars who in recent years have produced so much research on science. Most of this work, however, has added to my general knowledge, but not directly helped me in my work. I have, for example, read *The Structure of Scientific Revolutions*[3] with profit and pleasure, but it will not be further mentioned in this book. This is not because I regard it as unimportant but because it deals with different problems. In this it is typical. Most of the recent work has been done by people whose basic orientation is sociological, while mine is economic. There is no necessary conflict between sociologists and economists, but they do ask rather different questions. The work, particularly the empirical work, by the sociologists has enlightened and informed me, but it is generally not directly relevant to the problems investigated in this book.

1. The eventual outcome of my work was *The Politics of Bureaucracy* (Washington: Public Affairs Press, 1965).

2. In addition to *Personal Knowledge* (Chicago: University of Chicago Press, 1958), Polanyi has written numerous articles on science. His *Logic of Liberty* (Chicago: University of Chicago Press, 1951) contains much of interest to the student of science.

3. By Thomas S. Kuhn (Chicago: University of Chicago Press, 1962).

Although the study of the history of science is not new,[4] its present development is so much greater than at any previous period that it can almost be regarded as an invention of our present generation. This fact has both helped me and raised a minor but difficult problem. I have used numerous examples drawn from the history of science to illustrate theoretical points. The problem of whether I should footnote them all, thus insulting those of my readers who know their history, or whether I should assume that anyone who reads a book on the organization of science will need no authority for statements such as that Einstein was unable to get an academic job when he graduated was difficult. I have ended up with a compromise which will probably satisfy no one.

My colleague, Dr. James Buchanan, has assisted my work in many ways. In addition to many direct suggestions and comments, I have profited from his general methodological approach. His insistence on both imagination and rigor in the construction of theories has been an invaluable stimulus. One of the anonymous readers of the Duke University Press also must receive a good deal of credit for the final version. He (or she) made almost sixty specific suggestions for changes, of which I accepted over fifty, with a resulting major improvement in both the style and matter.

Last, having distributed credit where it is due, I must allocate some blame. The Duke University Press is solely responsible for any errors in spelling, punctuation, etc., which may occur in the book. I have never been any use at all as a proofreader, and the Press should have taken this fact into account in preparing the book for publication.

4. Adam Smith himself wrote a "History of Astronomy" in his youth. See Nathan Rosenberg, "Adam Smith on the Division of Labour: Two Views or One?" *Economica* (May, 1965), 127–39.

THE ORGANIZATION OF INQUIRY

CHAPTER I

THE SOCIAL ORGANIZATION OF SCIENCE

The purpose of this book is to answer, or attempt to answer, certain questions about science. I should like to be able to say that these questions have deeply interested scientists and that my solutions will be widely welcomed as settling important problems. Unfortunately I cannot do so. Leaving aside the problem of the correctness of my answers, the fact remains that I have been unable to find any indications that scientists have asked the questions to which I address myself. The unwary might take this as proof that the problems are unimportant, but scientists, fully conscious of the importance of asking new questions, will not make this mistake. Personally I think that the questions are important, and the answers, if not earthshaking, at least significant enough to justify adding one more to the fifty thousand or so books that will be published this year. In the first paragraph I can hardly expect the reader to share my faith, but I think that I can ask that he maintain that open but skeptical frame of mind which characterizes the best scientific thought.

In order to set the problem in its framework, let me begin with a lengthy quotation from a speech by Lord Brain.[1]

> . . . scientists often have no more in common with each other than that they are all seeking knowledge by means of scientific methods. Professor A uses these methods to investigate the light from receding nebulae, while Professor B is interested in the physiological clock which regulates the habits of shore-inhabiting crustaceans in relation to the tides. Dr. C is investigating the atomic nucleus and anti-matter, and so on through to Professor Z, who is studying the virus-carrying capacity of mosquitoes in a tropical forest. These scientists have probably never met one another. They may differ in age, sex, race, language, religion, and their general mode of life, and none of them may be interested in what the others are doing. As for the remote effects of their scientific activities, what Professor A does may be of importance for our ideas about the origin of the universe, while Professor B's work may have some implications for the stor-

1. As former president of the British Association for the Advancement of Science, Lord Brain gave this speech December 27, 1964, at a meeting of the American Association for the Advancement of Science at Montreal. It was published in *Science,* 148 (April 9, 1965), 192–98.

> age of information in the brain, and possibly for our understanding of the relationship between the brain and the mind. Dr. C deals with a subject which has already had profound importance in relation to the development of nuclear energy and today is likely to interest the philosophers of physics who are concerned with the ultimate nature of matter and the relationship between the observer and what he observes. And Professor Z's investigation of viruses concerns a scientific topic of great importance for our understanding of cell behavior, information at the molecular level, the nature of the gene, and the cancer cell. The immediate social effects of his work may well be the elimination of a particular group of diseases in tropical areas, and a resulting increase in the local population, which is already too great for its food supplies. Unless they are rather exceptional men in their particular field of work, none of these scientists may be much interested in its more remote implications. At any rate, they can all be first-class scientists without such an interest.
>
> I chose these examples at random, but I could well have chosen any other of the varieties of scientific work being practiced by the hundreds of thousands of scientists in the world. Scientists, of course, meet one another to exchange ideas, to promote their own particular branch of science, or science in general, or because they are aware of its social implications. Nevertheless, such collective activities, important though they may be in themselves, play a small part in their lives. Scientists, though they must always be aware of the work of their fellows in their own fields, are essentially individualists; and the body of knowledge to which they are contributing is an impersonal one. Apart from contributing to it, they have no collective consciousness, interest, or aim.

Note that Lord Brain never asks how it happens that these scientists who "have probably never met one another" and "may differ in age, sex, race, language, religion, and their general mode of life" are nevertheless contributing to an essentially co-operative activity. It happens that the particular examples he has chosen are in different fields of science, but if he had chosen men in the same field, say nuclear physics, they would still differ radically in "age, sex," etc. They are "essentially individualists," and "unless they are rather exceptional men in their particular field of work, none of these scientists may be much interested in its more remote implications." Clearly, however, the scientists are contributing to these remote consequences. What is the mechanism which leads the scientist "by an invisible hand to promote an end which was no part of his intention?"[2] There is no central co-ordinating organization, and few scientists consciously try to make their research contribute to remote and distant goals. Further, there is no more reason to believe that there is some sort of divine guidance for science than for economic activities.[3]

Obviously, however, the work of these highly individualistic scientists is not really independent. It is co-ordinated by something, so that Lord Brain can, quite correctly, say that the individual parts do fit together and lead to remote and unintended consequences. The scientists have never inquired into the nature of the social mechanism which provides this necessary control. Almost every scientist in the world would agree that cancer is more likely to be overcome by giving research funds to a large number of separate scientists without any central control over their research than by setting up a major hierarchy to plan each step of the scientific advance. The most effective way of "organizing" science seems to be the most perfect laissez faire. This, however, is a superficial view. Science is not unorganized. There exists a community of scientists, and this community is a functioning social mechanism which co-ordinates the activity of its members.

Another question which Lord Brain did not ask relates to the accuracy of the work done by the individual scientists. How does it happen that we can depend upon scientists not only to refrain from faking research results, but to exercise the most extreme precautions to insure accuracy? Although fraud and/or carelessness are not completely unknown among scientists, they are remarkably rare. The reliability of scientific reports is probably higher than that of any other form of literature. This phenomenon is so much a part of the existing system that most scientists simply take it as a given. Like Lord Brain, they do not ask the reasons for this extraordinary level of accuracy. Here, again, the answer lies in the organization of the scientific community.

This community is a most peculiar one, with its members living in different countries and speaking different languages. Further, it is not even geo-

2. Adam Smith, *The Wealth of Nations* (New York: Modern Library, 1937), p. 423. Smith continues: "Nor is it always the worse for society that it was no part of it."

3. The probable explanation for the fact that the phrase "invisible hand," which occurs only once in Smith's book, has been so widely quoted is the misapprehension that it refers to divine control. Smith as a follower of Leibniz probably felt that any well-functioning system in nature reflected the design abilities of the "divine clockmaker," but the purpose of *The Wealth of Nations* was to explicate the quite mundane mechanisms which controlled economy.

graphically organized. A French scientist studying a certain virus may find that the other scientists whose work is most important to him live in Japan, Italy, Russia, the United States, and Argentina. In a real sense they are his neighbors in the scientific community, but the professor of astronomy who lives next door to him is almost a foreigner in terms of their scientific relationship. Membership in this community is completely voluntary, and the scientists do not think of themselves as controlled by the community or as participating in the control of other scientists. As Lord Brain says, "apart from contributing to . . . [the body of knowledge], they have no collective consciousness, interest, or aim." Nevertheless, their search for knowledge is far from random. It is extremely dubious that even the most careful planning of research could lead to half the rate of progress we readily attain by our present organization.

Most scientists, while quite willing to agree that planning of their work would be unwise, have never given any real thought to the reasons for the success of the present system.[4] They are accustomed to it, and it certainly works well, so they worry about other things.[5] Taxpayers and voters, on the other hand, sometimes get upset by the apparently cavalier attitude taken by scientists. They feel that the casual handing out of research funds to a large group of people, most of whom do not seem to be working on anything of much present interest and all of whom are violently opposed to presenting a detailed advance budget, is a risky procedure. If the scientist were really uncontrolled, such a procedure would be dangerous, since scientists are much like other men and quite capable of misusing funds. In fact, however, the scientists are not unsupervised: they are subject to very strong social controls from the scientific community, and it is therefore quite safe to leave them free of other supervision.[6]

The principal purpose of this book is to investigate the nature of this scientific community and to make a start on explaining why it is such a success-

4. Michael Polanyi is, of course, a most distinguished exception. His lecture "The Republic of Science," delivered at Roosevelt University, January 11, 1962, is an excellent discussion of the resemblances and differences between the scientific community and the market economy.

5. During the thirties and early forties this was not entirely so. Scientists who were Marxists or who believed in "planning" for other reasons quite commonly were in favor of having scientific "plans" too. Happily this view no longer seems to have much importance.

6. Subject, of course, to the usual auditing procedures. Presumably there are as many potential embezzlers among ten thousand scientists as among ten thousand bankers.

ful social instrumentality—to explain why the individual scientist, who feels quite free and unconstrained, is nevertheless led to investigate problems of interest to others, and how, without any conscious intention, he exerts influence on the research done by other scientists. These are, I think, questions that the scientists have not heretofore asked, but problems that they will recognize as important.

Clearly the present organization of the scientific community, cutting across the lines of nation states, bureaus, and almost all previously existing institutions, cannot be the result of conscious planning. There is, today, a good deal of organizational planning, but all of the instrumentalities which engage in this activity were founded after the development of science was well under way. Further, most of these organizations are parochial in nature, concerning themselves with only some special part of the scientific community like mathematical biophysics or Russian science. There is no general institution which has shaped or now can shape the development of science, only a mass of institutions which provide little more than liaison (and sometimes funds) for the scientific "producers."[7] The scientific community must therefore be a sort of natural growth, an institution which developed out of the felt needs of the individual scientist and which continues to exist and develop because it still meets these needs.

> In the simplest terms, the only effective world community that now exists is the community of science. In this respect, if in no other, the vision of 18th century liberal philosophers has been achieved. For the progress of science, as they saw . . . is the progress of a set of rules and procedures which allow men to co-ordinate their thinking and to co-operate in the search for truth.[8]

Another problem concerns the limits of this community. Here Lord Brain does offer an indirect answer, but in my opinion an erroneous one. The scientific community's boundaries would, presumably, be co-extensive with those of science, and hence a definition of science would delimit the scientific community. In an earlier part of the speech quoted above, Lord Brain defined "science" as "knowledge obtained . . . by the use of scientific methods."

7. The rather uneuphonious term "producers" is used in order to cover both the individual scientist and the larger scientific organizations which co-ordinate the activities of a number of scientists in a single research project.

8. Charles Frankel, *The Case for Modern Man* (New York: Harper, 1956), p. 143.

Knowledge is the principal product of science, and it does no harm to define science so that it includes both the activity of seeking knowledge and the knowledge obtained, but not all knowledge is "scientific." By drawing a book out of my library and opening it, I find that the fifth word in the sixth line of page 185 of Volume 1 of A. Henry Savage Landor's *China and the Allies*[9] is "shelter." This is knowledge, but surely it is not science. Lord Brain, of course, specifies the use of "scientific methods," but I do not think that he would stick to his definition if pressed. Outside my office there is an irregular clump of Korean azaleas. At this time of the year they are in bloom and are a spectacular sight. Suppose I became curious about the total weight of the blooms and, by the use of the most advanced methods, found out that on May 11, 1965, at 2:10 in the afternoon the flowers weighed exactly 3.38649 pounds. Regardless of the "scientific" nature of the procedures which I used to reach this conclusion, I doubt if Lord Brain would accept the fact as a contribution to science.

The converse also holds true. The invention of the three-element vacuum tube will be generally accepted as a scientific achievement of the utmost importance, but it is hard to argue that it was achieved by scientific methods. De Forest was "a lone-wolf kind of Robin Hood: likable, shrewd and knavish, intent on speculative patents and on stock certificates as a means of robbing the rich in the wondrous world of wireless." One of his principal ways of making money was to copy a device invented by someone else, with some minor variation in the hope that the courts would hold it a new invention and thus allow him to avoid the original patent. The three-element vacuum tube was the only one of these changes which had any value. The discovery that the variation was not minor but important was made several years after De Forest first produced it and came largely by accident.[10] "That in the course of infringing the Fleming valve patent he should have hit on the magic intervening-grid form of control, although without really understanding its *modus operandi*, was the marvel of the age."

It is certain that many such discoveries are basically accidental, and hence

9. New York: Charles Scribner's Sons, 1901.

10. See Robert A. Chipman, "De Forest and the Triode Detector," *Scientific American*, 212, No. 3 (March, 1965), 92–100. The article set off a discussion between Lloyd Espenschied and Dr. Chipman which appeared on pages 8 and 9 of the May issue. The quotations are taken from Espenschied's letter. Espenschied first met De Forest and his assistant, John V. L. Hogan, in 1907 and later became a lifelong friend of both.

that they are not the result of "scientific method." The scientists will normally say, quite correctly, that luck may help but that a prepared mind, ready to understand the unexpected experimental result, is also necessary. Fleming fully deserved his Nobel prize even if the contamination of his slide by *Penicillium notatum* was completely accidental. The same accident must have happened to hundreds of other researchers, but only he realized its importance. Still, his discovery of the first antibiotic was not the result of "scientific method," but of the fact that he was a little unscientific in handling his slides, with the result that one was contaminated. Thus science sometimes advances through a failure to apply the best methods, not as a result of "scientific method."

In addition, there is the problem of recognizing "scientific methods." Lord Brain does not offer any explanation of how such methods are to be recognized. In practice, scientists do not have any great difficulty in differentiating between scientific and non-scientific methods, but the use of this fact to differentiate science from non-science would introduce a hopeless circularity. Scientific methods are simply those methods thought suitable by members of the scientific community, and thus we must be able to recognize that community by some other criterion. The provision of a systematic description of the scientific community which will make it possible to differentiate between scientific and non-scientific fields will be a further objective of this book.

The scientific community grew up without a conscious plan because it met a need. This need was a desire for knowledge, but knowledge of a certain type. The early scientists were looking for natural laws, laws which were the same everywhere, and which might interest people of every nationality. Further, most of these regularities which they called "laws" were both difficult to discover and likely to be of little direct interest to the mass of the population. The scientific community developed out of this search. The movement, which was simultaneously the greatest of adventures and a very unromantic drive for improved well-being, grew naturally into the present gigantic scientific enterprise. Today we have great laboratories and individual research projects employing thousands of scientists, but the interrelation between these giant laboratories, and between them and the myriad of individual investigators, is still one of voluntary, and almost unconscious, co-operation. It is not based on central planning or hierarchic organization. But as any economist knows, the fact that there is no one who can give commands does not mean that there is no social organization.

CHAPTER II

WHY INQUIRE?

"The scientific process has two motives; one is to understand the natural world, the other is to control it."[1] Putting the same thought in slightly more mundane language, we undertake investigations because we are curious, or because we hope to use the information obtained for some practical purpose. These two motives roughly correspond to the general fields of "pure" and "applied" research.[2] The correspondence is not exact, partly because human motives are seldom completely unmixed, and partly because the terms "pure" and "applied" themselves are not clearly distinguished in common use. What is "pure" research to one scientist may appear "applied" to another. In the interests of clarity, I shall use the term "pure science" for research which is motivated primarily by curiosity and "applied science" for that which is motivated mainly by a desire to obtain practical objectives.

It is the general opinion that pure science is somehow superior to applied science. This feeling, paradoxically, is usually justified by claiming that the long-run results of pure research are apt to be of practical value. It will be pointed out that various practical inventions are the result of pure discoveries at some time in the past, and it will be implied that similar results will follow from further pure research. This argument sometimes seems to point toward the conclusion that pure research is really a superior form of applied research. In fact, the general argument rests on something like an optical illusion. If we take any present-day discovery, practical or in the field of the most abstract theory, it will normally be based on a great number of previous discoveries. Some of these discoveries will generally be from the field of applied science and some from the field of pure science. It is always possible to select one of these previous discoveries and say quite truthfully that the new discovery could not have been made if this older discovery had not been made first.

The argument for pure science in terms of its practical results generally takes advantage of this fact. Some recent practical development will be

1. Charles Snow, "The Two Cultures: A Second Look," *Times Literary Supplement,* October 25, 1963, pp. 834–44, at p. 840. Lord Snow does not, of course, claim any originality for this thought. He is simply presenting the orthodox doctrine in his usual lucid English.

2. Sir George Thomson, "Two Aspects of Science," *Science,* 14 (October, 1960), 996–1000.

singled out, a bit of pure research in the past which was part of the basis for the new discovery will be pointed out, and the correct statement made that the new discovery could not have been made without the earlier bit of pure research. In a sort of logical leap, the argument will then simply generalize this correct bit of particular description. It will be implicitly or explicitly assumed that this is the way all practical improvements are made. The same system, of course, could be used to "prove" the importance of applied science to pure science; there is a Marxist school of thought which does just that. All of the early advances in bacteriology, for example, were dependent upon the practical improvements made by lens grinders who built progressively better microscopes.

Consider some area of science. At some time in the past a number of discoveries were made—some pure, some applied. On the figure below these are shown by the nodes at the top. With the progress of knowledge, further discoveries were made—designated by the nodes in the network—and eventually we arrive today at the discoveries at the bottom. The lines connecting the discoveries show interdependence; that is, each discovery is dependent upon all previous discoveries with which it is connected.

The normal practice is to put in only part of the diagram; thus discovery A'_3 will be connected to P_3 by the heavy line, or perhaps a tree, such as shown by the dotted lines, will be drawn connecting P_3 with all of its "descendants." From this partial diagram it may then be argued that pure science is really more important than applied science. It would make just as much sense to

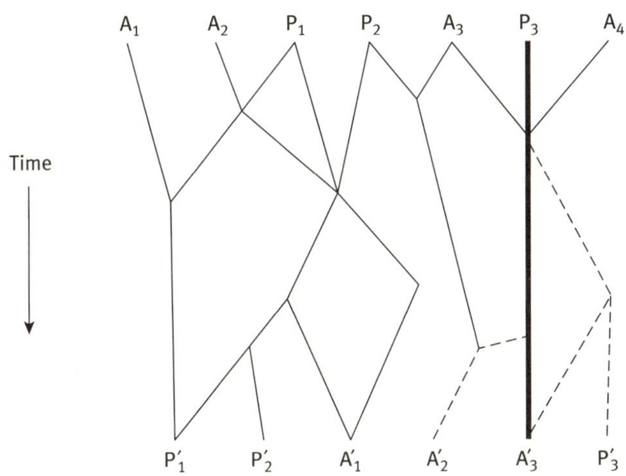

connect discovery P'_1 to A_1 and thus "prove" the superiority of applied science. In fact, the tree of knowledge may be drawn with almost any discovery as its root and can be used to "prove" that pure discoveries, applied discoveries, or discoveries made by men named Brown are more important than any others.

It is undeniably true that new discoveries are based on older discoveries. Further, if all previous discoveries of a certain class, whether that class be pure science, applied science, or discoveries made by men whose name begins with *C*, had not been made, then the absence of these discoveries would significantly reduce our present rate of progress. Transistors, for example, were originally invented and developed by applied scientists.[3] In their work, of course, they utilized previous discoveries, both pure and applied. Once transistors were available, they rapidly became important components of innumerable laboratory devices. These devices, in turn, made it possible to make still further discoveries, both pure and applied. Any of these discoveries made through the use of transistorized laboratory or computing equipment can be traced back to either the invention of the transistor or to some preceding discovery, pure or applied. Tracing the ancestry of the discovery back to any one previous discovery, however, is essentially illegitimate. Any discovery is the heir of innumerable previous discoveries, many of them applied and many of them pure.

Furthermore, the importance of individual older discoveries is less than is sometimes thought. Many things which were hard to discover in 1900 would be easily discoverable today. A researcher who finds himself in need of some given bit of information will normally be pleased to find it in some old scientific journal, because simply looking it up is usually easier than working out the matter experimentally in the laboratory.[4] On the other hand, our present equipment, both physical and theoretical, is so much superior to that of 1900 that a present-day graduate student may be able, in a few hours of work, to duplicate discoveries which were major scientific advances in 1900. Thus, if some bit of research which could have been undertaken in 1900 was, in fact, omitted, a modern researcher who needed the information in his

3. See note 21 below.

4. The so-called "data explosion" has made it sometimes very difficult to get information out of the "literature." The time taken to search through the library for some bit of knowledge may be less than the time taken in rediscovery. This problem will be discussed in Chapter IV.

work would be handicapped by the omission, but might well be able to overcome the problem with little difficulty.

The practical importance of research in previous periods is exaggerated by the process of tracing back the history of important present-day discoveries. Research in previous periods which did not lead to anything which turned out to be important is automatically excluded from the sample by this procedure. The correct test of the practical importance of research would be to examine all of the discoveries in a given field, say chemistry, in a given year, say 1900, and see what percentage have had important further discoveries as "heirs." For a test of the importance of pure research in developing practically important discoveries, it would be necessary to confine the original sample to cases of pure research. The experiment has not been performed, but I suspect that the percentage of discoveries of pure science which have not been made use of in any practical way would be high.[5]

The percentage would, naturally, vary from field to field. Astronomy, which can fairly claim to be the oldest natural science, has had practically no applications from its earliest discovery to the present.[6] Mathematics, rightly called the queen of science, also has had relatively little application.[7] At first glance this statement may seem absurd, in view of the domination of much of science by mathematical equations, but this is looking at the matter backwards. Physics requires large amounts of mathematical manipulation, but it does not follow from this that any large part of the total research in mathematics is utilized in physics. In fact, of all the work done by mathematicians, applied science has used only a fraction. As an example, consider Euclid's elegant proof that there is no largest prime number. This is now over two thousand years old, but no one has made a practical application of it, and it is hard

5. Professor B. R. Williams, in a paper read to the economics section of the British Association on September 4, 1956 ("Science and Industrial Innovation"), estimated that even among those scientific ideas which "are adjudged worthy of industrial research ten or less will be proved worthy of industrial application."

6. In a sense, astronomy was, from the first, used for practical matters in the form of astrology. More significantly, navigation and timekeeping have used minor parts of astronomy, and astrogation may shortly use more. Chemistry and nuclear physics have also owed minor debts to astronomy. Nevertheless, only a tiny bit of the work of the astronomers has had any effect on human affairs.

7. See Michael Polanyi, *Personal Knowledge,* p. 186, and G. H. Hardy, *A Mathematician's Apology* (Cambridge: Cambridge University Press, 1940), pp. 71–83.

to see how anyone ever will. In fact, considerably less than half of Euclid's propositions have ever been used in practical applications.

It is, of course, always possible that a practical man trying to do something practical will find that a mathematical system worked out by a mathematician is of great use. Leibniz developed binary arithmetic because he thought it proved the existence of God. It continued to be thought of as an impractical curiosity until the development of computers made it of the utmost practical importance. History would appear to indicate, however, that the development of pure mathematics will proceed more or less independent of practical use and that only a small fraction of the work of the pure mathematicians will ever find such a use. We can easily point to other fields where little or nothing in the way of practical applications can be expected. Archaeology, physical anthropology, and paleobiology are all perfectly respectable sciences, yet they have few practical applications. Even in such apparently practical sciences as physics and chemistry, there are numerous areas where few practical applications have been made.

The arguments justifying pure science by its practical results are really very weak. It seems reasonable that a given amount of resources will have more practical effect if it is put into applied research rather than into pure research, although pure research is likely to have at least some practical results. This does not, however, indicate that pure research is undesirable. Curiosity is a legitimate motive. Personally, I am very curious about conditions on the moon and the various planets and would favor their exploration even if I were convinced (as I am not) that no single discovery capable of practical application would result. It should merely be kept in mind that pure research is an effort to learn more about the universe just because we want to know. It is not a superior way of obtaining practical results.

Nor is there any real justification for the general tendency to consider pure research as somehow higher and better than applied research. It is certainly more pleasant to engage in research in fields that strike you as interesting than to confine yourself to fields which are likely to be profitable, but there is no reason why the person choosing the more pleasant type of research should be considered more noble. It is probably true that there are some differences between the personalities of people engaging in pure research and those in the applied fields. Most scientists are interested both in their own living conditions and in their work. The relative weight given to those two considerations will vary from person to person. Those who put the greater emphasis on the material returns from research are likely to enter the applied field, while those more interested in the research as a thing in itself will likely engage in pure research. Persons who regard concern with things here below as somehow mean and earthy will thus tend to feel that pure researchers are superior. On the other hand, it can be argued that pure researchers are more egotistical, pointing their research toward satisfying their own curiosity rather than benefiting humanity. There is, in fact, no reason[8] for feeling that either group is superior to the other. Einstein and Edison were both great men; let it go at that.

There is one sense, however, in which pure research is probably more productive than applied. In our present-day world very large amounts of resources are put into applied research, while pure research attracts considerably less money, particularly because a good deal of applied research is currently misclassified as pure. Granting that returns on research effort *on a given subject at a given time* are subject to diminishing returns, the marginal return on a given amount of effort in the pure field (in terms of discoveries, not in terms of monetary value) should be greater than in the applied field. It is probable that the pure fields of research are always a little behind the applied fields, and thus that progress is somewhat easier there. The spearheads of advance are probably normally in the applied fields rather than in pure science.

The popular belief that the reverse in the case is another example of one-sided reasoning. Both pure and applied researchers are normally working in fields which are separate. Both tend to use discoveries made in the other field some time ago. By pointing only to the indisputable fact that the pure scientist is engaged in research which is not being duplicated by applied researchers and the equally clear historic fact that applied scientists frequently make use of prior discoveries made by pure scientists, an apparent argument for the primacy of pure science can be made. But, since the applied researchers are also engaged in work which is not being duplicated by the pure sciences, and it is historically clear that pure scientists have frequently made use of discoveries by applied science, the reverse argument would be equally cogent. Reasoning from such sets of individual examples thus leads nowhere. It seems likely, however, that the marginal productivity of research effort in the two fields would vary inversely with the amount of effort in each. Thus, if we concentrated 99 44/100 per cent of our scientific effort in the field of pure science, the applied results of the remaining 56/100 per cent of the effort

8. The publisher's reader put a note on the margin here: "There are many strong reasons on both sides." Perhaps that is a better way of putting it.

would probably be disproportionately great. Under present conditions, with the greatest efforts going into applied science, the reverse is probably true.

The simplest and clearest example of the dependence of pure science upon applied is the great boon which pure science has received from developments in the field of measuring devices.[9] In addition, the production of laboratory equipment is now a major industry. The November 8, 1963, edition of *Science,* for example, contains over two hundred pages of advertisements of laboratory equipment. This is, of course, one of the periodic "Instrument Guide" issues of that journal, but the pages of almost any scientific periodical of good circulation will be filled with the advertisements of the equipment manufacturers who have engaged in applied research in the development of laboratory equipment. It ill becomes the pure physicist whose work is possible only because a group of engineers employed by High Voltage Engineering have developed and put into production a tandem Van de Graaff to deny his indebtedness to applied research.

Note that this is not an argument for more resources for pure science. The decision as to how much we put into satisfying our curiosity and how much into improving our technology can be reached only on extrinsic grounds. If the American voter is actually not very curious and is interested only in the practical advantages of scientific advance (and the efforts to justify pure science on practical grounds might be taken as evidence that the advocates of pure science believe this is so), then we are investing too much of his resources in pure science. Decisions as to whether a given amount of resources should be put into pure or applied science can be solved only in terms of the ends which the persons making the decision wish to reach.

Turning, however, to the effects of these motives on research, applied research immediately confronts a major problem. Inquiry is, by definition, concerned with the unknown. A man instituting an inquiry can never know for certain what will result or even if anything will result. Thus, it might appear impossible for anyone to undertake research aimed at some given end, and hence that applied research is impossible. Actually, most economic actions are taken under conditions of imperfect knowledge and under circumstances where the outcome cannot be known with certainty.[10] In this respect applied research does not differ from other forms of economic activity. De-

9. For a discussion of the early development of scientific instruments see Charles Joseph Singer, ed., *A History of Technology* (Oxford: Clarendon Press, 1957), vol. 3, pp. 582–646.

10. See Frank Knight, *Risk, Uncertainty and Profit* (Boston, 1921).

cisions on necessarily imperfect information must be made, and those who tend to make such decisions in such a way that they are successful will make large gains; those who tend to be wrong will have losses.[11] The problem is simply that facing any person deciding how to expend resources. Whether a filling station on a given corner would be a wise investment and whether it will be feasible to produce a plastic with certain characteristics are questions of the same sort. Both involve some known and some unknown facts; both require guesses as to the unknown facts; and our historic experience would indicate that there are some people who are better than others in making such decisions. In this field the research director is, like any entrepreneur, simply a well-informed man making decisions without complete information. Certainly he will be wrong on occasion, but so will any other person who tries to decide on the best use of resources.[12] In recent years a specialized type of entrepreneur who is good at guessing what can be invented and sold has developed, and whole companies, particularly in the electronics field, are built upon this type of entrepreneurship.

Of course, many practical inventions and improvements are made as a sort of by-product of the production process without any significant advanced planning or investment of resources. A workman will occasionally find an improved way of doing something or a way of making an improved product even if he does not invest any serious amount of time or effort in the search. More importantly, the management and supervisory personnel are likely to think of new ways of meeting their problems. Thus a continual, although slow, trickle of new techniques and devices can be seen throughout the whole history of the human race. This almost automatic process of invention, however, has been supplemented in recent centuries by the conscious process of directed research. Time and material resources are devoted solely to the process of making new inventions. Today this special form of "investment" takes up a significant part of our capital investments.[13]

11. This would be true in a planned or governmentally controlled economy as well as in a free economy. Only in this case, the decision-making unit might be very large so that the rewards and losses would not be apportioned to the individuals responsible.

12. W. I. B. Beveridge, *The Art of Scientific Investigation* (New York: Norton, 1950), is largely written from the standpoint of an applied researcher, specifically, from the standpoint of an investigator of the diseases of animals. Clearly Beveridge did make errors, but equally clearly the lines of investigation which he decided to pursue tended to be the right ones.

13. In bookkeeping terms this is not true. Under the tax laws most research expenditures can be treated as current expenses and are so handled in most accounting systems. Although I

This change, and it could be called a revolution, in the genesis of invention is largely the result of the development of the patent system. A patent is simply a legal monopoly granted by the state to the inventor of a new device. It has always disturbed economists because it has all of the disadvantages of an ordinary monopoly.[14] The argument for it has always been that the advantage which it gives in rewarding invention much more than counterbalances the disadvantage inherent in monopolies. The issue is not easy, but most economists rather unhappily vote for the patent system while hoping that someone will invent a better social device. This is not, however, a book on economics, and I will leave this debate to the economic journals. For our purposes we need only note that patents exist and then turn to a discussion of their role in promoting applied research. It is a notable one.

Consider the situation prior to the development of patents (in the modern meaning of the term). Governments then normally approved inventions and technological improvements which resulted in new products. Sometimes the new product might be thought undesirable for some reason, but generally it was accepted with gratitude. On the other hand, inventions which simply eased the method of production of existing products were usually frowned upon. The fear that labor-saving inventions will result in widespread unemployment is as old as history. Its continuance today may be taken as one more indication that what we learn from history is that we do not learn from history. The Emperor Claudius's rewarding an engineer who had developed some machines for reducing the manpower needed in construction and, at the same time, his prohibiting their use may be taken as a humane application of this fatuous policy. One of the great advantages of the modern patent system lies in its failure to distinguish between these two types of invention.

Without patents, a man considering investing time and money in some sort of economic enterprise would seldom consider applied research as a

---

do not question the tax advantages to be obtained by this procedure, the expenditures are actually investments.

14. The patent monopoly has another disturbing feature, the almost comic confusion of the laws in this field. Leonard Lockhard put these complexities in fictional form in four most amusing stories published in *Astounding Science-Fiction:* "Improbable Profession," September, 1952; "That Professional Look," January, 1954; "The Curious Profession," April, 1956; and "The Professional Touch," February, 1959. For a careful statement of the problem from an economist's viewpoint see Fritz Machlup, "Patents and Inventive Effort," *Science,* 133 (May 12, 1961), 1463–66. The economic literature prior to 1959 was carefully surveyed by Richard R. Nelson in "The Economics of Invention," *Journal of Business,* 32 (April, 1959), 101–27.

likely alternative.[15] Any new product or process he discovered could be immediately copied by others. Thus the innovator would have spent his time and money in producing something which largely benefited others. Only if the new process was such that it could be kept secret (products, of course, could not be kept secret if they were to be sold; but a new product might involve a new process which could be kept secret) would research directed toward producing it be likely to be profitable. Under the circumstances research would be almost entirely devoted to the development of processes which could be kept secret. Only a small fraction of all possible inventions fall in this category. Consequently, there was little planned investment in research in the age before patents.

Even if some early entrepreneur did undertake research leading to the discovery of a process which could be kept secret, the necessity of keeping it secret would generally greatly reduce its utility. It could normally not be used on any great scale, because that would require letting too many workmen know how it was done.[16] Normally, also, the process could not be dispersed to a number of geographically remote producing centers for the same reason. Thus the profit derived even from some process which could be kept secret would likely be less than the profit obtained from a patent on the same idea, and the incentive to undertake research would be proportionately less.

The disadvantage of the pre-patent system of keeping new inventions secret, however, has still not been fully pointed out. The advantages gained from any new invention can be divided into two categories: the direct advantage gained from its application and the indirect advantage gained from the increase in knowledge. The new device or process or one of its underlying principles is likely, in the long run, to have even greater effect through its intellectual descendants than through its direct application. Each discovery makes further discoveries just that much easier. If, however, the discoverer keeps his discovery secret, then no one else is able to use it in making other

15. *Prescriptions, Drugs and the Public Health,* "a digest of the presentation of the Pharmaceutical Manufacturers Association before the Senate Subcommittee on Antitrust and Monopoly," presents the businessman's view on this problem. See also "Patents as a Research Tool," a speech by Robert L. Hershey, vice president, E. I. du Pont de Nemours & Co., before the ninth annual conference of the Patent, Trademark, and Copyright Research Institute of George Washington University, given June 17, 1965.

16. Venetian glass was produced on a considerable scale for quite a while before the secret leaked out, but the normal entrepreneur could not expect to have the dread Committee of Ten to help him keep his process secret.

discoveries. Thus the simple act of keeping it secret deprives the human race of much of its advantage.

The patent system is not, however, used in all fields of applied science. There are many areas where it is impossible to collect royalties from the users of new discoveries. In agriculture, for example, many discoveries simply take the form of improvements in such things as crop rotation, spacing and arrangement of plants, and proper mixture of fertilizers. It is not feasible for a man who has engaged in research and discovered that corn crops may be increased if fertilizers are mixed in a certain proportion under certain conditions of soil and climate to collect a royalty on the use of his idea. Individual farmers need merely order the various fertilizers from other dealers and put them on the crops in the desired proportions in order to get the full benefit of his idea without paying any royalties. Even if our patent laws permitted patents on such discoveries, the policing problem would be impossible.

The consequence is that private individuals who invest in research in such an area are not able to regain the costs of their research and therefore will not undertake it. Their situation is the same as that of any inventor without the protection of patents. The only way of obtaining new discoveries in this field is by some kind of collectively financed research paid for by all the farmers. As a rule, this means state-paid-for and -directed research. The fact that research in the agrarian field is largely governmental rather than private is perfectly logical.

It should be noted, however, that the dividing line between the areas where some kind of governmental research is necessary and the areas where private research may be relied upon does not exactly correspond with the division between agriculture and industry. Farm machinery, for example, has been largely developed by private inventors. Further, although most new and improved strains of crops or livestock come from government laboratories, there are occasional exceptions. Hybrid corn, for example, was certainly the most significant new "strain" of modern times, and it was developed entirely by private entrepreneurs. The difference is easily explained. Most improved seeds for a given crop will breed true. The farmer who has bought seed for one year is in a position to use his whole crop to compete with his original supplier in the second year.[17] In the case of hybrid corn, however, this is not

17. Sometimes, even when the strain will breed true, the precautions necessary to prevent accidental contamination of the breeding stock may be costly. In these circumstances, special-

true. A farmer who was so foolish as to plant the crop he got from hybrid seed in the expectation that it would give equally good results would be sadly disappointed. The hybrid seed for each crop must be produced by a separate hybridization process, and the developers of hybrid corn, therefore, could and did make a large return on their investment in research. The profit was much less than would have resulted from a patent, however, since other breeders could duplicate their "strain."

Outside agriculture, too, there are areas where applied research would appear to be called for but where the result would be unpatentable. Management techniques and sales methods provide examples. Under present conditions, relatively little serious research is devoted to these problems. Government-sponsored research does not provide an answer here, since the people who would initially benefit from the research do not have the political influence of the farmers and cannot hope to get large appropriations for this purpose. In these fields we are little better off than in the period before the invention of the patent. We do, of course, make progress, but we would make much more if some better way of rewarding the inventor could be developed.

A man interested in some particular bit of applied research may hire someone else to help him or even to do the whole thing. Under these circumstances very difficult problems of supervision may arise, but there is nothing which is particularly distinctive to research about them. A man desiring to accomplish anything who hires someone else to do it must remember that the other person is motivated not by a desire to carry out the project, but by a desire to earn his salary (in favorable cases, he may share the employer's interest in the basic project). If he can continue to earn his salary while switching his work over to a field which interests him more or which will require less work, he is likely to do so. Some types of jobs, and research is among them, offer exceptional opportunities for this kind of thing, but all we can say is that supervision under such circumstances will be difficult and probably not wholly efficient. Scientific research does not differ from many occupations in this respect.

The major industrial laboratories, full of hired scientists doing various applied projects, are a major and important part of our scientific resources.

---

ized breeders may develop, but the price they receive for their seed reflects the difficulty of raising it, not the cost of the developmental research.

Nevertheless, many of the scientists are dissatisfied and want to improve their social status by being pure scientists.[18] The managers of the laboratories, interested in getting their research done at the least cost, may provide facilities for genuine pure science, if this permits them to hire scientists at a wage rate low enough that the savings will pay the cost of the pure projects. Sometimes, also, managements impressed by the propaganda about "social responsibility" will actually feel that pure research is their duty and undertake a little of it. Normally, however, the pressure of the stockholders, who want dividends, and competitors, who are continually coming out with new products or cutting prices, will force industrial laboratories to keep pretty close to research having direct practical applications. This pressure is weaker in companies having substantial monopoly powers; pure research is more likely in such areas.[19]

Another technique which has been frequently resorted to involves a slight change of definition which makes certain types of applied research "pure." Thus, a laboratory trying to improve some device will find that further work requires information which is not now available—let us say a table of values of some physical constant. The compiling of this table, in spite of its eminently practical motivation, can be called pure research and thus may raise the social status of the men working on it.

Another type of applied research likely to be termed "pure" by people doing it involves the investigation of some particular field of research in hopes that something useful will be found. Thus DuPont, in the 1920's, hired a distinguished chemist to go through a certain class of chemicals looking for something useful. Since he found nylon, this can be listed as one of the most spectacularly successful pieces of applied research in modern history. The whole process, however, was called pure research. It was called "pure" partly to raise the status of the researcher, who would probably have insisted on a

18. Similar considerations may lead to publishing data rather than keeping it secret. "The big company . . . has to publish enough to make itself attractive to the scientific community, whence will come its future strength. Yet the old sense of property, the basis of the firm's very existence, inhibits it from tossing to the four winds those few nuggets of practical information for which gold has been traded." Kodak reports, *Science,* 148 (May 14, 1965), 890.

19. Sometimes morale may be raised by simply announcing that a branch of the laboratory which has been devoted to improvements in gadgets will, from now on, carry out pure research (in the development of gadgets). This type of thing will achieve maximum effectiveness if it coincides in time with one of the periodic reorganizations of the laboratory.

higher salary if he had been told he was to do applied work, and partly because he was, in fact, given no very specific instructions. The management (and the chemist) felt that there were probably commercial products somewhere in the class of chemicals and were willing to pay for an investigation. If the chemist had found nothing useful, he would most certainly have been switched to another area (or fired), no matter how significant his discoveries were in terms of increasing our knowledge of the universe.

In 1958 Dr. John Grebe, director of nuclear and basic research for the Dow Chemical Company, presented a basic theory about the nature of the nucleus. The theory has attracted relatively little notice, probably because it turned out to be incorrect. For our purposes, however, it is interesting that he did his work on it at home on his own time.[20] This was genuine pure research, inspired by his own dissatisfaction with the existing state of knowledge, and he realized that it was not the kind of thing which he could include in the company's research budget.

Another related type of applied research which may sometimes be designated pure involves hiring some scientist who is believed to be particularly likely to make commercially useful discoveries and simply letting him do what he wants as long as the results are good. The Bell Telephone Laboratories seem to operate on this principal to a considerable extent.[21] Excellent personnel are hired and very good facilities are provided. In theory, the scientists (or at least some of them) are free to investigate anything which strikes them as interesting. To read some of the descriptions of this laboratory, one might think that the fact that the overwhelming majority of the results have something to do with communications was purely coincidental. In fact, of course, the heads of the laboratory know that they must justify their budget appropriations in terms of output, and individual scientists know that they must make discoveries which are of enough use to pay their salaries. The whole thing is an exceptionally well-run applied-science laboratory.

Turning now to pure research, i.e., research undertaken to satisfy curiosity, we can distinguish two extreme cases. Robert Boyle, a wealthy man, equipped a laboratory and pursued highly important research as a sort of

20. *New York Times,* March 12, 1959, p. 3.

21. Richard R. Nelson, *The Link Between Science and Invention* (RAND Corporation, P-1854-RC, December 15, 1959), gives an account of the most important single discovery of the Bell Laboratories, the transistor, and makes it quite clear that the researchers had practical applications in mind at all times.

hobby. We may regard this as an example of pure curiosity research. At the other extreme, all universities have on their faculties people who do research and produce articles simply because that is the way they earn their living. They may actually have very little interest in the subject of their investigations and will abandon their researches without a single pang of regret if they are offered a better paying job doing something else. This is an example of *induced* curiosity. Most real-life pure research lies somewhere between these two extremes, of course, but we can simplify our discussion if we consider the two extreme cases separately. The intermediate situations which are commoner in the real world can then be thought of as varying mixtures of the two pure cases.

Induced research is a relatively recent development, and we can profitably follow the historic order and discuss pure curiosity research first. An investigation of the psychology of a selected list of eminent scientists resulted in the following description of their motivation:

> Once it was fully understood that *personal* research was possible, once some research had actually been accomplished, there was never any question. This was it. . . . There has been no question since. From then on absorption in the vocation was so complete as seriously to limit all other activity. . . . Although a few of them have cut down on their hours of work as they have grown older, it is still the common pattern for them to work nights, Sundays, holidays, as they always have. Most of them are happiest when they are working. In all of these instances, other aspects—economic return, social and professional status—are of secondary importance.
>
> Being curious plays a major role. . . . It is of crucial importance that these men set their own problem and investigate what interests them. No one tells them what to think about, or when, or how. Here they have almost perfect freedom.[22]

Most of these scientists, of course, were making their living by their scientific activity. For the truly curious, however, this is a relatively minor consideration. They have found an occupation in which they are paid for doing what they would do on their own if they happened to have inherited a for-

22. Anne Roe, "A Psychological Study of Eminent Psychologists and Anthropologists, and a Comparison with Biological and Physical Scientists," *Psychological Monographs,* 67, No. 2 (February, 1953), 49. These remarks refer to all of the scientists, not just the psychologists.

tune. In a sense they are hired to play. If we take the normal economic concept of opportunity costs, they may in fact be "paying" sizable amounts for the privilege of engaging in research. Some[23] of them, certainly, could make considerably larger incomes by applying their abilities with equal diligence to some other line of work. Thus they actually do make a monetary sacrifice to engage in research, just as Robert Boyle reduced his expenditures on luxurious living in order to support the specially trained artisans who produced his equipment. Since they obviously enjoy their work, they are maximizing their utility, but not their income. Their basic motivation is curiosity, not making money.

We can divide the curiosity which motivates a pure researcher into two general types: general curiosity and particular curiosity. Most scientists will be found to be generally curious (at the least in the general field in which they operate, but more normally about the whole universe), but particularly curious about the solution of some problems upon which they are currently working. It is my belief that the particular curiosity which leads a scientist to undertake a given bit of research is always the outcome of his general curiosity. His general curiosity leads him to arrange to have a sizable information input, through reading journals, attending meetings, etc. This information input resolves some of his curiosity, but it will also occasionally suggest to him research which he could undertake which would further satisfy his curiosity. The result is the development of particular curiosity in a given problem and a specific research program. Thus the scientist's curiosity is subject to social guidance. The information inputs from other scientists are important in shaping the problems which he will investigate. Similarly, he is normally interested in the approval of his peers and hence will usually consciously shape his research into a project which will pique other scientists' curiosity as well as his own.

The situation can be readily explained with the aid of an economic analogy. A stock market speculator is, presumably, interested in making money through buying and selling stocks. He usually has little concern with which stocks. Nevertheless, opportunities for profit normally occur in various individual stocks, and the speculator must make his money out of such opportunities. He thus keeps well informed on conditions in the market and looks for opportunities to make money in individual stocks. His specific operations

23. To offer a subjective guess, considerably more than half.

will always involve only a few stocks, but they arise naturally from his interest in using the whole market as a source of gain. Similarly, the man seeking to satisfy his curiosity will keep informed of developments in the whole field about which he is curious, but will undertake specific investigations only when he thinks he sees an opportunity for particularly fruitful discoveries. Like the stock market speculator, he may be wrong, but he generally receives a sort of consolation prize in the form of at least some new information.

This, it should be noted, is a major advantage the pure scientist has over the applied scientist. The applied scientist may fail. It may turn out that he cannot make the device or carry out the process toward which he aims, and that his effort, therefore, does not reach its goal. The pure scientist can hardly fail in this sense. His research will always lead to some result which satisfies his general curiosity even if it is completely unsuccessful from the standpoint of the particular curiosity which inspired the particular project. Thus, the famous Michelson-Morley experiment was an effort to discover certain characteristics of the movement of the earth with respect to the "ether." The results simply did not make sense in terms of the physics of the day; they implied that the earth was stationary. The long-run effect of these completely unexpected results was the elimination of the "ether" from the "world view" of the physicist.[24]

Although particular curiosity comes from general curiosity, it may develop a life of its own. Thus a man who is curious about nature in general is likely to specialize his curiosity into some selected segment of the whole universe of potential knowledge. This segment itself will normally be pretty broad, although its width will vary from person to person. It may shift considerably during the life of any investigator. Within this segment, an ingenious and highly motivated investigator will see specific opportunities for increasing his knowledge and undertake corresponding specific investigations. This involves the particular curiosity which we have been discussing. In most cases, this particular curiosity is transitory, being readily replaced by something else if the investigation is successful or if it turns out to be a failure. Sometimes, however, the investigator becomes emotionally involved with a particular problem and subordinates all other interests to it. Usually, such in-

24. The experiment was carefully discussed by Dr. A. Grünbaum in his vice-presidential address to the history and philosophy section of the AAAS on December 29, 1963, at the Cleveland meeting. The speech was published under the title "The Bearing of Philosophy on the History of Science" in *Science,* 143 (March 27, 1964), 1406–12.

volvement occurs only with difficult problems and, consequently, some of the most important advances in science have come from such a situation. Kepler's work[25] will do as an example. Simple problems can usually be solved quickly enough that the investigator does not have time to become obsessed. The more difficult problems usually take more time and are thus more likely to trap their investigators. Since the solution of such difficult problems is of greater importance than the solution of the easier ones, the emotional involvement of the researcher with his problem has, perhaps, received undue emphasis in accounts of the development of science. Not only have some important scientific advances occurred when the investigator was not deeply involved in the particular problem (the special theory of relativity, for example), but the bulk of the minor advances which make up so much of science have occurred without any deep emotional involvement between the scientist and his subject.

Once he has made a discovery, the scientist who is primarily motivated by curiosity is rather apt to want to tell people about it. He is probably proud of the discovery, and like the rest of us, he enjoys the approval of others. The successful investigator will normally discuss his discovery with all whom he can get to listen and may carry his enthusiasm to the point of acute boredom for most of his listeners. In most cases the circle of people who will be interested is quite narrow, but this narrow circle is composed of the people best qualified to judge the discovery.[26] From the standpoint of the development of our knowledge of the universe, this is of great importance. It is highly important that new discoveries be circulated rapidly. Further, the desire of the scientist for the approval of his peers provides a slight but real social control over his choice of problems. Unless the discovery he makes is of interest to at least the specialist, he will find it hard to get people to listen and approve his results. Sometimes this element of social control is unfortunate. Gregor Mendel was surely one of the greatest scientists of the nineteenth century. He is famous for only one set of experiments, however, his discovery of the foundations of modern genetics. After making these truly epoch-making discov-

25. Charles Joseph Singer, ed., *A Short History of Scientific Ideas to 1900* (Oxford: Oxford University Press, 1959), pp. 236–41.

26. A mechanical method of approximating the circulation of a new idea has been developed in the "citation count." By counting the number of times a given article is footnoted in other articles, an idea of its importance can be obtained. For a sample of the method, see J. H. Westbrook, "Identifying Significant Research," *Science*, 132 (October 28, 1960), 1229–34.

eries, he gradually moved out of science and became abbot of a small monastery. Surely his complete inability to interest the biologists of his day in his discoveries[27] was one of the major factors in this shift in his activities.

A man engaged in satisfying his curiosity may hire assistance just like anyone else. We may distinguish two cases. In the first, the employee is hired to engage in specific research. Thus a junior scientist may be expected to make various minor investigations which his senior directs. The situation does not differ very much from that found in many industrial laboratories. The ultimate end aimed at, the increase of knowledge for its own sake, is different, but the means and the relations between the participants are the same. Another method of getting people to do specific research in return for monetary rewards is simply to offer a prize. The most famous example of this technique was the prize offered by the British Admiralty for an accurate chronometer after the destruction of Sir Cloudesley Shovell's fleet off the Scilly Isles.[28] This was an example of applied research, but the same technique could as well be used in the pure field. Occasionally someone interested in some specific problem does offer a prize for its solution.

The use of monetary rewards to get scientists to investigate specific problems which the provider of the money is curious about, however, is of no great significance in modern pure science. More commonly, an effort is made to stimulate the curiosity of the hired researcher. Since this technique is so important to the organization of modern science, I will give it a special name—"induced curiosity." There are two general methods to use. The first, and less important, is simply to offer a prize for the best work in some field. Thus there is an annual prize for the best paper concerned with gravity, and the *Journal of Political Economy* used to offer a prize for the best published article each year. The Nobel prizes, in a sense, are examples of this technique. It is important to distinguish this from the offering of prizes for specific discoveries. I am particularly curious, let us say, about the chemistry of silicon. As a way of satisfying my curiosity, I offer a series of prizes for the synthesizing of certain designated possible compounds of silicon. This is using the prize system to obtain research in specific fields which I have selected. The alternative would be to offer the same prizes for the "best" research in silicon chemistry. In the second case, I do not designate the specific research to be carried out. The researcher hoping to win a prize must not only carry out research,

27. Singer, *A Short History of Scientific Ideas to 1900,* pp. 485–90.

28. Singer, *A History of Technology,* vol. 4, pp. 410–12.

he must first decide what research is most likely to be important. Thus I have "induced" curiosity in him and hope to benefit from it in having my own curiosity satisfied.

Unfortunately, this method of inducing curiosity is relatively little used. The more common method consists of hiring an investigator and making his continued employment contingent upon his obtaining significant discoveries.[29] As compared with the prize system, this device has disadvantages. The curious person who has decided to spend funds in satisfying his curiosity must choose his investigator. Thus his efficiency as a personnel manager and the various chance factors which always affect the hiring of individuals will be reflected in the results. Advertising a prize and letting anyone who wishes make investigations in that field will normally lead to a sort of self-selection by a very wide group of people, and only those who think themselves[30] specially qualified will make the attempt.

In practice the system has become entangled with the educational system, which has its disadvantages. Before discussing this, however, it is necessary to turn to a special situation which does not depend upon induced curiosity, but which appears to. Let us suppose that a wealthy man (or institution) is curious about colloids. He (or it) finds a poor man who is also much interested in colloids. The wealthy man (or institution) gives him an honorarium so that he can devote his full time to satisfying his curiosity. Under these circumstances, which may be considered ideal for research, there is no induced curiosity because the curiosity was already there. It is a case where both parties are permitted to do as they wish and find that, through accidents, their wishes coincide.

In many cases of induced curiosity, an effort is made to pretend that the above situation exists. It will be maintained with every appearance of sincerity that research workers work because of their interest in the problems with which they deal and that they are employed not simply for that end. Doubtless most scientific workers, like most workers in other fields, are in fact interested in their work. Most men act out of a series of overlapping motives, but that the dominant one in this case is the system we have described as induced curiosity can be readily seen by examining the real situation. In the first

29. See Norman W. Storer, "The Coming Changes in American Science," *Science*, 142 (October 25, 1963), 464–67, for a discussion of the changes which have come about in science as a result of the rapid growth of this type of research.

30. And they necessarily know more about themselves than any employer.

place, the people who hire academic personnel in scientific fields where research is turned out make no bones about using research results as a major criterion in hiring and deciding whether to continue the employment of their subordinates. The faculty members themselves seem convinced that academic success is highly correlated with "publication"[31] and will usually explain promotions and demotions largely in these terms.

The system, however, is in other ways badly designed to get the best out of inducing curiosity. In the first place, the research is subsidized as a sort of by-product of education. Instead of hiring people who are thought to be good investigators to do research, they are nominally hired to teach and are required to devote a good deal of time to that end. The organization of the researchers and the number employed are entirely controlled by the needs of the university system. Thus the national balance between investigators in economics and physics is heavily influenced by the number of students who elect to enroll in courses in these two fields. The geographical distribution of various types of physicists is also controlled by the needs of the educational system. They are spread across the country in a pattern determined by the needs of universities rather than the needs of research, and men in the same branch of work may see each other only at the yearly meetings of the societies to which they belong.

Furthermore, the people who hire them are not directly interested in their work. The number and length of published papers are highly important, but the authorities responsible for hiring and firing are frequently not sufficiently interested in the subject covered to even bother to read them.[32] The whole responsibility for evaluating research, in essence, is left to the editors of the learned journals. If research is good enough to be published in a respected journal, it is assumed to be valuable on that evidence alone. This delegation of authority by the real employers to editors, who, to say the least, are of widely varying abilities, would appear to be unlikely to lead to good results.

The present university administrators themselves, however, would be rather poor people to put in charge of deciding what research is important. Most are little interested in the results of research, although they feel that good research is necessary to maintain the prestige of the university, and

31. See Theodore Caplow and Reece J. McGee, *The Academic Marketplace* (New York: Basic Books, 1958), for a detailed discussion of the part research papers play in the hiring of academic employees.

32. This is brought out particularly clearly on pages 126–31 of *The Academic Marketplace.*

many have the common man's attitude of respectful admiration for "science." If the administrator has come up from the research side, he may retain his interest in his particular field but is unlikely to be much more concerned with increasing knowledge on the interrelation of American Indian languages than is the average man. His real interests are administrative, particularly getting more money (he may be able to develop great enthusiasm for "science" if he thinks that this will increase his take). All of this is not to denigrate such men. They are necessary for the advancement of science, and their continual concern for getting more funds is of the utmost importance for the advancement of research. It is simply to say that the present scheme under which they do not have much to say in determining the relative merits of various investigators is not as irrational as it might appear.

Who then does decide? At first glance, it would appear that the editors of journals fulfil this function. In fact, although they are important, they fill a subordinate role. I could not turn myself into a power in chemistry by the simple expedient of starting a journal. The ultimate control lies in the hands of the readers. Every scientist who is really curious about his field reads a good deal of material in it. Although he probably does not read any one journal from cover to cover, he reads in a good many. Thus, although he may not have read any individual piece of research by a given other investigator, he can tell something about his ability by noting what journals have published his work.

The scheme works in somewhat the same manner as the market economy.[33] The individual scientists are both producers and consumers of research, producing on a specialized basis the results of their particular curiosity and consuming results of others' particular curiosity in order to satisfy their general curiosity. Each one, by subscribing himself, or influencing institutions to subscribe, to journals and by making the type of statements which build or demolish reputations, contributes his mite to the importance of each journal. The editors of the journals are thus motivated to do their best to select the best articles from among the contributions they receive. Since the most prestigious journals usually get first choice of articles, a sort of hierarchy of excellence is established, and the general scientific worth of a man can be, in fact, approximated by simply counting the number of publications he has had in various journals.

33. For an account of the strictly commercial side of the process, together with some examples, see *Time,* January 12, 1962, p. 36.

This chapter started with the assertion that we inquire to satisfy our curiosity or to obtain useful information. I should like to point out that the two motives are not mutually exclusive. A man can be motivated to the same investigation by considerations of both types. The relative weight of the two motives obviously varies vastly from case to case. Further, though these two motives are the characteristically scientific ones, most investigators have also been motivated by various other subordinate considerations. Some of the early scientists were under the impression that they had been directly ordered by God to undertake their investigations. More importantly, a good many researchers get a good deal of amusement out of their investigations. The aesthetic side of science should not be ignored. Mathematicians in particular seem to be heavily motivated by the beauty of their work, but most scientists get at least some aesthetic satisfaction from their subjects. All of this is to say that man is a complicated animal and his motives are many and varied. The two motives of curiosity and a desire to make practical application of new knowledge, however, will be found to be more intense among scientists than among the rest of the population and may therefore be used to distinguish science from other activities.

CHAPTER III

THE SUBJECT AND METHODS OF INQUIRY

The subject of inquiry is, quite simply, anything which anyone might be curious about or which might be practically useful. This formula sounds simple almost to the extent of simple-mindedness, but in fact it conceals a number of difficult problems. Let us start with curiosity, which is defined as "the desire to learn or know about anything."[1] It has been quite seriously questioned whether it is possible really to learn or know about anything. This position, which originated in religious speculation, has a number of variants. The extreme position, solipsism, is logically invulnerable. I cannot really prove to any adherent of this position that either I or this book exists and naturally have no chance to prove that anything else exists. All I can say is that I very much doubt if anyone really believes in solipsism.

A less extreme position, best stated by Bishop Berkeley, does not doubt the reality of the world, but points out that there is no proof that this real world corresponds to the sense impression which we receive from our necessarily imperfect sensory equipment. Again, the position is logically invulnerable; there is no way of demonstrating that the appearances and the realities coincide, since any evidence we present will refer only to the appearances. It should be noted, however, that the opposite position, that this paper is, in fact, white and that the ink is black, is equally invulnerable logically; it also cannot be disproved by any conceivable test. To the practical man the problem seems to be of little relevance. It makes no real difference whether the statement "If we do A then B will result" or the statement "If we do something which appears to be A, then something which appears to all of our senses to be B will happen" is true. To the pure scientist, however, the question is a relevant one.[2]

How, then, does he handle this important but apparently unanswerable question? It is hard for us to tell what someone else really thinks, but certainly all scientists act as though they believe that the appearances and the realities

1. *American College Dictionary* (New York: Random House, 1955).

2. For a general discussion of the importance of such philosophical problems to science and the importance of science to philosophy, see K. R. Popper, "The Nature of Philosophical Problems and Their Roots in Science," *British Journal for the Philosophy of Science,* 3, No. 10 (1952), 124–56.

coincide. To most laymen this will appear so obvious that they will wonder at my spending so much time on it, but to some scientists it will appear to be wrong. Ever since the time of Galileo there have been scientists and philosophers of science who have held some variant of the views so well expressed by Bishop Berkeley. In the latter part of the nineteenth century this view rapidly expanded its influence, and in the first half of the twentieth it was very widely held. Poincaré, Duhem, and Mach are probably its most important modern proponents.[3]

The basic view of reality shared by these scientists can be illustrated by Toulmin's condensation of Mach's views:

> Mach wanted to insist, rightly, that a scientific theory draws its life from the phenomena it can be used to explain; furthermore, the idea that the scientist needed insight into the causal connection of things smacked to him of metaphysics, and he tried to do without it. In view of this, it was natural for him to suppose that, if a law of nature was to contain no more than the phenomena it was used to explain, it must be thought of as a summary of them, i.e. as an abridged description or comprehensive and condensed report of the experimental observations: "This," he concluded, "is really all that laws of nature are."[4]

Suppose we heat an enclosed vessel containing a gas and record the gas pressure at various temperatures. If we are careful in making our observations, the pressure will vary in proportion to the (absolute) temperature of the gas. The statement "The pressure varies as the absolute temperature varies" is certainly more compact than a table showing a vast number of readings of our instruments, but is it any more than that? The layman would immediately answer that it represents a scientific law and that its discovery was

3. The philosophical issues are very well presented by J. Agassi in "Duhem versus Galileo," *British Journal for the Philosophy of Science,* 8, No. 31 (1957), 237–48. The version of operationalism upheld by P. W. Bridgman comes very close to Mach's position, "the proper definition of a concept is not in terms of its properties but in terms of actual operations. . . . concepts can be defined only in the range of actual experiment, and are undefined and meaningless in regions as yet untouched by experiment." *The Logic of Modern Physics* (New York: Macmillan, 1951), pp. 6–7.

4. Stephen Toulmin, *The Philosophy of Science, An Introduction* (London: Hutchinson, 1953), pp. 105–6. The whole of Toulmin's Chapter IV (pp. 105–39) is a concise and lucid critical discussion of the general view of reality we are concerned with here. The four or five pages devoted to Mach give his position far more clearly than Mach ever did.

an appreciable increase of our knowledge. For a proponent of Mach's position, however, it is really only another way of presenting the table of instrument readings, superior only because it takes up less space and is easier to remember. The real discovery, in this view, consists of the initial instrument readings.

The position of the believers in this version of Bishop Berkeley's philosophy, although they generally do not realize it, is that of the Jesuit cardinal who was Galileo's principal intellectual opponent. St. Robert Bellarmine wrote:

> It seems to me that your reverence and Signor Galileo act prudently when you content yourselves with speaking hypothetically and not absolutely. . . . To say that on the supposition of the Earth's movement and the Sun's quiescence all the celestial appearances are explained better than the theory of eccentrics and epicycles is to speak with excellent good sense and to run no risk whatever. Such a manner of speaking is enough for a mathematician.[5]

Galileo's crime consisted in not taking the hint in the cardinal's first sentence. He refused to act "prudently" and maintained that he had discovered a real law of nature rather than a simple system for tying a set of observations into a neat bundle.

In fact, of course, all scientists act as if they believe they are engaged in uncovering the real world. They show no signs of real doubts about the application of their theories to reality. "Albert Einstein has remarked that if you want to know what a scientist really believes, don't listen to what he says, but observe what he is working on."[6]

If the theories were merely devices for conveniently summarizing experimental results or mnemonic devices to make it easier to keep the results in mind, the interest of all scientists in improving them would be inexplicable.

5. Giorgio de Santillana, *The Crime of Galileo* (Chicago: University of Chicago Press, 1955), p. 99. The Catholics and the scientists have, in a way, exchanged positions on this issue. Since 1893 Galileo's position has been the doctrine of the Catholic church. As a result a modern Catholic scholar can say: "It is a curious and paradoxical circumstance . . . that as a piece of scriptural exegesis Galileo's theological letters are much superior to Bellarmine's, while as an essay on scientific method Bellarmine's is far sounder and more modern in its views than Galileo's." J. Broderick, *The Life and Work of Blessed Robert Francis, Cardinal Bellarmine, S. J.* (1928), vol. 2, 360, quoted in de Santillana, p. 101.

6. Joseph Berkson, "Smoking and Lung Cancer," *American Statistician*, 17, No. 4 (October, 1963), 15–22, at p. 19. I have been unable to find the original statement.

There are only a few experimental observations which can be treated more simply by the Einsteinian system than the Newtonian. If they were not interested in the truth of their theories, obviously the scientists would recommend the Einsteinian solutions for these few problems and use the Newtonian system everywhere else. The question of which was true would not arise, and the work of Einstein would be regarded as simply a minor step forward. The actual attitude of scientists on this problem is clearly contrary to Mach's position. Einstein's work is held to have disproved Newton, a conclusion obviously impossible if we assume that theories are simply abbreviated statements of observations. Nevertheless, the vast majority of all computations undertaken by physicists are strictly Newtonian. Only in a few special fields[7] has the work of Einstein actually had any significant effect on the everyday work of the physicists.

Any economist can testify that many highly successful businessmen have great difficulty in explaining how they behave, even to themselves. They are apt to grab hold of various ill-conceived theories, but they obviously do not really understand their own behavior in an analytical sense. In part, this is simply an illustration of the principle of division of labor. The manager of a plant making small electric motors has all sorts of difficult and urgent problems, and working out a careful and consistent explanation of his own behavior in solving these problems is not among them. That is a matter for another specialist in the system of division of labor, the economist. If, after the problem has been solved by the economist, he presents the results to the businessman, he should not be surprised if they are rejected. The businessman has spent the day worrying about whether he should buy a set of new core-winding machines and still has not made up his mind. If his attention is directed to the problem of why this worries him, he is likely to seize upon some simple solution which will not distract him from his preoccupation with the core-winders and to maintain that economists are impractical theorists.

The same phenomenon may affect scientists. A man who is extremely interested in the results obtained by high-energy accelerators and who is working night and day to put these results into some kind of theoretical framework is not likely to be highly motivated to study the problem of why he is so interested and why he chooses the particular methods he uses to solve his problems. Like the businessman, he is likely to pick up some apparently

7. The fields, such as particle physics, where Einsteinian computations are regularly made, tend to have higher social prestige among physicists.

simple solution as a way to economize on his time. We need not object to this; the division of labor is one of the indispensable requisites for human life, but we need not, also, pay much attention to either the scientist or the businessman when they analyze their own activities.

A second reason for some scientists' denying the possibility of truth in their own theories arises from the rather peculiar real situation of those theories. The history of science has been a history of the disproof of theories.[8] Observations have tended to stand the test of time quite well (although even here we make improvements which sometimes disprove rather than improve an earlier observation), but theories seem not to last. As a result of this experience, scientists are trained to be skeptical of their theories.[9] They are thought of as hypotheses, always living in the shadow of potential disproof. Every scientist must keep continually in the back of his mind the possibility that the theory on which he is currently working may simply be wrong. But if this is true of generally accepted theories, new theories are subject to even more suspicion. Until a theory has been in existence for some time and has been subject to considerable testing, the scientist can have little real confidence in its validity. Nevertheless, frequently the most fruitful line of search open to a man interested in a given field is to apply a new, and hence dubious, theory. Under these circumstances, it is clear that scientists can have little psychological confidence in their theories and that the development of a "theory of theories" which simply denies the validity of theories as anything other than a simplified set of observations is not an unexpected result.

The hollowness of this "theory of theories," however, can be readily seen if we consider the situation when a new theory is proposed. If neither the new or the old theory which it purports to replace represents any deeper truth, why should we choose one over the other? The conventional answer is that we choose the simpler. When, however, this explanation is used to explain the demolition of the Newtonian system by Einstein, it is clear that the

8. "The new . . . does not rise on the back of the old; the two are incompatible and incommensurable; and transfer of allegiance means working in a new world." "What Are Scientists Made Of?" *Times Literary Supplement,* October 25, 1963, p. 850.

9. The discovery that the "noble gasses" could combine, first reported in the October 12, 1962, issue of *Science* (p. 136), was a particularly striking example of the insecurity of present knowledge. In the lead editorial, Philip H. Abelson pointed out that "For perhaps 15 years, at least a million scientists all over the world have been blind to a potential opportunity to make this important discovery. All that was required . . . was a few hours of effort and a germ of skepticism."

word "simple" must have some meaning in this context other than its dictionary definition. By almost no stretch of the imagination can the Theory of Relativity be considered simpler than Newton's system.[10]

The scientists' acceptance of the Einsteinian approach as "simpler," however, can be justified if "simple" is given some other meaning than it bears in common speech (or that intended by Occam when he propounded his famous "razor"). If in this context "simple" means something else than it does in ordinary speech, then it would appear that anyone using it to justify the choice of one theory over another should tell us what he means by the word. He should also tell us why "simplicity" in this special sense is desirable. A theory which is simple in the normal meaning of the word clearly has some advantages over one which is complex, although whether this is a decisive advantage is a question to be determined in each case by considering other matters, too. If "simplicity" is assigned some other meaning, however, then we may ask whether this other "simplicity" is desirable. No decision on this matter can be reached, however, until we have an explanation of what "simplicity" means in this context.

It has been suggested by Michael Polanyi that what is really meant by the scientist when he says that one theory is simpler than another is that he feels it is closer to the truth.[11] According to this view, the scientist is behaving like a businessman who explains that his prices are determined by adding a percentage mark-up to the cost. In both cases, the man is producing an erroneous rationalization for his own behavior, but his behavior is, in fact, highly rational. If Polanyi is correct, and I believe he is, then the scientists are not searching for something obscure which they choose to denominate by the word "simplicity" but are searching for truth.

The theory that scientists are in search of truth raises certain logical problems. One such which I regard as false has to do with the definition of "truth."[12] I do not believe that anyone really has any difficulty understanding

10. Clearly the simplest way to explain the experimental results reported by Dr. Rhine and his followers is to accept ESP as a fact. Most scientists, however, have insisted on much more complex explanations involving allegations of various complex experimental errors on the part of Dr. Rhine. For a survey of the viewpoint held by most scientists, see Waldemar Kaempffert's "Science in Review" column in the *New York Times* for July 22, 1956, sec. E, p. 9.

11. This is one of the major themes of Michael Polanyi's *Personal Knowledge*.

12. J. Agassi's review article "A Hegelian View of Complementarity," *British Journal for the Philosophy of Science*, 9, No. 33 (1958), 57–63 discusses a particular variant of the problem, the

what this word means, and I think that people who appear to have such difficulty are actually worried about other problems, particularly whether there is any real thing which corresponds to the concept and how we recognize truth. Both of these are real problems and worth discussing briefly. We may begin with the problem of whether science can hope to reach any real truth about the universe.[13]

We have seen that most theories now in use are regarded by scientists as of dubious validity, and we cannot, therefore, allege that they are true with any high degree of confidence that our own statement is true. But the view that present theories are to be viewed with skepticism does not necessarily imply that *all* are untrue. Mathematical propositions, to take an extreme case, are normally accepted as being really true. It is possible that some proofs and demonstrations will be found to be flawed in the future, but the bulk of mathematics will stand up to future critics as well as Euclid has stood up to his critics in the last two thousand years. Theories about the real world are obviously more subject to suspicion. Most of the theories propounded by the Greeks have been discarded. Some, however, have been retained. The theory of the lever remains as the Greeks left it, and a few other examples could be found. The theory of the lever may, of course, be disproved tomorrow, but the fact that it has withstood two thousand years of critical examination, much of it using tools which the Greeks could not even dream of, does raise some presumption that here we have a bit of theory which is absolutely true. It seems likely that somewhere in our present vast collection of theories there are others which are, in fact, true, that is, which will not be disproved at any time in the future. It is, of course, impossible to say which they are.

We must be skeptical about each theory, but this does not mean that we must be skeptical about the existence of truth. In fact, our skepticism is an illustration of our belief in truth. We doubt that our present theories are in fact true, and look for other theories which approach that goal more closely. Only if one believes in an objective truth will experimental evidence contrary to the predictions "disprove" the theory. We are skeptical of our present theories

---

statement that "truth is relative," and demonstrates the impossibility of producing a consistent explanation on this ground.

13. In a personal letter dated July 25, 1956, on scientific philosophy, Waldemar Kaempffert, science editor of the *New York Times,* expressed the then fashionable skepticism in an extreme form. "We must not forget that the universe is a hypothesis. . . . There is no certainty; hence there can be no approach of reality."

because we suspect they do not coincide with the truth. The progress of science consists of developing ever newer theories which approach ever closer to the truth. For the logical reasons we discussed earlier, we can never really be sure that the truth is there, but we have no choice but to act as if it is. Further, the success of our theories in predicting new observations is evidence, albeit not conclusive evidence, that they do have some relation to reality; and steady improvement in this respect can be taken as indicating that they are continually getting closer.

The second problem connected with our position that science is based on a belief in the existence of a real universe susceptible to human understanding and knowledge concerns the test of the truth of any given proposition. The logical problems connected with this question have been exhaustively discussed by various philosophers; Karl Popper's *The Logic of Scientific Discovery*[14] may be taken as a summation of the present position. We need not, therefore, go into these problems, but it is necessary to discuss two possible "tests of truth": "workability" and "consensus of the informed." Before discussing the workability test, we must devote some time to the subjects investigated by applied science, for this test is closely connected with the practical use of science.

If pure science seeks truth, applied science seeks useful information. The difference may be seen most clearly by noticing how often engineering magazines run articles discussing ways of approximating various functions. Serious research is put into developing formulas which, although known to be wrong, are simple and give results approximating the correct result. Frequently an engineer, in undertaking a particular piece of research preliminary to designing some useful device, will be able to choose among three or four formulas, all of which approximate the correct formula with varying degrees of fit under various conditions and which are of different degrees of difficulty.

Nevertheless, note that these "theories" are referred to as approximations. Although they work very well and are simpler than the "true" theory, even the practical man who uses them agrees that they are incorrect. The situation may be considered as analogical to the following figure. The numbered points indicate observations; the small letters minor theories which bind together these observations into a coherent system; and the over-theory *X* connects these minor theories into a rational whole. Reversing our explanation, from *X, a, b,* and *c* may be deduced; from *a,* 11, 12, and 13 follow. Note, however,

14. New York: Basic Books, 1959.

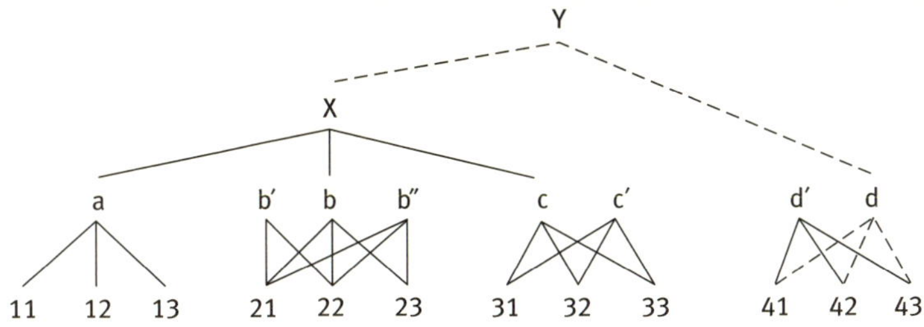

that there are other alternate minor theories available. Anyone interested only in 31, 32, and 33 could also use *c′*. If it was simpler, the applied scientist (or even the pure scientist) would have no hesitancy in so using it.[15] Similarly in the 20 area, a scientist has his choice between theories *b* and *b″*, which cover the whole area, and *b′*, which covers only part of it. For practical purposes, he chooses the most convenient.[16]

From the standpoint of the applied scientist, this raises no particular problem. He chooses the "theory" which works best in his individual problem, but note the theoretical situation. A number of theories fit each given set of facts, and for practical purposes they may be interchangeable.[17] Workability, then, cannot be a decisive criterion in determining the correct theory. Nevertheless, the applied scientist using theory *b′* for some practical purpose will be perfectly willing to agree that theory *b* is better. He will refer to *b′* as an approximation, but in this meaning "approximation" is a little different from its ordinary usage. Scientific experiments are frequently difficult, and a certain vagueness in result is normal. Graphically, the results, instead of falling on a simple curve, vary around a sort of zone. Under the circumstances several equations are likely to be about equally good fits. Normally, in fact, a scientist in possession of a computer can get the best fit by instructing the

15. See W. Ross Ashby, *Design for a Brain* (2nd ed.; New York: Wiley, 1960), pp. 17–19, for an excellent example.

16. "The general point then, is that even when it is possible to formulate a physical problem in exact mathematical language it is often practical for an engineer or scientist to neglect some terms in the mathematical formulation in order to expedite the solution. The mathematician would not make this simplification and would persist in attempting to solve the original problem even if he had to hand the problem on to successive generations of mathematicians." Morris Kline, *Mathematics and the Physical World* (New York: Crowell, 1959), pp. 62–63. This attitude is characteristic of all pure scientists, not just mathematicians.

17. In some cases, there may be only one theory available, *a* on our diagram, for example, and this may be interconnected with the higher-level theory *X*.

machine to use one equation on one part of the data and another elsewhere. Applied scientists frequently do just that. Thus the "true" theory, to which the others "approximate," may (or may not, of course) actually deviate from the measured data more than the "approximation." What the scientist means, in this case, is that b' cannot be deduced from X while b can. He therefore believes b to be correct and b' incorrect regardless of the question of which fits the actual data (within limits) more closely.

The same attitude can be seen more clearly in those not uncommon situations in which a series of experiments have produced some data which an applied scientist needs, but which cannot be deduced from any existing over-theory. Under these circumstances, shown at the right of our diagram, the applied scientist may use an equation d' in his work, but refer to it as an approximation in spite of the fact that there is nothing for it to approximate. In essence, he is assuming that it is incorrect in spite of its agreement with his observations because it does not fit into the general theoretical picture. He believes that another theory, d, will eventually be invented which fits the data in the 40's and which can be connected to the over-theory X or, as in our diagram, to a new and higher over-theory Y. This belief is obviously not empirically based and can be considered either as an act of faith or as based on the same general picture of the universe held by the pure scientist.

The pure scientists sometimes do the same thing. Gregor Mendel introduced the "genes" into his theory of heredity not because he believed that they existed, but because he thought they made it easy to understand the data. They served much the purpose of d' in Figure 2. In this case Mendel, who was right in so much else, turned out to be wrong. The genes do exist, although it took almost forty years for the biologists to realize this.

The applied scientist agrees with the pure scientist that it is impossible to reach the truth and that the great general theories represent a closer approach to that truth than the small theories which bind together small parts of experience. With regard to the small theories, he uses them more or less regardless of their relation to the grand theories and with heavy emphasis on their simplicity. The grand theories may well have no close relation to practical work. The minor theories deduced from them may, of course, but these are not really dependent on the higher theories. Practical engineers have gone on using the Newtonian mechanics for fifty years now in spite of its destruction by Einstein. They are not perturbed by the lack of any formally worked out relationship between the minor theories they use, which work well, and the new mechanics.

This is not said in a spirit of criticism. Both applied and pure science have important roles to play in our struggle to improve our position. The roles are, however, different. The applied scientist is mostly interested in minor theories covering the small segments of reality in which he is operating. The pure scientist is interested in the grand amalgamations which bind all of these little theories together. This difference arises naturally from their different basic motives, but the two tasks supplement rather than contradict each other. The applied scientist will attempt to deduce minor theories with practical applications from the grand synthesis of the pure scientist, and this is a valuable check on the accuracy of the theories. Similarly, the numerous minor theories developed by the applied scientist provide data and stimulation for the theorist. Thus "workability" is a necessary, but not a sufficient, condition for a valid theory.

Turning now to methods of recognizing the truth, the consensus of the informed is often urged as decisive. This is a natural result of the fact that men are not infinitely capable. We can hardly hope to investigate more than a very small part of reality ourselves and therefore must rely on the division of labor for the bulk of our information about the universe. In areas where we have not taken the trouble to become good judges ourselves, we must, of necessity, accept someone else's judgment. Naturally, we should try to select the best authorities for our information about the area which we do not intend to investigate ourselves, but we should keep in mind that the experts have often been wrong.[18] But let us inquire how the "informed" themselves judge the truth or falsity of a position. Clearly, they cannot base their judgment on their own position, which is what consensus of the informed would mean in this situation. They must, then, have some other, superior, method of determining the truth, and this method is simply themselves investigating and reaching personal judgments on the truth of the matter. An intelligent outsider who has the time and interest in the problem should investigate, himself, since only in this way can he reach the level of certainty of the experts themselves. Personal knowledge is always superior to hearsay, and, paradoxically, the fact that we seek out the best experts in each field for information is itself proof that we consider it to be so.

To elaborate further, it is safe to assume that each investigator would like information (whether his basic motive is curiosity or the desire to make use

18. They are sometimes also very badly biased. See Walter Hall Wheeler, "The Unitatheres and the Cope-Marsh War," *Science*, 131 (April 22, 1960), 1171–76.

of the information in a practical way is irrelevant here) on a vast number of matters. We can arrange this desired information in an array so that the most desired information is at the top and the least desired is at the bottom. This would roughly represent the proportionate amount of effort he would be willing to put into a search for each type of information. To this schedule we must attach a second which shows the individual's view of the difficulty of obtaining each bit of information. From this schedule, if it were at all realistic, it would be immediately obvious that any individual in his lifetime could investigate only a comparatively few problems. Further, leaving aside mathematics, obtaining absolute certainty would probably be outside the real possibilities even if a full lifetime were devoted to the task.

Returning to our earlier discussion of general and particular curiosity (the same point can be made for applied science), a man has a general curiosity in a certain area; as a result of this curiosity and his estimate of the difficulties of investigation, he develops a particular curiosity in some given subarea and undertakes an investigation. This is unlikely to lead to theories which are absolutely true in our present state of knowledge, but normally at least some improvement will result. The improved knowledge in this area changes the schedule of priorities for the remaining problems and also changes the estimates of difficulty (it will possibly also add some new problems to the schedule). On the basis of this new schedule, the investigator now turns to another problem, which may, of course, be a development of his previous one.

So far, however, we have described the behavior of an investigator dealing with problems near the top of his priority schedule.[19] Only a few problems, even only a few of the problems relative to his particular research, are within the scope of the possible investigation of one man. He must therefore depend on others for much information.[20] As we work down the priority schedule, we proceed from information which the investigator ranks high enough to determine for himself to information that he is willing to take on trust. This latter field, however, is also ranked. Here the relevant criteria are the impor-

19. It should be noted that the difference between a scientist and a non-scientist is largely the relative position of the desire to know, i.e., our priority schedule for investigation compared with other desires. The man who puts great weight on such things will likely become an investigator. The man who puts relatively little emphasis on obtaining further information will turn to other lines of endeavor.

20. This reliance must, of course, be based on the assumption that the others upon whom he depends are in fact themselves doing research and not simply relying on still others.

tance of the information to the investigator and the ease of obtaining someone else's findings. Here again, the investigator will economize on the effort he puts into obtaining different types of information. In some areas he will read numerous reports and carefully judge their merits. In others he will simply consult a single "standard authority." And in the ultimate case, he simply accepts what information happens to come his way without effort or verification on his part.

All of this is a fairly good description of how scientists really act. The fact that such a description can be derived from our basic postulates is evidence that they are true. The similarity to economics is, of course, very strong. In both, men are treated as attempting to reach desired ends with limited means. Thus science has a relation to economics above and beyond the trite observation that it must be paid for and is one kind of economic activity.

We are now in a position to discuss the methods actually used by scientists in deciding which theory is to be provisionally accepted. Out of the infinite universe of possible theories, those which clearly conflict with the evidence are first ruled out. This is simply requiring that the theory fit the real world. Unfortunately sometimes no theory has been invented which does not conflict with at least some data. In such cases a judgment must be made as to which existing theory is closest to the real world. If a number of theories which fit the real-world data are now available—and this also will frequently be the case—the one (or several) of the higher order of generality will be selected. If we still have more than one theory, we will choose the simplest. Thus simplicity returns to our picture of the behavior of scientists, but in the ordinary, everyday meaning of the word. Further, simplicity appears in subordination to resistance to disproof and generality.

This pattern of behavior can be most readily explained by a belief on the part of the scientist that the universe is logically ordered, and that both the nature of the universe and its order are comprehensible to the human mind. Scientific progress thus would approach, although not necessarily reach or even get very close to, a single grand theory explaining everything in the universe. In the late nineteenth century this ideal was actually held by most scientists, who thought of each theoretical or experimental advance as bringing us closer to the distant goal. Now, in the latter half of the twentieth century, few scientists consciously think of their work in these cosmic terms, but their behavior patterns still match those of the earlier investigators.

In addition to pure curiosity and the desire to make practical use of new discoveries, there is another reason for undertaking research, which we have denominated "induced curiosity." An investigator wholly motivated[21] by induced curiosity is different in many ways from one motivated by either curiosity or a desire to make practical application of new knowledge. In the first place, from the standpoint of the man whose curiosity is induced, scientific concern with the real world is secondary to other matters. If he could establish and maintain his reputation, and hence his job, by reporting completely fictional discoveries, this would accomplish his end. While an investigator motivated by curiosity or practical utility must, of necessity, concern himself with real phenomena, the man motivated by induced curiosity could, if the risk of discovery were not great, simply ignore reality.

This, of course, presents a problem for those administering a system of induced research. They must make certain that the investigators are induced into research. They must make certain that the investigators are induced to pay attention to the real world. As we have seen, the actual system used by administrators in our present setup is simply to count the number of papers published by a man in journals of various degrees of reputation. The reputation of the journals, again as we have seen, is determined by their readers. Now, a man motivated by induced curiosity reads a journal not because he is interested in the facts reported, but because he hopes to find a suggestion for work of his own. It will be seen that a self-perpetuating process might be set in motion in which a journal read only by people motivated by induced curiosity gradually slipped away from reality in the direction of superficially impressive but actually easy research projects.

In most sciences this does not happen, and we may profitably consider why. First, journals are normally read by applied scientists as well as by pure scientists. The applied scientists are apt to seize on any idea and try to make some use of it. If the failure of their application to work leads them to doubt the original research, they may protest strenuously. On a lower level, the applied scientists are likely to be mostly interested in articles which promise some real advance in the area in which they work. They are normally under considerable economic pressure to confine their reading to things which might lead to practical advances. They are therefore less likely to be interested

21. It is probably worth repeating that human motivation is usually complex and that people with a single motivation are probably uncommon. We can, however, discuss the effects of some single motivation and draw conclusions as to the effect it may have on the behavior of a man who also has other motivations.

in ideas and formulas for purely aesthetic reasons and more interested in reality than are less practical people.

The curiosity-motivated investigators also are a major hazard to any man who is simply trying to make money through having articles published and who would rather not do the research. The barriers to false research would thus appear to be high, and a man whose only motive for research is induced curiosity is usually held to fairly high standards. We can, however, see certain conditions which might conduce to a sharp reduction of the quality of induced research. The first of these conditions would be a lack of likely practical applications for research in a given field. If people whose sole objective is to find something out of which they can make money are not likely even to read the journals, then the investigators in that field are subject to much less pressure.

Further, if the field is one in which there are vastly more people (as a result of the necessity of staffing teaching posts in each field according to the number of students) than would appear justified by the likelihood of making discoveries of any significance, then there will be more pressure to make false discoveries or to present trivial discoveries as major. This kind of situation is one in which all of the people in the field are apt to be looking primarily for an opportunity to do something which can be made to look like research, and the reputation of journals is consequently likely to be dependent on the aid they give in this endeavor. One symptom of the existence of this condition is the development of very complex methods of treating subjects which can be readily handled by simple methods. Calculus will be used where simple arithmetic would do, and topology will be introduced in place of plane geometry. In many fields of social science these symptoms have appeared.

The people really interested in the truth could, of course, prevent this development if they were present in sufficient numbers. If, however, they are a small minority in any given branch of investigation, then they are not likely to be able to set the tone of investigation. In areas where the number of teaching positions is vastly greater than the apparent likelihood of discovery, people who are simply curious tend to be a small minority, since they are generally attracted to areas where discoveries in the real sense are likely. It also seems probable that people who are genuinely curious are apt to have higher IQ's than those who are only induced (and by comparatively small salaries in the present-day United States) into research. Those areas of research which tend to have lower average intelligence among their workers also should be suspected of having relatively few persons who are genuine pure scientists.

Lastly, in an area where motives other than seeking the truth are important, the induced researcher is unlikely to be held to a high standard. If it is widely believed that the function of the researcher in a given field is to uphold some special point of view or if it is doubted whether anything approximating "truth" is really existent in a given field, then the standards to which an induced researcher must conform may be deplorably low. Simply presenting a rationalization for some position chosen on other grounds may be acceptable as an objective of research, and the principal criterion in judging journals may become their points of view. The concern with reality which unites the sciences, then, may be absent in this area, and the whole thing may be reduced to a pseudo-science like genetics in Lysenko's Russia. Again, these symptoms may be found in some of the social sciences.

So far, I have discussed science and inquiry as though they were the same thing. In one of the general uses of inquiry, this is true, but in other meanings of this term they are different. Investigations may be started which are not motivated by either curiosity about reality or the desire to make practical use of knowledge of the real world, but by some other motive. A lawyer building up a brief for his client, for example, may be much more intelligent, more learned, and more ingenious in his research methods than most scientists, but his investigation is not scientific, because he is not searching for the truth. He looks for an argument, based on factual information to be sure, which he thinks will persuade. Whether it is true or not is not of his concern. In fact, in the Anglo-Saxon adversary type of legal proceedings, he is prohibited from expressing his personal opinion on this point in court.

Consider, for another example, an advertising man trying to produce copy which will sell toothpaste. The higher ranking advertising copywriters, certainly highly intelligent and ingenious men, devote large amounts of time and effort to the search for good slogans, but this again is not a search for truth. Truth-seeking, however, may be found even here. If we have several slogans, none of which, shall we say, is true, the question of which of these will convince the most people is subject to investigation which aims at obtaining a truth (i.e., which of these false statements will sell the most toothpaste).

Even if we limit ourselves to investigations aimed at reaching the truth or at least an approximation of it, it is obvious that many such investigations would not normally be called scientific. A jealous husband who hires detectives to determine whether his wife is adulterous is engaging in an investigation aimed at reaching the truth, but this is hardly part of science. Popular usage, however, is of little help in distinguishing between scientific and non-scientific fields. Archaeology, for example, is considered a perfectly respectable science, while history normally is not. Since the difference between archaeology and history is precisely that we have better information in historical fields,[22] it would appear that the popular definitions are unclear.

Left to myself, I should like to define science in such a way that only fields in which fairly elaborate theoretical structures have been developed, like physics or economics, would be included. Other areas, like biology (minus genetics and a few other specialties), would not be called sciences, because they have not yet attained the theoretical stage.[23] This, however, would be a sharp deviation from customary usage, and I will, accordingly, confine myself to distinguishing between two types of science, the theoretical and the empirical. Since both of these words are "plus" words, I hope that scientists in the two categories will not object.

It must be pointed out that the distinction is one of degree, although most disciplines are mainly in one category or the other. Even mathematics in practice concerns itself to some extent with the real world. Recently, in fact, a sort of experimental method has been introduced under which various problems, such as commensal work, are tried out on computers instead of solved in the conventional manner. At the other extreme, even a biologist engaged solely in collecting specimens in a previously unsurveyed area does have some theories and hypotheses. The difference between a "theoretical" science like physics and an "empirical" science like most botany is a difference in emphasis. It is also, probably, a difference in stage of development. The "theoretical" sciences can, I think, justly claim to be more highly developed than the "empirical" ones. We can hope that the future will bring general theories into the presently empirical areas.

Although we now have a principle for distinguishing between two kinds of science, we are still lacking one for distinguishing between science and other types of inquiry. It is rather widely held that the difference is one of

22. A common distinction holds that the presence of written records is the difference between history and archaeology.

23. Evolution is sometimes considered as a "theory of biology." That evolution is one of the grand theories can hardly be denied, but in the present state of knowledge, it is impossible to connect most biological information with this great theory. There is an almost complete absence of the chain of minor theories which should connect the grand theory with the individual observations. In the circumstances, the existence of this particular grand theory has little effect on the concrete research of individual biologists. See Anthony Standen, *Science Is a Sacred Cow* (New York: Dutton, 1950).

"method," but this seems unlikely. There is no evidence that the brains of scientists work differently from those of other men. So far as we can see, the primitive caveman had as good mental equipment as the modern man, and some of the cavemen certainly had the inherent equipment to become Nobel prize laureates. Not all of the most intelligent men of modern days are engaged in science, and there is no particular reason to suppose that highly intelligent men engaged in investigating some matter without the scope of science would refrain, either from ignorance or desire, from using any technique of investigation known to the scientists. It would appear, then, that there must be something special about the situation in which the scientist finds himself which resembles other, non-scientific structures.

Our language, at this point, has a false implication. The place where a scientist works is generally called a laboratory and his work research, regardless of what he is doing. Since the word is the same, a feeling that the work is also somehow the same has developed. Actually this is quite untrue. Scientists carry on the most diverse activities. Probably the category of "all things done in laboratories" is larger than the category of "all things done in structures which are not laboratories." Certainly, the two classes are of the same order of magnitude. Laboratories where radically different problems are being studied will normally resemble each other no more than they resemble other, non-scientific structures.

Similarly, "research activities" is very likely a wider category of action than "non-research activities." There is a sort of order and tendency to repeat in non-scientific activities, but the active and ingenious scientist is always thinking up some completely new approach to a problem which has never been tried anywhere else. The view that the nature of the activity engaged in is the defining characteristic of science is a fairly widely held one, but is clearly wrong. It is perfectly possible for two men, one a scientist and the other not, to do exactly the same things, but the scientist will still be doing scientific work while the layman will not.

But if science is not distinguished from other activities by the methods it uses or by the fact that it seeks the truth, what does so distinguish it? There are, I think, two answers to this question. The first, which is a little doubtful, is that the scientist seeks *general* truth.[24] He is not interested in the truth or falsity of a proposition about some specific person, place, or thing, but of

24. The point is particularly well made by H. C. Loguet-Higgins, "Portrait of the Scientist as Artist," *Times Literary Supplement,* October 25, 1963, p. 856.

more general propositions. The biologist is basically uninterested in the particular monkey he is studying; what he is trying to unveil are general "facts" which are true of all monkeys (or, all male rhesus monkeys one year of age who have been infected with a certain virus). Even when he concerns himself with individual variations, he will turn out to be interested in general measures of the range of variation to be expected in the species, not in some specific individual.[25]

A close look at what scientists actually do, however, indicates that while they are normally interested only in general truth, they will sometimes be concerned with particular truth. If we accept archaeology as a science, it is almost always concerned with the particular rather than the general. Geology, which is clearly a science, is quite frequently concerned with the particular truth of the underlying structure in some specified region. Even the more general sciences like physics and chemistry may occasionally be concerned with singular facts. Recently astronomers and physicists became much interested in the discovery of bright and temporary red spots on the surface of the moon. These were thought to indicate some sort of volcanic activity. Clearly the presence or absence of volcanos on the moon is a particular fact, albeit one of considerable interest. Nevertheless, most scientists, most of the time, are searching for general truth, not specific truth.

The second distinguishing characteristic of science is, in my opinion, the membership of all scientists in the scientific community. It is not anything special about the individual scientist, or his work, which distinguishes him, but the special human environment in which he operates. This environment is, in many ways, most peculiar. A scientist specializing in some narrow field may almost never meet the other members of the community with whom his intellectual contacts are most intimate. His important colleagues may live in other countries, be the products of violently different cultures, and speak no language that he knows. Nevertheless, his activities are controlled and shaped by these others, while the people whom he meets regularly, his family, friends, and colleagues on the local university faculty (if he teaches for a living), have almost no effect on his work.

Consider a scientist interested in a given problem. He may be the only man interested in it anywhere in his geographical neighborhood. There may, of course, be other people also interested in the same problem who live or

25. For an excellent example, see Roger J. Williams, *Biochemical Individuality* (New York: Wiley, 1959).

work near him, but in any event, the vast majority of all the other people interested in this general field will live and work far away. Many of them will be foreigners. Nevertheless, he will depend on information about their previous work in his research, and his work will ultimately be judged and made use of by them. It is this far-flung community which is important to him as a scientist, not the local community in which he works and which has such a dominating influence on his non-scientific activities. The presence of this community distinguishes the scientific from the non-scientific world.

The rest of this book is devoted to a discussion of this community, the organization which controls inquiry, and although I cannot briefly define it, it is possible to point out certain of its characteristics here. In the first place, it is a system of voluntary co-operation. Every individual simply seeks his own ends, but the organization is such that this leads him also to serve the ends of others.[26] As we shall see, the organization is not as precise and elegant as that of the market, but the problems dealt with are even more diffuse than the economic problem of properly distributing scarce resources among innumerable desirable ends.[27] Under the circumstances, it is highly unlikely that a greatly improved system can be developed. It is my hope that scientists with a greater understanding of the community can use it better, and I have appended at the end of this book a few recommendations for minor improvements in the organization of the community, but the present system is clearly an efficient one, and I see no real prospect for major improvements.

It is the existence of the scientific community which distinguishes between science and non-science, and this fact is implicitly relied upon by scientists in judging whether some field of study is or is not "scientific." Thus a physicist is able to realize that Karlgren's reconstruction of the pronunciation of archaic Chinese is "scientific," not because he is able to judge either the correctness of the conclusions or the evidence or the methods used by Karlgren, but because he can see in the work and in its discussion by various other linguists the existence of a scientific community. We here can explain the ap-

26. In *The Origins of Scientific Economics* (New York: Doubleday, 1965), William Letwin shows that the precursors of modern economics were not dispassionate scholars, but very practical men who were mainly engaged in making propaganda for various special points of view. Frequently they were motivated by a prospect of the crassest sort of material gain. The discussion process, however, forced gradually rising standards of information and coherence upon them, and the eventual outcome was a genuine science.

27. To be more precise, it is a special and especially difficult subproblem within that area.

parent riddle that archaeology is a science while history is not. The social studies, of which history is one, have their own communities, but they operate rather differently from those in the sciences. The problem is discussed in detail in Chapter VI, but the difference in the attitude and approach is clear to even the casual observer (and the physical scientists tend to be very casual observers of the social sciences).

I may, perhaps, be permitted to introduce a personal experience to indicate the extent to which this suspicion is carried. Once in conversation with a minor member of the physics fraternity, I happened to mention the law of diminishing returns. He replied, "I don't believe in general laws." When I expressed surprise at such a statement from a physicist, he modified it: "I mean laws like that." The "that" obviously referred to laws in economics, and his expression of distrust had nothing to do with this particular law, but with a general feeling that economists are not to be trusted. It proved quite impossible to shake him at all in argument; in fact, it was clear that he simply was not listening. He knew that my position was "unscientific." He also knew that there were many plausible arguments for various false positions in his field which an amateur could not answer; so he simply assumed I was wrong because I was not a scientist. The situation is particularly ironic because the law of diminishing returns is really a physical law, and the evidence for it is very much stronger than that for most of the laws of physics.

As an introduction to my discussion of the scientists and their functioning in the scientific community, I must say a few words about scientific method in the strict sense. This is really a branch of logic or philosophy, not of the social sciences, but a little background is necessary for the rest of the book.[28] The advance of scientific knowledge involves the accumulation of more data and the development of new theories. The relationship between the facts and the theories is a complex one. Normally, it is easy to demonstrate that a theory is based on facts which were known to its originator and that most of the information that we have was developed as the result of a hypothesis held by the original discoverer. Thus we gain little by asking which came first, the hypothesis or the data. In all relevant cases, a chain of data-hypothesis-data-hypothesis stretches back to our earliest records.

28. Karl Popper's *Logic of Scientific Inquiry* provides the best general statement of the view I hold of scientific method in the strict sense. This is natural since I learned the subject under his guidance. It would be possible, however, to accept either Dr. Popper's position or the position of this book without accepting the other, since they really refer to different aspects of science.

In this chain I have chosen to start with data collection, proceed to formulation of hypotheses, and then turn to data collections; but this is merely a convenient order for exposition. Logically, I could have started with the hypothesis just as readily. My present arrangement puts the hypothesis in the center of the process, which gives it the importance which I think it deserves. It also has the advantage of giving me a separate chapter in which to make one more assault on the problem of induction. Because solution of this problem has escaped investigators since Hume first propounded it, the odds are against success in my attempt, but I can at least try.

In the view of scientific method which I learned from Popper, the method by which we reach our hypothesis is less important than the question of whether the hypothesis is true, and this latter question can be answered only by testing it. Thus the logical problems of scientific method revolve around testing hypotheses, not around how we get them originally. This scheme is, I think, a realistic description of the actual behavior of scientists. It neatly solves as well a host of logical problems raised by "inductive" reasoning. Efforts to prove that we can reach conclusions about general laws by induction from specific instances have always failed. Popper points out that the truth of the general laws depends not on how they were derived but on how they pass tests once they have been invented. The crucial problem of science is not: Was this proposed law derived according to proper procedures, but: Is it true? This question can be most readily answered by testing it.

CHAPTER IV

DATA COLLECTION

That data collection is a major scientific activity and that it leads to formulation of hypotheses will hardly be denied. It is frequently pointed out, however, that most data have been collected as the result of pre-existing hypotheses. This is true, but it does not affect our reasons for treating data collecting separately. With regard to any specific hypothesis, a good deal of data was present in the mind of the inventor when he made it. The sources of the data may not be directly relevant to the new hypothesis. The hypothesis which led to the accumulation of the data on which the new hypothesis is based may be either trivial or irrelevant. For an example of the trivial, we may take the multiplication table, a basic element in much scientific reasoning. It can be said that the scientist has this in his mind because of two hypotheses: a hypothesis on the part of those responsible for his education that it would be useful for him to know how to multiply, and a hypothesis on the part of the young scientist that he would be disciplined if he did not. For an example of the not directly relevant, we may consider information which a scientist obtained as the result of a previous hypothesis unrelated to the new one. For example, he may have switched from one branch of his field to another, but may have found some fact that he discovered in his first field to be of great importance in his new one.

The data which are important to a scientist when he forms a hypothesis are the data which are present in the scientist's mind. We have vast libraries of accumulated facts, but until they get into someone's mind, no hypothesis will be developed therefrom. The collections of facts in the library "only stand and wait."[1] We collect these vast masses of data partly because we think them interesting in themselves, but principally in hopes that someone will use them to develop a general law of some sort. Before this happens the someone must learn of them, i.e., he must get them into his mind. Since the capacity of the human mind is smaller than that of even a rather small

1. They may wait a long time. One of the members of the founding congress of the Chinese Communist party wrote a master's thesis on the early development of the party for Columbia in 1924. Deposited in the Columbia University Library and forgotten, it was not rediscovered until 1960. *New York Times,* October 30, 1960, p. 13.

library,[2] this may seem a hopeless task, but, as we shall see, social co-operation provides a partial solution to the problem.

We shall therefore discuss how information accumulates in the minds of individual human beings. The libraries and indexes will be considered only as aids to this accumulation. We shall also, however, consider the pattern formed by the information-collecting activities of a number of people and try to answer the question of what an optimum organization would be. Throughout we shall think of data collection primarily as a preliminary step to the development of hypotheses, but the data collector may be collecting simply to put his findings in a library somewhere for another to use in framing a hypothesis.

A good deal of the information contained in any human mind is simply the result of accident. Anyone will accumulate lots of facts which are of no real interest to him, but which his memory will retain for some period of time. I know, for example, the general arrangement of furniture in the apartment across the hall from my own although I do not know my neighbors more than by sight. They have a habit of leaving their door open, and I therefore sometimes see into their apartment when leaving my own. This is an extreme example, but that we all have a good deal of information which has come to us through pure accident is obvious. To a scientist, this may be more important than to the ordinary man, since he is apt to accumulate information about his field this way. He sees things in the laboratory, finds his work interrupted by colleagues who insist on boring him by discussing their work, and hears a great deal of gossip. It is quite possible that some bit of information obtained by these accidental means may be of great importance to him.

Far more important, however, is the information picked up through the formal educational process. Preparing people to advance human knowledge is not, of course, the only objective of the educational system. Potential researchers are only a small minority among those receiving educations. It is probably not even among the three or four most important objectives, but it is a purpose of education, and a good deal of the data possessed by the average scientist comes from his education. Strictly speaking, there are two types of education: self-education and formal education. They tend to go on together, but for reasons of simplicity we shall discuss them seriatim. If prepar-

2. Not as small as one might expect, however. John E. Pfeiffer, "How the Mysterious 'Memory Traces' Outperform Microfilm," *National Observer,* May 13, 1963, p. 20.

ing for scientific work is a rather minor part of the educational system, it is not unimportant from the standpoint of the man who eventually does end up as a scientist. We can therefore consider the educational system solely as it affects the potential scientist in his preparation for his work and ignore all the other aspects of the subject. Our discussion may give a rather distorted picture of education as a whole, but will be a useful abstraction from our present standpoint.

We can represent the results of our present method of education on the knowledge of a scientist by the following diagram.

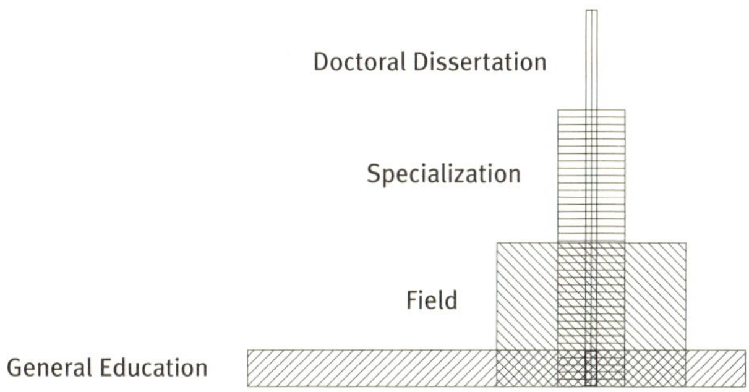

At the bottom we have a smattering of information from many fields, which is called general education. It seems to be the opinion of some educators that this covers *all* of human knowledge, but this is obviously absurd. Many things taught in elementary school in other parts of the world are learned in the United States only by a very few specialists near the end of their education, if at all. This is not, of course, a criticism. If "general education" really tried to cover everything, its coverage of the subjects now included would have to be sharply reduced. Whether the particular combination of subjects now covered in our educational system under this head is ideal, I have no way of telling, but that selection begins at this level is clear.

Students usually also undertake special studies in some given field, say history or physics. Normally, but not always, this field is one to which the student has already been introduced by his general education (as on our diagram). In this field, he becomes much better trained than in the other areas where his education is only general. Normally, also, the student will be expected to specialize in a small section of his field, let us say the feudal period in England or crystallography. In this special field, his education will be pushed even further. Eventually, he will usually write a doctoral dissertation based on research into some problem, and, theoretically, this itself is a contribution to knowledge.[3] These projects tend to be fairly trivial, but they do improve the student's knowledge of one field.

Debate on educational policy is largely confined to discussion of the relative weight to give to the different rectangles on our diagram. Greater specialization, or a better general education, is stressed by various writers, and a better "broad" background in an entire field is frequently advocated. To this dispute I have nothing to contribute. My only point is that increases in one area must be offset by decreases in others. The total areas covered by our rectangles cannot exceed the learning capacity of the student. Any argument for more general education is, at the same time, an argument for less knowledge of the student's particular special field of concentration. Obviously, there will be advantages in both "generalism" and "specialization," but we cannot have both and must make some sort of compromise. To repeat, I have nothing much to say about what compromise is desirable in any one case, but I think that I can say that the compromise should differ radically from student to student.

Let us consider the problem of making scientific advances in the abstract. The new ideas which this advance requires come largely from the brains of men who know some of the facts. These new ideas then stimulate the further research which proves or disproves the ideas and which produces further facts upon which further ideas develop. Consider a situation in which the whole of human knowledge is eight facts: A, B, C, D, E, F, G, and H. A scientist appears with a theory based on A, B, D, and H and suggests that further research be undertaken to discover whether S, hypothesized by the theory, really exists. At this stage, we need not consider this further research, but can simply discuss the formation of the original theory. First, note that although C lies between B and D, it is not included in the theory, while H, at the other end of the spectrum, is. This clearly is no objection to the theory. There may be another theory which includes C and excludes H, but until it is propounded, we will never know.

This is an illustration of the elementary fact that until a new theory is developed, we can never know what field it will cover. If education in the soci-

3. In some cases the work leading to the doctoral dissertation should be classified as self-education, but in many, it should, I think, be listed as part of formal education. Graduate students now frequently undertake dissertation projects not as the result of more or less unguided choice, but by negotiation with various organizations which have funds for research. These negotiations frequently control the subject and general treatment of the research.

ety we are considering had been divided between two specialties, A–D and E–H, then the new theory would never have been proposed, since no one would have simultaneously had facts A, B, D, and H in his mind. In this very simple society, the whole of human knowledge could readily be held in the mind of one man, so this problem would not be likely to be serious, but in real life the total available knowledge is vastly beyond the capacity of one mind. If we cannot tell in advance which combinations of information are the necessary basis for new theories, how can we organize our educational system so as to maximize the production of new theories?

The obvious answer appears to be a system of random assortment. We might aim at having all possible combinations present in the brains of different people. The problem here is mathematical. Assume that the total information available to the human race, stated in its most compact form,[4] would be enough exactly to fill the minds of four people. If we wish to assure that any two bits of information are present in the mind of at least one man, we can follow the process of dividing the total information into eight equal parts and then directing the education of various people so that all possible combinations are present in at least one head. This would require a minimum of twenty-eight people.

Suppose we want to insure that any three bits of information are present in the mind of at least one person. Here again, we can divide the information into twelve equal parts and then direct the education of students so that each of them masters three of these, and all possible combinations are represented. Unfortunately, we find that it would require 220 people to cover all possible combinations. Since the total information available to the human race is vastly greater than could be mastered by four people, probably more than could be mastered by forty thousand, and since our theories are normally suggested by complexes of facts considerably in excess of three, it is obvious that the total number of people necessary to insure that any combination of presently known facts which might lead to a new theory is known to at least one man would be one of those vast numbers which exceed anything in nature and occur only in probability mathematics.

Even if we did have this incredible supply of human beings and could direct their education so that all possible combinations of information were

4. Normally, the most compact form in which data can be presented is a theory covering it. Thus the view that theories are merely convenient ways of writing down our observations has this to be said for it: it is clear that they do serve this purpose, among others.

present, there still would be no assurance that every possible theory would occur to at least one person. The human mind is a chancy thing, and we could hardly take much assurance from the fact that one person was educationally qualified to perceive a given possible interrelation of facts. We would need several thousand such people to feel even modestly secure in the belief that all possible interrelations would be perceived. It seems clear, then, that we cannot hope to distribute the sum of human knowledge in such a way that all possible interrelations are likely to be perceived, and that even a near approximation is out of the question. Our objective must be restricted to making the best of our very limited resources.

The method now in use by the educational system is essentially based on an implicit prediction of the areas in which new discoveries are most likely. Such predictions, like any effort to anticipate the direction and pace of the growth of our knowledge, are extremely difficult. If we could predict with certainty in this field, this would amount to knowing today the things which we predict for tomorrow and, hence, would not involve prediction. In addition to this logical difficulty, the record for such predictions is very bad. Scientists frequently offer predictions of the future based on their view of the probable development of technology, and these predictions are as poor as other predictions of the future. Even in narrow fields major mistakes are made. When penicillin was discovered, the chemists thought they could synthesize it and get it into mass production in about eighteen months. Fortunately, another program to produce it by biological means was put in hand to cover the eighteen-month period. It turned out that the synthesis was vastly harder than anticipated. Even today almost all penicillin in general use is biologically rather than synthetically produced. Research is, by definition, search for the unknown, and we can hardly know in advance what the unknown will turn out to be.

Guesses can be made, however, and our present scientific educational system is implicitly based on such guesses. Let us consider again the system of education outlined above. Only, this time, let us put several different people on our chart.

Each of the nine people, A–I, has received a general education which is identical. A, B, and C have also received identical educations in the first general field; D, E, and F in the second field; and G, H, and I in the third. Each person also has his own specialty.

I have also drawn in three sets of "facts" which might, to the prepared mind, suggest a hypothesis, the set of the X's, the set of the O's, and the set

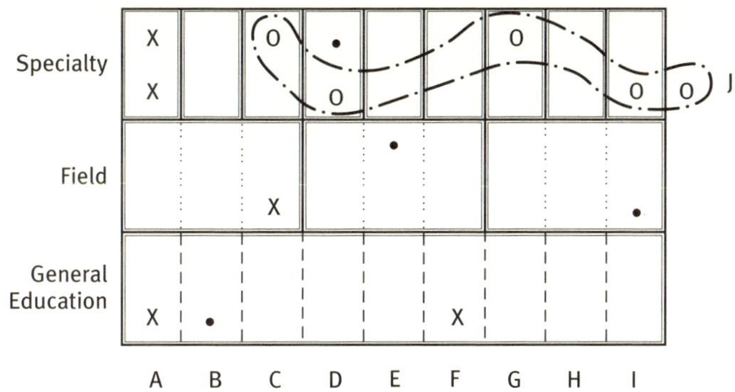

of the dots. Note that scientist A would have all of the information necessary to discover hypothesis X. Part of this information is directly in his specialty, part comes from his general knowledge of his field, and part comes from his rather low-level knowledge of F's field which he got as part of his general education. This type of theory, then, would be likely to be discovered with the educational distribution shown. With the theories which the O's or the dots would suggest, however, this is not so. No single member of the group of scientists has control of all of the facts which would suggest these theories. Education organized in this way, then, would appear to be justified only if it is believed that more theories are of the X kind than of the O or dot kind.

Presumably, most people engaged in administrative planning of scientific work have given the problem little conscious thought. Nevertheless, they do probably reach fairly good results by use of another line of reasoning. The various subjects learned by a student today are grouped partly by categories which are simply historical developments and partly by categories of things which appear to be related. I can suggest no better organization for education, but we should realize that it is far from ideal. Further, even if more theories can be discovered by this organization than by any other, this does not imply that we should confine ourselves to one system.

Unfortunately, we cannot plan to set up educational systems which will bring together in one mind all the facts which will lead to some given hypothesis, because, until the hypothesis is discovered, we do not know what these facts are. A second system of organization of studies crossing the basic one might, however, lead to improved possibilities of discovery. Thus, the person J, following the course of study enclosed by the curved line, might discover hypothesis O. It must be noted, however, that the crossing system of education will necessarily reduce the manpower available for the basic one.[5] Further, for the mathematical reasons given above, we cannot hope to set up an elaborate system which insures complete coverage of all possible hypotheses. Still, classifying knowledge according to two distinct systems for the purpose of educating researchers is very likely to be worthwhile.

This is what our present educational system does. In addition to the budding scientist studying such fields as physics and chemistry and their subdivisions, there are the engineers studying such fields as civil and mechanical engineering and their subsections. These fields cut across the scientific ones. A student preparing to be an automotive engineer, for example, must know something of both organic and inorganic chemistry, metallurgy, gas and liquid dynamics, thermodynamics, electricity, mechanics in the strict sense, and even some human anatomy and psychology. Although he is unlikely to know as much about any one of those fields as a scientist in that field, none of the scientists will know as much as he does about all of the fields and about their interrelations in the design of an automobile.

The *raison d'être* of the two systems can be readily perceived. The scientific disciplines are defined in terms of the traditional fields of knowledge, which are felt to conform somehow to the underlying order of nature. We might say that theoretical unification of each of the scientific fields is thought to be likely, although none has yet achieved this status.[6] In any event, we feel that the division between physics and biology, say, does reflect a basic difference in the nature of the phenomena studied. The scientific fields, then, are unified by hypotheses about the nature of the structure of the universe.

The engineering fields, on the other hand, are defined in terms of utility. Each covers a given type of activity to which knowledge can be applied. The civil engineer learns to build bridges and is not much concerned with the question of whether his rules for required strengths of materials and for avoiding resonance may someday prove to be deducible from some single theory. He may select ideas from the most diverse fields of knowledge, if they permit him to make something useful. Engineering fields are thus defined by the type of knowledge which has been used in some type of practical activity.

The difference between the two approaches may serve to point out the difference between the hypotheses of "pure" science and those of applied science. The pure scientist searches for some way of integrating knowledge into

5. The terms "basic" and "crossing" are arbitrary. There is no reason to believe that one is more basic than the other.

6. Physics almost reached it in the last part of the nineteenth century.

a larger whole which will explain some given area. The applied scientist searches for some way of integrating knowledge which will permit the construction of some "device." The underlying unit of the universe is sought in one case, in the other, a completely different type of unity. In the case of the pure scientist the unity sought is a pre-existing natural unity. In the case of the applied scientist it is a deliberately contrived unity in which diverse things are brought together to serve some end. One type of unity may be represented by the Newtonian mechanics and the other by a diesel engine.

Our educational system, by producing researchers from two different sets of schools, the schools of science and the schools of engineering, thus makes sure that two different systems of classification will be used in deciding what knowledge is held in the brains of the different investigators. This may result in more hypotheses being susceptible to discovery than would a system using one or three classifications. On our graph, however, one theory, the one of the dots, remains undiscoverable because no individual has the necessary knowledge in his mind. This may, of course, be much the most important hypothesis of the three. We can do nothing about this, because, in order to put the necessary knowledge in the mind of an investigator, we would first have to know what knowledge was needed, and this can be discovered only after we have the hypothesis. All of our present classification systems operate as implicit predictions of the knowledge which will, in the future, inspire hypotheses, but they are based on history. Extrapolations into the future are notoriously dangerous, but it is hard to see how major improvements can be made.

One change might be attempted in the organization of our scientific education.[7] The concentration of students in the regularly defined fields which have led to discoveries in the past is clearly rational, but the present organzation of our teaching system probably raises this concentration above the desirable level. Analogically, we may say that our present scheme follows line A instead of the proper line B (as shown in the following diagram). While it is sensible to have the bulk of our students working on the particular combina-

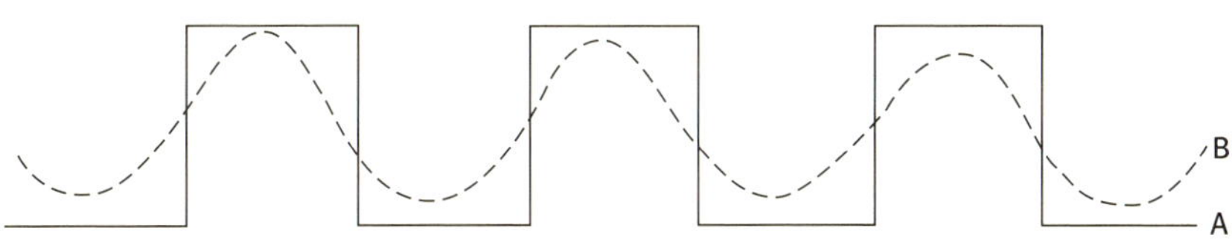

7. The same improvement might be made in engineering training, but the engineering schools approach the ideal in this respect much more closely than the scientific ones.

tions of information which make up the traditional fields of science and their subdivisions, it would be desirable to have some pursuing differently organized knowledge. To take an extreme case, we probably have no man in the world who has devoted half of his time to nuclear physics and half to marine biology. I doubt if it would be wise to develop any sizable education system to produce such men, but I think one such man might be worthwhile.

The problem, of course, is the faculty organization of most universities. A student is normally required to choose a department and frequently a subdivision within that; and a good deal of pressure, sometimes quite unconscious pressure, is put on him to take a standard set of courses. Similarly, universities in hiring staff look for people who are qualified for certain departments. There are few appointments for men who do not really fit into any one of the departments. Since this system seems to work well for the bulk of scientific research, the problem is to provide for another system for a minority of our scientists. This could probably be done if a fraction of the universities, say 10 per cent, emphasized interdepartmental work on both the student and faculty levels. The danger would be that our practice of following educational fads and fashions, combined with the strong tendency to conform, would lead to either a too large or a too small number of "interdisciplinary" scientists.

Turning now to the self-education of the scientists, we should once again note that the distinction between formal education and self-education is a hazy one. Further, the distinction between self-education and regular research is even vaguer. Nevertheless, we can usefully devote some attention to this rather vaguely defined field. Its importance is obvious to anyone who looks at all carefully into the biographies of major scientists.[8] In a surprising number of cases their most important work was not even in the same specialized field as their formal education, and, in the overwhelming majority of cases, their discoveries arose as a result of information obtained after they left their universities. The tendency to do work outside the field of training appears to be particularly strong in the applied fields and with those pure scientists who are actually motivated by curiosity. The scientists induced to be curious are more likely to stick to their original speciality.

The reasons for the importance of self-education are, of course, quite ob-

8. Michael Faraday, one of the greatest scientists of the nineteenth century, was an extreme example. The son of a blacksmith, he was apprenticed to a bookbinder and read the books sent to be bound. L. Pearce Williams, *Michael Faraday* (London: Chapman and Hall, 1965).

vious. In the first place, knowledge tends to get out of date. A distinguished chemist has just retired from my university. Most of his recent research has involved radioactive tagging of chemicals. When he published his first article, in 1911, this technique was not even dreamed of. Even if the student leaves school with the very latest information, shortly he will find his school-taught education sadly deficient. It is probable that the simple process of keeping up with developments by itself will result in the average scientist ten years out of school having more self-taught information than school-taught. The scientist who fails to keep up will probably make no significant discoveries; the ones who do make discoveries are likely to have a large part of their knowledge as the result of self-education.

This is by no means the only reason for the importance of self-education in the development of scientists. It is the self-education of a scientist which differentiates him from the other scientists. His value comes largely from the fact that the particular combination of information which he has mastered is different from that held by any other scientist. Obviously, this kind of information could not come from a formal education. In fact, the process of self-education followed by most scientists is at the same time more specialized and more general than any formal educational system. The pattern of reading he will follow will be unique in the sense that no other individual is doing exactly the same. On the other hand, it will not be as bound by the formal division of science into fields and specialties as is the educational process.[9] Since the self-education of the scientist is more carefully fitted to his personal interests than the formal education he has received, it is likely to play a larger role in his work than does his formal education.

The difference between the significance of self-obtained information and formally taught material to most scientists, particularly the greatest, is so large that we may even question whether the importance of a scientific education lies in the subjects actually taught or in the habits and contacts formed in the schools. The student leaves his university with a good deal of factual and theoretical information, but it may be that other things are really more important. He has a formal entreé, a sort of union card, which permits him

9. This is less true of the scientists motivated by induced curiosity than of those motivated by practical considerations or plain curiosity. The "induced" investigator may, in fact, simply read everything he can in some narrow field defined in strictly formal terms. This is a rather good test to find out the real motives of a university-employed pure scientist. Those who stick very closely to some formally defined field of study will normally be "induced."

to get a scientific job. Not least important, he has a web of contacts with other people who are obligated by the current scholastic ethic to assist him in getting a scientific job but not any other kind of job. He is convinced, partly as a result of his original choice of profession, partly as a result of his great commitment of time which he does not want to waste, and partly because of his associations during his education, that he is a scientist and that the rest of his life will be devoted to investigation. He has probably also been convinced by the process of indoctrination carried on in most scientific educational institutions that science is a high and noble profession (I do not quarrel with this appraisal; I only say there are other high and noble professions) and that its practitioners are somehow superior to other men.[10] Once he has become a practicing scientist, he will educate himself to a very great degree.

The self-education of a scientist turns largely on three sets of institutions: the learned periodicals, scientific publications which are not periodical, and conventions.[11] We shall take them up in turn, starting with the learned periodicals, but first we must briefly discuss two less important channels of information, the non-scientific press and gossip, which are important as fast, albeit inaccurate, channels of information. Important scientific developments not infrequently get on the front page of the *New York Times,* and this insures them wide circulation. Recently the regular scientific journals, particularly in physics, have become annoyed at being "scooped" and have been putting considerable pressure on scientists to give them the "first publication." In some cases this pressure has gone to the extreme of threatening to deny publication to any work which has previously appeared in the press. While the jealousy of the editors of the scientific journals is perfectly understandable, it is unlikely that they will be able to censor the press successfully.

Gossip is usually faster than the popular press in transmitting new discov-

10. Possibly I overemphasized the importance of these non-content aspects of a scientific training because my own training was in the law. The most important things a lawyer needs to know are not taught in law school, and most of the things taught in law school are of little use to a practicing lawyer. See Jerome Frank, *Courts on Trial* (Princeton: Princeton University Press, 1949), particularly chap. xvi, pp. 225–46. The principal reasons for law school graduates' going into law, then, are those I have listed which have no connection with the content of the courses. While these extracontent aspects of the educational system are undoubtedly important in other fields, possibly my own experience leads me to overemphasize them.

11. Some scientists have been experimenting with a radically different method in which the distribution of "reprints" is the major factor. See Seymour S. Cohen's letter, "Reprints Again," in *Science,* 148 (May 28, 1965), 1173.

eries around the scientific community, and even more inaccurate. It should be emphasized, however, that gossip more often takes the form of a letter than a face-to-face conversation. Scientists are highly dispersed, and their communication is likely to be, even today, largely through the written rather than the spoken word. They do write each other, however, and they frequently pass on rumors about various people's work. Usually the reports are fragmentary and highly casual, but a scientist often hears of important new developments in his field first through such channels. An effort to formalize this channel of communication in the field of Sinological studies was made by George Kennedy in the form of a sort of intermittent newsletter called *Wen Ti*. A more recent example is the "information-exchange group set up to provide better communication among scientists in the related fields of electron transfer, oxidative and photosynthetic phosphorylation, ion transport, and membrane structure and function."[12]

Turning to the scientific periodicals, their importance to science is so great that it is possible to argue that modern science really began when the first such periodical was published. They generally serve two distinct functions: to disseminate news of new discoveries through the community and to serve as a file to which researchers who wish to find what is already known about a given subject can turn. The two functions would normally lead to somewhat different editorial policies, but since both will be served reasonably well by selecting the most important articles out of those submitted, it is possible to combine them. The research function of the magazines will be discussed later; we will now confine ourselves to their function as news-magazines.

The system on which they operate is simple. A scientist who has made what he considers an important discovery writes it up and mails it to a journal. If the editor agrees with him, it is accepted, which normally means that it will be printed, but its publication does not result in any direct payment to the scientist. It will, of course, increase his prestige, and this may indirectly increase his income.[13] If the editor does not like the article, he rejects it, and the scientist is free to submit it to some other journal. Eventually it is either printed or the scientist gives up. The fact that each journal considers the article separately is of the utmost importance.[14] It is less likely that a new and

12. *Science,* 143 (January 24, 1964), 308–9.

13. Some very primitive calculations I have made indicate that the indirect monetary gain made by economists from publishing is of the order of $2,000.00 per article.

14. John R. Baker, "Freedom and Authority in Scientific Publication," in *Science and Freedom* (London: Secker & Warburg, 1955), pp. 58–68.

different idea will be rejected by each of seven men acting independently than that it would be rejected by a board of the same seven men or even by the most brilliant among them. Some other institutional arrangement might well lead to the average quality of articles being better, but from the standpoint of giving new ideas a hearing regardless of how radical they are, the present system is hard to improve on.[15]

Normally the scientist himself will decide to which magazine to submit his article on the basis of two criteria, the special field covered and the prestige of the magazine. He starts with the magazine he thinks most suitable and, if his article is rejected, works his way down. We have already mentioned the prestige aspect, and no further discussion is necessary, but the field of specialization raises certain difficulties. In the first place, the definition of the field itself raises the problems of classification of knowledge which we have discussed. An article which does not fit the field covered by any given magazine may be very hard to publish. Returning to our diagram, if the fields of knowledge are shared by magazines, as shown on the following figure, potential research projects would be outside the scope of all of them. (Magazines actually tend to occupy overlapping fields, but this would only marginally affect the reasoning on which the diagram is based.)

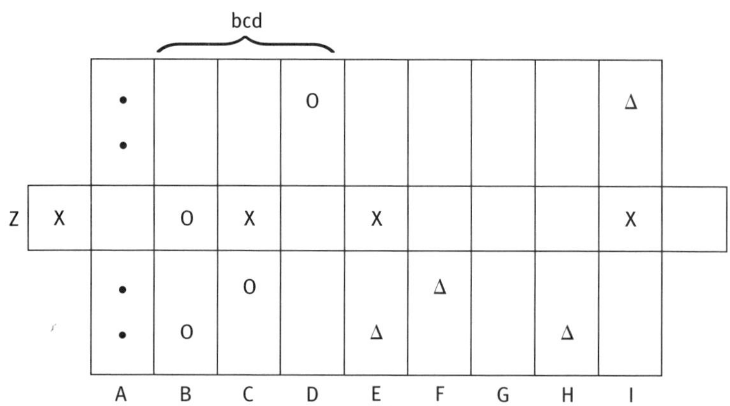

15. In reality the role of editors may be less than I have indicated. A good deal of the work of selecting articles may be delegated to others. In this event, the "other" or "others" who make the selection play the role of editor in my discussion. This whole subject will be discussed in the final chapter.

Magazine A would welcome the research represented by the dots, but any of the magazines A–I would tend to feel the work represented by the X's, the O's, or the triangles was mostly outside its field. It would be very hard, therefore, to get articles covering such work published. The problem is partially solved, again, by the engineers. The classifications used by the engineering publications are completely different; articles which would not fit into any given "scientific" field may fit neatly into an engineering magazine's editorial scheme. The June, 1965, issue of *Astronautics and Aeronautics,* which I happen to have on my desk, carries mainly articles which cannot even be classified by scientific fields. They involve the discussion of devices which incorporate elements from almost all the fields of physics. Thus, returning to our diagram, the engineering periodical Z might publish the work based on the X's, although none of the strictly scientific periodicals would.

We can also classify journals according to level of specialization. In the last figure, journal bcd covers three different fields from the standpoint of journals B, C, and D. For a man doing work which does not fall into any one of these three small fields, this would be highly helpful. Project O, for example, falls neatly into the scope of bcd although outside the scope of any of the more specialized publications. Thus, more generalized publications may also help to provide an outlet for work which does not fit into a narrowly defined specialty. This is of limited use, however, because the magazines of wider scope frequently think of themselves largely as "popularizers" of the material published in the narrower journals in their fields. To take an extreme example, the *Scientific American* does not publish articles which are not contained in one of the scientific specialties. Its editors consider themselves to be engaged in informing scientists of what is going on in other fields, not in publishing original research which does not fit into any given field. Even the journals which do publish original work spreading across several fields normally print work that is less "advanced" than the work in the individual specialties.

Returning to the figure, we can consider that the research is arranged from bottom to top in order of its historic discovery. Thus, the newest advances would be at the very top. Theory O, then, would be the kind of original research actually published by most non-specialized journals. It combines a very advanced discovery in one subfield with information long known in others. A theory based on the latest advances in each of the subfields would probably not be published. This is possibly not a serious drawback, since as science is now organized, few such projects are carried out. Still, once again we find science organized to confine research in a predetermined mold of existing special fields. I deplore this existing situation, but I can offer no proposals for improvements.

If the journals are to have the effect of spreading news through the profession, they must be read. Since the scientist will want to satisfy his curiosity or to find something which can be made use of, he has an incentive to read them. He cannot, however, hope to read all of them. Not only does he lack the time; the more specialized ones are written in a style which is intelligible only to specialists. He must therefore choose some among them to read, some to skim, and a much larger number to ignore. For this function, he need not take account of the prestige of the various publications, except in the very early stages of his training. He should read the ones which interest him most, while skimming those which occasionally carry an article which appeals to him. The choice of scientists who operate on this principle establishes the relative prestige of the various magazines.

This system of deciding what to read is not only the easiest from the standpoint of the individual scientist, it is the system most likely to promote the advancement of science. If, however, the various individual scientists confine themselves to narrow specialties in their reading (which would simply reflect their interests), then the discoveries which require knowledge of several specialties will not be made. Radio astronomy, for example, is largely a post–World War II development, although the technical foundation for it had been available at least since the early 1920's. The long delay in its development obviously arose from the fact that no astronomer knew or cared much about electronics, and the electronics specialists were equally uninterested in astronomy. The eventual development of radio astronomy was largely initiated by a radio engineer of no outstanding talent who simply became interested in the applications of his subject to extraterrestrial radiation. This tremendous step forward in astronomy was made by a man whose education and native intelligence were doubtless far inferior to those of numerous astronomers and physicists whose contribution to the advancement of knowledge was much less than his. His sole advantage was an unusual combination of information and interests. The "marginal return" on this combination was much higher than on the more normal combinations.[16] As a re-

16. Lest I be suspected of putting too much emphasis on cross-disciplinary research, I should like to mention that another great advance in the recent history of astronomy was the invention of the Schmidt telescope. This was the result of a lifelong devotion by Mr. Schmidt

sult the Smithsonian now proudly displays the world's first radio telescope: a machine built in his backyard by a middle-class engineer.

Scientists must choose what they will read as part of their general self-education, keeping in mind their limited capacity to absorb more than some given quantity of information. Some should select that given quantity from among the traditional specialties (some of the traditions may be of very recent origin, perhaps only a few years); others possibly should decide to combine two fields, knowing that this will lead to their being less well-informed in both than a specialist, but hoping to get something out of the interrelationship of the fields. Others may concentrate on one field but have a "minor" in another, or perhaps several others. For mathematical reasons, it is not possible to have all of the possible combinations and permutations present, but there are far more individual scientists than there are scientific organizations or journals, and this gives more possibilities for coverage of unconventional combinations of knowledge to individuals than to the more organized groupings.

Scientific periodicals operate on varying levels of generality. At one extreme is the *Scientific American,* obviously written solely for the layman about each branch of science. One can hardly read any article without realizing it is written for the benefit of people who do not know much about the subject matter. Everything is carefully explained, and there is none of that reliance on the specialized knowledge of the reader to fill the gaps which makes the more professional periodicals so unreadable to non-specialists. Each article is written, not for the benefit of the experts in that field, but for the benefit of people who are specialists in some other field, but ignorant in this one. The result is that any intelligent man with the average college "liberal arts" background in science can follow it easily.[17]

Between the *Scientific American* and the narrowest specialized periodical there is a whole gradation of magazines of varying levels of generality. The degree to which scientists read articles outside their specialized fields varies, of course, from person to person, but all of them read at least one. The fact that they follow this course means that the less specialized magazines have a larger

---

to the extraordinarily narrow specialty of telescope optics. I do not quarrel with the present organization of science with the bulk of the workers engaged in narrowly defined specialties; I merely suggest that the concentration in traditional fields is higher than optimal.

17. Scientists, of course, normally have no more knowledge than this of the fields in which they have made no special study.

readership and greater influence than the highly specialized ones. This leads to more careful editorial work, the possibility of commissioning special articles on a fee basis, and better make-up in the more general magazines. In this as in so many things, the *Scientific American,* with its fine printing, numerous advertisements, and specially written articles, presents the extreme case. This editorial superiority of the more general magazines probably leads to their being more influential in shaping the developments of science than might be imagined from their numbers. It is possible that this partially counterbalances the highly specialized nature of the rest of the scientific community.

The non-periodical literature plays a subordinate, but nevertheless important, role in the diffusion of knowledge through the scientific community. The most important type of non-periodical literature is, of course, books. Large numbers of books are written and published (sometimes commercially, sometimes on a subsidized basis) in the various scientific fields. Books naturally cover much broader fields than articles. The article typically reports some investigation which resulted in some specific discovery. The book will almost always cover the equivalent of a number of articles, but will also involve an effort to integrate them into a general scheme. The "big picture" is more clearly presented in the book field than in the periodical system.

In many cases the book makes no real effort to present new discoveries, but confines itself to reviewing what is already known.[18] While I do not wish to discuss the question of the relative merits of writing articles and writing books, it is clear that books, by reviewing what is known in some field, perform an important function. By putting the data in a coherent order, they may considerably assist the individual investigators in ordering their thoughts. Even more important, a man from some other field who decides that he needs information on the field covered by a given book and by many articles will normally turn first to the book. Thus the book-writer is, in part, educating people outside his field and contributing to interfield co-ordination. The absence of a "standard work" in any given field poses a considerable barrier to the dispersion of knowledge from that field.

Intermediate in length between articles and books are the monographs. Prima facie one would assume that there would be many more monographs than books, but the reverse is true in the United States. Relatively few monographs are circulated, and the ones that do appear have a strong tendency to

18. If history is to be counted a science, then it constitutes an exception to this rule. A great deal of new work in history appears first in book form.

be ignored. This is, I think, a significant defect in the organization of science in the United States.[19] There is no apparent natural law which provides that discoveries will always either be readily presentable in article form or justify a full-length book. It seems likely that more "available" discoveries would require 40–120 pages to report than would require a full-length book. The forcing of actual publication into the article-book mold, therefore, must both direct research toward "article" and "book" projects and away from "monograph" research, and result in what research of "monograph" size is done being reported in an inconvenient form.[20]

There does not appear to be much, however, that can be done about this. If scientists in America prefer to confine their reading to books and magazines and to pay little attention to items of intermediate length, then the "market" for monographs will remain limited and the incentive to produce them slight. The current situation, where most monographs are produced largely for substantially free circulation by various sponsoring organizations, will continue until scientists change their reading habits. Since the circulation of such monographs is essentially free of editorial control, it is not surprising that vast numbers of short items are now also distributed free by individual scientists and scientific organizations.

In reading books (and monographs), scientists can hardly fall into the habit of using the same source, as they do with magazines. They must make conscious choices, instead of simply taking the latest issue of their favorite magazine. They are likely, in fact, to be heavily influenced by the reviews in the magazines in making such choices. This fact would appear to dictate great caution to the magazines in reviewing, but this is normally handled in a rather slipshod manner.[21] As a consequence, the readership of new books may be largely determined by the accident of who is selected by an overworked editor to do the reviewing. Fortunately, most scientists read several periodicals and are likely to see several reviews of any given book.[22]

19. The problem is much less severe in Europe, where many monographs or booklets circulate, but even there it is unlikely that a proportional number of monographs are produced.

20. For a similar complaint with the suggestion that journals solve the problem by making space for very lengthy articles, see Peter Gruenwald's letter, "Too Much of Too Little," *Science,* 148 (June 11, 1965), 1412.

21. For a discussion of the difficulties of writing a good review, see George Sarton, "Notes on the Reviewing of Learned Books," *Science,* 131 (April 22, 1960), 1182–87.

22. As a personal experience, *The Calculus of Consent* (Ann Arbor: University of Michigan Press, 1962), by Dr. James Buchanan and myself, was reviewed by four of the five principal eco-

In reading books, one of the major objectives which seems to guide most scientists is reviewing what they already know. There is no reason to object to this, of course, but the reading of books in fields which are new to the scientists is more interesting. A good, interesting book which attracts the readership of a number of men who would not otherwise have learned much about its subject is likely to have a most stimulating effect on the development of knowledge.[23] Almost certainly some of the readers will find some knowledge in this book usefully combinable with their previous knowledge.

In addition to reading a great deal, the self-education of scientists normally involves meetings and conventions. It is my impression that these meetings are generally more social than scientific, but that they have a scientific component is undeniable. The exchange of gossip, the miscellaneous drinking and socializing which go with the conventions of the various learned societies have been widely commented on, but I see no reason to object to it. Most scientists live rather isolated lives intellectually. They have no one near them who is much interested in their specialties. When they finally get a chance to talk with people who are so interested, it is not surprising that they relax a bit. A good deal of the socializing "small talk" is scientific. Scientists genuinely interested in their subject are not likely to waste much of their limited opportunities to talk to others so interested. To the layman, it may not seem likely that a "disorderly" party of scientists in the next room are all talking about colloids, but if that is their speciality, quite probably that is just what they are doing.

In any event, a good deal of professional discussion does go on at these meetings, and, although it is the fashion to deplore the papers read at the formal meetings,[24] they undoubtedly do perform a function in spreading newly acquired knowledge through the profession. The meetings are the only occasions on which a scientist, presenting his work to his peers, is immediately subject to oral critical discussion. A scientist who is writing an article may feel that potential critics will write letters to the editor only if they have fairly se-

---

nomic journals; the fifth does not publish reviews. It would be a rare economist who was not exposed to at least two of these reviews.

23. Unfortunately some of the "standard" books contain enough errors so that they may actually retard the growth of science. M. King Hubbert, "Are We Retrogressing in Science?" *Science,* 139 (March 8, 1963), 884–90.

24. Letter by E. H. Ahrens, Jr., "Conference Literature," *Science,* 148 (April 16, 1965), 313. For a contrary view see John H. Schneider's "Conference Literature: Rebuttal" in the June 18 issue (148: 1542).

rious differences with him. In oral discussion of a paper, on the other hand, much finer objections may be raised. This undoubtedly is good discipline for the scientist.

We have so far discussed the problem of self-education, which we might consider as the pursuit of information to satisfy the general curiosity of a pure scientist. For an applied scientist, it performs somewhat the same function, except that he will always aim his self-education at getting practically useful ideas. We will now turn to the stage at which the scientist, whether pure or applied, begins to engage in research on a particular problem. This, however, raises a special problem of the sort which is a continual irritant to anyone trying to consider seriatim a general process which can, in reality, follow many different courses. Our process is from data accumulation to hypothesis to checking to dissemination of discovery. We have broken the data-collection stage into two parts: education and specific investigation. Unfortunately—and we will meet similar problems later—some hypotheses are formed without any specific investigation. It is not uncommon for an investigator suddenly to perceive a pattern among the data as a result of his general reading. Under these circumstances he proceeds directly from the self-education, general-curiosity stage to the hypothesis.

As an example, we may cite the legendary discovery of the Newtonian physics. If the story is to be believed, the basic idea occurred to Newton when he was hit by a falling apple. Widely learned in the physics and mathematics of his time, he suddenly realized that a large number of phenomena previously believed to be independent could be united by one theory. That such things happen and that they are sometimes of great importance to the advancement of knowledge is clear. If such instances of skipping stages seem a little irregular, they raise no particular difficulty for the general theory of this book. We follow a descriptive scheme from accumulation of facts to hypothesis to checking and disseminating the hypothesis. Normally the accumulation of facts divides into two stages, general and special accumulation, but if the hypothesis is formed on facts accumulated in the general stage, we simply skip the process of particular investigation. The other stages also may sometimes be skipped. Shortly, we will discuss a situation in which the hypothesis itself is skipped.

Turning now to the particular investigation, we must carefully distinguish between the type of investigation which is begun to check a hypothesis and that which is undertaken in hopes that it will lead to a hypothesis. Probably most scientists are little concerned with this problem, which, in fact, makes no practical difference to them, but it is necessary to talk about one thing at a time if clarity is to be achieved. We will take up investigation which it is hoped will lead to a hypothesis here and leave investigation undertaken to check the hypothesis till later. In a sense, of course, all investigation proceeds from a hypothesis. In the case which we are about to consider, the hypothesis is of this form: Investigation of problem A will develop factual information which will permit formulation of a general hypothesis. This is an investigative hypothesis, a guess about the advantage to science of pursuing a particular line of research, however, and should be strictly distinguished from a hypothesis which purports to be an advance in itself.

Supposing, then, that an investigator has become interested in a given problem or area of knowledge (or combination of problems or areas of knowledge) and proposes to increase his information in that area. Normally, his first step will be to examine the literature in order to find out what has already been discovered in the way of factual data and what has been proposed in the way of theoretical explanation. In the vast majority of all cases, he will find that his problem has already been adequately dealt with by someone else. This fact often tends to be overlooked largely because the cases in which the investigator cannot solve his problem by reading about someone else's work are of such great importance. Absorbing someone else's ideas does not contribute to the advance of science in the same way as producing new ideas.

Nevertheless, the advance of science has as its objective the steady increase in the number of problems which can be solved by the simple expedient of consulting the literature. Each new discovery by an investigator is one more bit of data or theory which will not have to be discovered again. The steady growth of our knowledge permits the economizing of time of investigators. Instead of personally rediscovering various things, they consult the previous work of others and then use the time so saved to investigate new problems. Thus, the medieval scholars who devoted so much trouble to the rediscovery of Aristotle and the other Greek scientists and to the correction and multiplication of their texts were performing a real service to human knowledge. Finding out what the Greeks had discovered was, in fact, the proper first step for any investigator in the thirteenth century, and maximization of returns from a given amount of effort required that the spreading of the recently recovered Greek knowledge be given higher priority than new discoveries. It is, of course, true that once the Greeks had been recovered, there was somewhat too much reverence for them, with a consequent de-emphasis on new work, but even here the time gap between the substantial completion of the work of recovering the Greek discoveries and disseminating them throughout the learned community and the work of the men who added to them is not very long.

If the social prestige of discovering something which you yourself did not know but someone else did is less than that of genuinely original work, such "research" is still of great importance. Unfortunately, it is not as easy as might be hoped.[25] The investigator interested in a certain problem must first find the previous work on it. He obviously cannot simply go through the whole of human knowledge in hope of finding something, since the total is much too vast for any one mind. This problem has resulted in the presently burgeoning interest in "information retrieval." To date, the research in this growing field, far from solving the problems for other fields, has itself developed into a field too large for an investigator to follow thoroughly. Still, the effect of this research can hardly avoid eventually making the "search of the literature" easier. The investigator normally cannot even hope to cover the whole of any reasonably wide field, since the advance of human knowledge has caused even quite narrow classifications to contain more information than one man could possibly absorb. Further, he is normally even more limited. He does not intend to devote his whole life, but only a small period of time, certainly not more than would be necessary to discover the same facts by direct investigation, to the search. The whole point, in fact, of having this vast body of knowledge available is as a sort of labor-saving device, an assurance that resources will not be wasted in rediscovery. The greater the speed with which a given investigator can find what is already known about a problem and the greater the security he can feel that he has actually found everything, the better the system works. Unfortunately, there are inherent limits on the efficiency which can be expected.[26]

These limitations depend on two facts: the obviously limited amount of resources to be invested in improved filing and crossfiling of data (it would be wise to increase the present level) and the impossibility of predicting accurately the information which will be wanted in the future. Thus it is impossible to group information under the heads which would be of maximum

25. Phyliss Allen Richmond, "What Are We Looking For?" *Science,* 139 (February 22, 1963), 737–39.

26. The problem of "data retrieval" is now the subject of a specialized journal, *Information Storage and Retrieval.* The issue of *Science* for May 8, 1964 (144: 581 ff.) contains articles by Richard See, Gerard Salton, John C. Green, and Eugene Garfield which will serve as an introduction to this growing field.

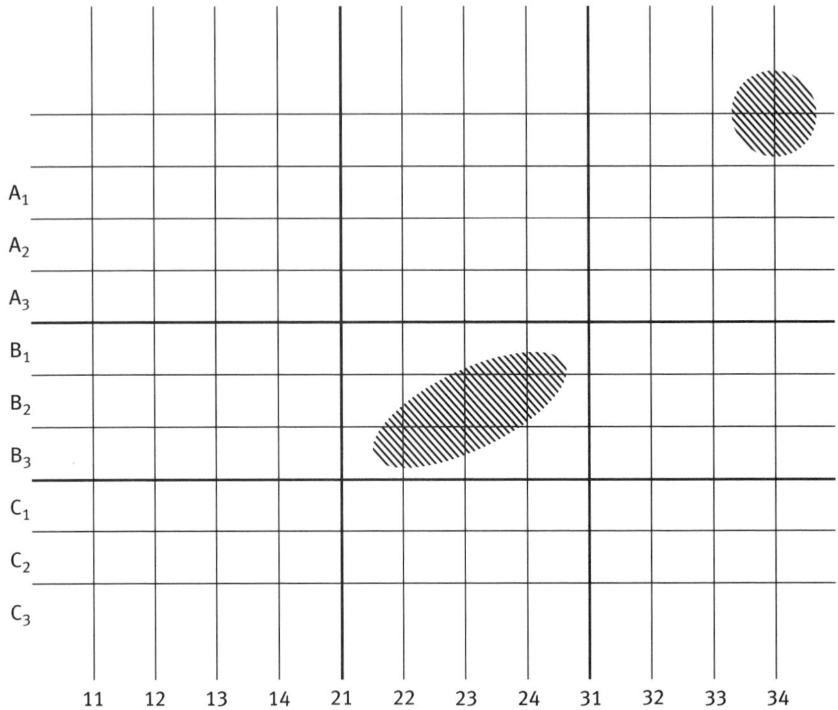

utility for as yet unpredictable research. Turning once again to our graphic representation of knowledge, let us suppose that all knowledge has been classified by two crossing systems, each of which has general categories, subcategories, sub-subcategories, etc.

Suppose a given investigator becomes interested in learning about the information in the area enclosed by the oval. Note that it does not fit any of the classifications, although both classification systems recognize the close relationship of the facts concerned by putting them close together.[27] None of the subcategories in either classification system would give him the information that he wants. Either the general category B or the two series would give him what he wants (there would be other areas of research, the circle, for example, where even this would not be true), but covering either field would involve a vast amount of wasted reading, only a tiny part of which would bear on his

27. The type of problem where a man is interested in information in fields widely separated in the existing classification system can be considered as a series of separate problems of the sort we are now discussing.

problem.[28] In actual practice, the amount of information absorption which would be necessary to cover the whole of human knowledge on the smallest conventional classification which contains the area under investigation would normally be quite a major project.

Sometimes, particularly in applied research, this problem can be solved by teamwork in which each of several men becomes expert in one phase of knowledge. The limitations on this procedure arise from the fact that not all research can be divided into independent segments. Quite frequently success requires that all fields be integrated in one mind. Consider, for example, a team designing a jet plane, and let us suppose that it is broken into three divisions: engine, electronics, and airframe. A change in engine design which reduced the efficiency of the engine might be desirable on general grounds because it permitted superior airframe design. Obviously, such a change would never even be considered unless the engine designers knew enough about airframes or the airframe men knew enough about engines to recognize the interrelationship between the two problems. Thus if the personnel were genuinely specialized, they would not produce the optimum design. On the other hand, possibly the improvement in airframe design is so subtle that only a man who has devoted his whole life to study of airframes could perceive it. In this case, the problem is insoluble.

If the teamwork solution is not possible, and in a very large number of cases it is not, then we must depend on the filing system to produce the necessary knowledge. The problem, to repeat, is not to get the information needed out of the library (which is easy), but to exclude the unnecessary information so that the investigator will have a manageable job of self-education. The system in use proceeds in two steps: first, a great deal of information is excluded from the classification system as a whole, and second, the classification system tries to so order the included information that the investigator may find what he needs while excluding what he does not need.

The two problems are interrelated in that the more efficient the classification of the included data, the less data must be excluded. Speaking analogically, if the average investigator is capable of mastering a thousand "bits" of information on a given problem, and the classification system divides knowl-

28. Our diagram is an analogy, and like all analogies, not exactly congruent with reality. It might appear that the simple solution would be to examine everything contained in the classification B which is also filed under the general field 2, but this would work only on our diagram. Seldom, if ever, would this be possible in reality.

edge into ten thousand parts, then the total amount of knowledge which could be included in the system could not be much above ten million if it was to be efficiently used. If the classification system could unambiguously distinguish a million categories, then the system could operate on a billion bits of information. This, of course, assumes that the exclusion process, on the whole, excludes the less important bits of information, although this is a rather heroic assumption.

The initial exclusion process operates essentially at the publication level. It would obviously be desirable, if the classification problem did not exist, to have every bit of information available to the human race permanently recorded and available to investigators. Every experimental result and every document should be available for future consultation. If, however, any effort was made to accumulate this vast mass of information, researchers would be confronted with unmanageable masses of data when they investigated even the simplest problem. It would not, of course, be difficult to construct a classification system which broke any given quantity of data down into parts of any given size, but setting up such a classification system on a non-arbitrary basis has so far been impossible. Perhaps the very active research now going on will shortly produce improved techniques. But classifications chosen must be such as to have at least a reasonable chance of assisting future researchers by presenting information in categories which will be useful for as yet undreamed-of investigations. It must also be understandable to investigators in the sense that they will not have any great difficulty in learning to use it to find data. All existing systems which meet these requirements, and probably all systems to be invented in the future, have strictly limited abilities to discriminate knowledge into classes, hence the necessity of excluding some information from the catalogues.

If information is to be initially excluded and thus made permanently unavailable to future investigators, then it is obviously desirable that the most important information be included and the least important excluded. This, however, requires prophecy, since "important" means "important to future research." That errors will be made is obvious; we can only hope that they are minor. The system now in use simply depends on the individual judgment of various editors. If a given work of research is thought unworthy of publication by all of the editors (including editors of monograph series, etc.) to whom it is submitted, then it is excluded from the information which will be classified. True, the investigator, if he thinks enough of his work, can pay to have it printed, but it is unlikely to be included in any standard classification system.

The classification systems utilize a further stage of exclusion. In the first place, there are a great many different ones operating on different principles. At the lowest level the periodicals publish cumulative indexes of their own contents, and libraries keep card catalogues of their holdings. At the other extreme, there are a great many special indexes published covering various classifications of knowledge. Even these special indexes, however, make no particular effort to be catholic in their coverage. Normally, they consciously limit their coverage to magazines and new books which they think are of a certain level of importance, rather than simply indexing everything in their field. Another form of indexing material is represented by such magazines as *Physical Abstracts,* which presents brief abstracts of what its editors think are the most important publications in its field.

The object of all of this reference guide material, of course, is to make it possible for a scientist pursuing some future research project to find quickly and easily everything already discovered on the subject without having to read any significant quantity of irrelevant material. In view of the impossibility of predicting the course of future research, this objective cannot be exactly reached, or even very closely approximated, but we can at least make an effort. The actual system used is only partially based on efforts to predict the future. History and the structure of our language are both more important to most existing classification systems than conscious efforts to guess what will be needed in the future.

The historical development of science is ever present in our methods of classifying knowledge. Anthropology, to take an extreme example, covers two completely distinct fields joined only by the historic accident of some early investigators who happened to be interested in both. The same type of thing will be found throughout science. In addition, with the progress of science, connections not previously known are discovered, and previous connections are dissolved. The definitions of fields of knowledge tend to be determined by the exact time in this process in which the term hardened. As a consequence, fields of knowledge tend to be rather arbitrarily defined. These fields, however, are used as the basis for much indexing of knowledge, which gives the indexing a similar arbitrary slant.

The language of science contains similar arbitrary elements, in spite of the committees for standardizing and rationalizing usage. Most scientific terms were invented some time ago, and thus some of them cover fields of information which, to our present knowledge, seem somewhat arbitrarily demarcated. This is of little importance in the actual work of research, since the precise meaning of a word in the particular context used will normally be clear, but it does mean that the words are less than ideal as classification media for finding data. This is particularly so since it is clear that the growth of knowledge in the future will make even the best usage of today seem arbitrary.

Nevertheless, the use of historically developed subject categories and scientific terms as the basic system for classifying knowledge is unavoidable. Even if we could think of some other system, it would be less useful than the present one, since the scientist must know where to look in any system. If he knows the traditional fields and the normal meanings of words, and it must be presumed that any scientist who is likely to make advances in human knowledge will be already well acquainted with them, then he is equipped to use a system based on them. Development of another system would mean that the scientist would have to learn that system, as well as learn the subject covered. Since the classification system could not be simple and brief unless the subjects covered were also simple and brief, this would impose a major burden on him.

One highly valuable type of classification system should be mentioned. The great unifying theories which the various sciences seek are, among other things, classification systems which order knowledge in their fields in a regular way. A scientist who must master the general theory for his regular work will find that he has also mastered the system on which knowledge in the field is classified and will thus find it fairly easy to find data. Unfortunately, grand theories are all eventually disproved (the ones discovered very recently, such as the special theory of relativity, have escaped this fate, but no one has much confidence that they will last forever); and we can, therefore, deduce that some information lies outside the classification system of such theories. Only the "final theory" which presented the whole universe in one grand equation would be a really perfect classification system.

The manifest defects of the existing classification systems, even for a body of knowledge which has been deliberately pruned, are met in part by the cross-indexing system. Each item of knowledge, ideally, should appear under a number of different heads so that it can be found by searchers using different methods. The heads themselves should be selected so as to group facts and theories together in clusters which have something in common. Generally speaking, the more cross-indexing, the better, but here again we come up against mathematical problems. With a given body of data, the physical size of the index will be directly proportional to the number of different heads under which the average item is catalogued. This principle will apply regardless of the fineness or roughness of the principles of classification used.

The physical bulk of the total index is probably of little importance, at least until any given index becomes much more complicated than any present index, but the extent of the cross-indexing also affects the number of items under each heading and thus reduces the exclusionary effectiveness of the indexing system. If the average item appears under ten separate headings, and the total number of headings remains the same, then there will be twice as many entries under each head than if each item appears only under five headings. A scientist searching for an item of information under a given heading would have to plow through twice as much irrelevant information. On the other hand, he would probably be more likely to find the item under the first heading he tried.

The obvious solution to this problem is to use finer classifications, with the result that there are more headings. Further, a cross-classification system may, analytically, simply add a whole new list of headings, thus avoiding the whole problem. In practice the total number of headings is limited by the financial resources of the indexing organization. The more numerous the classifications, the more skilled, and hence the more expensive the indexers. The limitation on fineness of classification is also largely financial. The finer the classification, the larger the number of total entries and the more skill required on the part of the personnel doing the classifying. The increase in the amount of cross-indexing is thus partially dependent on increased financial resources and partially dependent on finer classification procedures which themselves are largely dependent on greater financial support.

The improvement of the indexing of present knowledge is thus to a considerable extent a matter of increased financial support. Because this type of work lacks the glamour and interest of new discoveries, it has tended to attract less in the way of money and a good deal less in the way of talent than direct scientific research. It is, however, highly important and readily susceptible to organized improvement. It has always been doubtful if large organizations, like the government or the Ford Foundation, are really capable of advancing science very much. Discoveries are so much a matter of accident and/or personal inspiration that such large organizations can do little more than provide incentives and opportunities to individuals or, occasionally, small groups. The long sad record of Alexandrian science contrasted with the short brilliant record of pre-Alexandrian Greek science is often pointed out. The large-scale support of science available in Alexandria drew almost all of the best Greek minds there, and the central organization then stifled them in an atmosphere of cataloguing and minor advances. The possibility of a repetition of the experiment on a much larger scale should give any well-wisher to the human race nightmares.

Cataloguing, however, is an important part of science and, as the Alexandrian experiment illustrates, is a feasible objective for organized scientific activity. It requires organization and fairly large funds, but it does not require much independence or inspiration. It is therefore an ideal area for large-scale projects; large organizations trying to advance science can probably do their best work there. Improvements in filing and cataloguing would have, at least, a proportional effect on the growth of science and might well have a more than proportional effect. It should also be noted that improved classification procedures would permit the lowering of the present "threshold" of merit so that the total volume of information kept in our collective "memory" would also be increased.

As a sample project, the Linnaean system is obsolete. The development of biological knowledge since Linné's day has been so great as almost to overwhelm his basic system. A haphazard system of patching and extension has been used to add to his classifications, but the end result is both aesthetically ugly and practically inconvenient. The development of a whole new system, based on Linné in the same way that his work was based on Aristotle, would obviously be a major step forward and one which would require no new knowledge. It would be very expensive, of course, but where could the Ford Foundation better invest $20,000,000?

The recent tendency to turn to computers to solve all problems has also been seen in this field. In fact, the problem is not of the sort that present computers are adapted to solve. There would be no particular difficulty in designing a computer to go through a set of files and select out all items under a given head. It could even be attached to an automatic library which delivered the required volumes. Devices of this sort, albeit of limited capacity, actually exist. This is not, however, the basic problem which concerns the original headings and making of the index. This, under present circumstances, can be done only by human beings and will require as many of them if a computer is used in the later stages as if it is not.[29] The possibility of using computers several orders of magnitude larger than any now contemplated to "search" the whole body of knowledge for specified information does exist, but is not for the immediate future.[30]

The search of the literature will be continued by the investigator until one of three things happens: he grows tired of the particular project, he finds a testable hypothesis (the process of "finding" such a hypothesis, given adequate factual knowledge, is the subject of the next chapter), or he exhausts the recorded information on the field and turns to direct investigation. Little can be said about the methods of direct investigation except that the mind of man is almost infinitely ingenious. The number of apparently insoluble problems which have been solved is amazing.

The investigation of reality also proceeds until the investigator grows tired of it or a hypothesis is achieved. Since there is no further step available, these are the only two alternatives. The fact that an investigator grows tired of his project without obtaining any hypothesis does not prove that the project was fruitless. He may have discovered enough simple factual information to justify his work. This factual information may later, either by itself or combined with other discoveries, lead to an important hypothesis. Not infrequently, in fact, the whole purpose of the investigation was simply the accumulation of data. The recent major investigations in the Antarctic, for example, were largely aimed at the accumulation of geographic data. Exploration of new territory has always been basically concerned with simple data accumulation.[31]

29. Computers have been programmed to perform various routine tasks which would normally have to be done by the indexer. This permits the human "parts" of the system to work more efficiently but does not solve the basic problem. See L. Karel, C. J. Austin, and M. M. Cummings, "Computerized Bibliographic Services for Bio-medicine," *Science,* 148 (May 7, 1965), 766–72, for an example of such a system.

30. Even with computers of the desired size, the problem of specifying the information desired in terms which would permit the computer to recognize desired items and reject undesired items would be an extremely difficult one. Presumably the answer would be sought along the lines of searching for certain combinations of words and phrases, but this raises almost as many difficulties as it solves. Again, a great deal of research in this area is presently being undertaken.

31. This is something of an oversimplification. While the hypothesis "If I look on the other side of the hill, I will find something" has always been basic to geographic exploration, not infrequently some more specific and testable hypothesis has been an important motivating factor. Hypotheses about the sources of rivers seem to have been particularly fruitful.

Similar motives are not infrequently behind laboratory experiments. The development of more accurate tables of physical constants is a continuous preoccupation of scientists, and the development of a table of measurements of almost any new phenomenon is normally considered a quite respectable research project. It is, of course, quite possible that this new data will lead to a hypothesis, but developing the data would be considered worthwhile even if this were impossible. Scientists are curious about, among other things, exact magnitudes; the practical usefulness of tables of measurements is obvious. The development of information on such matters, therefore, is legitimate even though it leads to no hypothesis. In such cases, the research is continued until the investigator gets tired of the subject.

Sometimes research is aimed at simple data accumulation in fields other than those in which exact measurements are likely to result.[32] Geographical exploration, already mentioned, is an example, but a good deal of chemical research (especially in the nineteenth century) was concerned with mixing some things and seeing what resulted. In the applied field there is still a great deal of this sort of thing. Other illustrations can be found in metallurgy and parts of astronomy. Personally, I feel that science aimed at hypothesis and grand theories is of a higher order than simple data accumulation, but data accumulation has its place. Here, again, is an area where large organizations with sizable appropriations can operate successfully. The library at Alexandria did a good deal of this sort of work, and today it is done on a large scale by state-operated laboratories in various parts of the world.

So far I have discussed the problem of data accumulation in terms which might suggest that such research projects normally lead to a predetermined result (i.e., the achievement of a hypothesis or the attainment of a set of desired measurements) or lead nowhere. The problem is not that simple. Many scientific discoveries are accidental. A researcher is accumulating data with the objective of solving problem A, when suddenly he sees that the data are pointing to a solution to problem B. Such accidents are of the very greatest importance to the development of science and are one of the major reasons for not trying to predict its growth.

It should, of course, be realized that such an accident depends greatly on the alertness and intelligence of the investigator. He must recognize the importance of his new data for a problem other than the one he is investigating

32. For an amusing discussion of the danger of simple data accumulation, see the letter by Bernard K. Forscher, "Chaos in the Brickyard," *Science*, 142 (October 18, 1963), 339.

and must realize that his other problem is important. To say that a given discovery is the result of accident, then, is not to cast doubt on the ability of the investigator making it. It may well involve, as in the legendary case of Newton, the very highest scientific talents, but it is still in a large part the result of chance. It is probable, however, that most scientists have many opportunities to make such chance discoveries. Without recognizing the possible outcome, they undertake experiments which lead to results of great importance to fields other than the one they are investigating. The rare investigator who seizes on such an opportunity deserves as much credit as if he had originally aimed at the result he eventually obtained.

CHAPTER V

THE PROBLEM OF INDUCTION

C. D. Broad has pointed out that inductive reasoning, which is the glory of science, is also the "scandal of philosophy."[1] Scientists go happily along engaging in what they call induction in spite of Hume's destruction of the possibility of logical progression from the particular to the general. Philosophers, on the other hand, make attempts which have grown more and more desperate over the centuries to develop a logical basis for induction. This chapter, in a sense, is another effort in this direction, although it will take the course of trying to avoid Hume's problem rather than solving it.[2]

Strictly speaking, this is a digression from the main purpose of this book. The rest of our study is devoted to the operations of a social organization of a certain type. At this point we will consider a process which takes place in the mind of an individual man, although it can eventually influence the social organization. What interests us as outsiders about a new theory is not the process which the discoverer followed in reaching his theory, but whether it is correct. The correctness or incorrectness is determined, as has been pointed out by Popper, by testing the idea. If it survives difficult tests, then we have confidence in it and would have such confidence even if the discoverer confided that the idea had been revealed to him by Brahma in a vision. Even if the discoverer were revealed as the permanent resident of an insane asylum whose management tolerantly permitted him to bombard the editors of various journals with crackpot contributions, we would still accept his theory if it survived adequate tests.[3]

But if the real basic problem is "Is it true?" not "How was it obtained?" the second question is still of enough importance to warrant discussion. This

1. C. D. Broad, *The Philosophy of Francis Bacon* (Cambridge: Cambridge University Press, 1926), p. 67.

2. Jerrold J. Katz, *The Problem of Induction and Its Solution* (Chicago: University of Chicago Press, 1962), is the best recent discussion of the problem. It contains a strict proof of the impossibility of logically justifying "inductive" reasoning.

3. It would probably be hard for such a person to get his theory tested. Michael Polanyi has emphasized the role of an "orthodoxy" in the development of science, and our lunatic would probably find it most difficult to get orthodox scientists to pay attention to his idea. Once it had been tested, however, it would stand or fall in terms of the test, not of its origin.

discussion, ever since Hume's day, has turned on the problem of induction. In a sense, this represents an oversimplification, since a great many discoveries are the result of deductive rather than inductive reasoning. Efforts to explain both processes by the same theory are naturally handicapped. I shall first discuss the development of new theories and hypotheses by deductive reasoning and then turn to the cases which genuinely cannot be explained on deductive grounds.

The first method of producing a new hypothesis by deduction is simply to deduce a further consequence from an existing, accepted theory. Sometimes this process is initiated in order to test the theory. This is, in fact, the best way of "validating" any theory. More frequently the newly deduced hypothesis is developed for other purposes, and, in this case, it is not likely to be thought of as a hypothesis. Thus, the Michelson-Morley experiment was deduced from Newtonian physics, but the two experimenters were not trying to test the validity of the Newtonian system. On the basis of deductive reasoning based on a system in which they had complete confidence, they built an instrument to measure certain characteristics of light. The end result did not illuminate the problem which had been the object of the investigation, but instead cast grave doubt on the Newtonian mechanics.

The same type of deductive reasoning is very important in applied science. All sorts of improvements are developed as the result of deductive reasoning based on various received theories. Here, however, failure of an experiment is normally not considered as a disproof of the original theory, largely because of the modesty of the investigators. The applied scientists are perhaps more aware than the pure researchers of the likelihood of experimental failure due to outside factors. Partly, of course, this reflects real differences in the conditions faced by workers in these two fields. The applied scientist is trying to make something useful and must keep a careful eye on the likely costs of the ultimate product. Thus he cannot take such elaborate precautions to eliminate external influences as can the pure scientist. It really makes no great difference to the man trying to improve an automobile engine whether the failure of his experimental attempt to apply a deduced theory arises from the falsity of the original theory or from the existence of external influences which can be eliminated only through extremely costly modifications of the engine. Thus he is unlikely to undertake experiments to elucidate this problem and will normally simply assume the existence of external influences in his particular device. Sometimes, of course, he will decide that he has disproved the theory. He may also report his unsuccessful experiment in a form which attracts a pure scientist to test the original theory and thus at second hand provide for its validation (invalidation).

More important than this type of direct deduction, at least in numbers of hypotheses deduced, if not in the individual significance of the hypothesis, is the process of probable deduction. This is a system of perfectly ordinary deduction which proceeds from a probable premise to a probable conclusion.[4] Thus:

If A probably B
A
Probably B

The use of this device in research can be readily illustrated. It was discovered that certain chemicals belonging to the family of nitrogen mustards were usable in a small way in the treatment of cancer. From general chemical experience and the principle of the uniformity of nature, it had been previously deduced that chemicals which are generally similar, but not identical, will have some similar effects on biological organisms and some different. It thus appeared probable that other members of the nitrogen mustard family would be better or worse than the originally tested chemicals, and that at least one member of the family would be markedly better. This probable deduction could then be converted into the hypothesis, "Chemical A will be useful in the cure of cancer" (or, "will not be useful") and the hypothesis tested. This hypothesis is obviously the result of a probable deduction, with the final probable conclusion then converted into a certain statement solely for the purpose of rendering it testable. (Unfortunately, the hypothesis has so far been falsified.)

If none of the probable deductions survive tests, then we can turn to possible deductions which follow the same process, but with less likely results. A large part of cancer research has, in fact, followed this route. Slim and distant analogies have been searched out and testable hypotheses deduced from them. Although I have undertaken no statistical studies, I suspect that this type of probable/possible deductive reasoning is far and away the principal source of hypotheses for science; it is the normal route which research into any given problem follows. Data are carefully assembled, probable general-

4. J. O. Wisdom, *Foundations of Inference in Natural Science* (London: Methuen, 1952), pp. 132 *et seq*.

izations which seem to apply are searched out, and the data and the probable generalizations are combined to deduce probable conclusions. These probable conclusions are then shifted to testable form and tests are made. If the tested hypotheses are falsified, other less probable generalizations are applied to the same data and so on. Eventually, either the process produces a hypothesis which survives testing, or it plays out and the research project is abandoned.

Another, rather rare but highly important, use of deductive reasoning in the development of hypotheses involves the careful examination of an existing theory. Let us suppose an existing theory which from certain premises deduces properly a large number of physical phenomena. From premises A . . . E, we deduce the results of experiments 1. . . . N. An investigator deduces another experiment, N + 1, from the premises, and on testing, the experimental outcome contradicts the predicted outcome. Assuming there are no errors, this falsifies the original theory. The investigator then may consider carefully the experimental results, the original premises, and the logical chain connecting them. It may be possible, by straight deductive logic, to determine which of the original premises must be changed to explain the new results. It may even be possible to deduce what new premise must be substituted for the "falsified" old ones. This process played a great part in the development of the special theory of relativity. A careful examination of the logical basis of Newtonian physics led Einstein to realize that it was based in part on an implicit assumption of the invariance of time. He tried changing this premise (the particular change he used could not have been obtained by deduction) and got his theory.

It should be noted, however, that this process works only sometimes. Further, it produces only hypotheses. It is possible to produce an infinite number of theories fitting any given set of facts. Only if the theory "predicts" facts not involved in its development can it be regarded as tested and, therefore, as probably true. Thus, the new theory, although obtained by deduction from an old theory and new data, is not, by those facts, proved. It must survive further investigation before we can put much confidence in it.[5]

5. G. Polya, *Mathematics and Plausible Reasoning* (2 vols; Princeton: Princeton University Press, 1954), discusses the solving of scientific problems from a different viewpoint. He is interested in the procedures and attitudes of mind which are most likely to lead a scientist to success in research. This leads to a quite different approach, but his rules seem eminently sensible. "Flashing the subconscious," however, is left out of his analysis. See also Polya's *How to Solve It* (Princeton: Princeton University Press, 1945).

So far this discussion of possible deductive ways of obtaining hypotheses has failed to mention the principle of the uniformity of nature, although this will normally be involved in any deductive system of natural laws. Since there seems to be no method of deducing this principle, the fact that it is an indispensable step (although frequently unstated) in the logical chain from which any logical theory is deduced might seem to invalidate any deductive theory. Since the problem has been much discussed by the philosophers of science, I can confine myself to a few sentences. The question of whether the principle should be regarded as a testable hypothesis itself, or whether it is inherently untestable, and hence "metaphysical" in Karl Popper's terminology, would appear still to be an open one. For our purposes, however, it is largely irrelevant. Everyone believes in the principle of the uniformity of nature regardless of the basis of that belief. All our deductive processes in connection with the real world, and, indeed, most of our day-to-day activities, are based upon this firm conviction. Thus, regardless of the philosophical question of the justification of this principle, people do use it to deduce hypotheses, and that is all we need to know for our present purposes.

Another possible problem in connection with the deduction of hypotheses concerns the validity of deductive reasoning itself. The best answer to this question was given by Morris Kline: "Who decides . . . which forms of deductive reasoning are valid? There is a simple answer to this question. Those people who agree on what is valid deductive reasoning band together and call the others insane."[6] This may not be philosophically satisfying, but it suffices for the student of society who need only know how people act.

Much of what I have been discussing so far is customarily called induction. My argument that deductive reasoning is really involved may seem hair-splitting, but it has a real objective. After we have taken away all of the methods for obtaining hypotheses listed above, a residue will remain. There are hypotheses which were not obtained by these methods. Of the remaining hypotheses, some will be found to have resulted accidentally through errors of one sort or another, but some, I contend, are the result of another mental process, for which I wish to reserve the term "induction."

The usual definition of induction is the process of getting from the particular to the general. Thus an experiment has been repeated several times, and a given result has been obtained. The movement from this statement to

6. *Mathematics and the Physical World* (New York: Crowell, 1959), p. 16.

the statement "This experiment will always give that result" is the normal example of induction. From my standpoint, this is a deductive operation in which the general principle of the uniformity of nature and the experimental data form the two premises of a syllogism from which the conclusion can be deduced. To take an example, we observe that the incidence of lung cancer correlates highly with the smoking of cigarettes. From this observation and a general principle that if two things are correlated they are probably causally related with the probability proportional to the strength of the correlation, we deduce a causal relation. From my standpoint, there is no induction except, possibly, in the original development of our general principle. Induction, in my usage, involves the discovery of general principles or patterns in terms of which deductive logic can explain factual data. The steps of explanation, on the other hand, are strictly deductive.

To make the point even clearer, let us consider a graphic example. Experimental evidence indicates that consistent sets of phenomena b, c, d, and f exist; b, c, and d are all deducible from theory Z. It is thought likely that a new theory, Y, will be eventually developed from which it will be possible to deduce Z and another hypothetical subtheory which permits deduction of f and some other as yet undiscovered set of phenomena, e. Obviously, we cannot deduce Y from Z and f because that would be going from the conclusion of an argument to its beginning. This is possible only in special cases where the conclusions and some of the premises are given, and they are so chosen as to permit only one set of additional premises to fit the situation. We cannot expect nature to be so accommodating in the normal case. In fact, we can feel no security that we have even properly guessed the general area in which the new higher-level theory will operate. It is perfectly possible that no theory Y exists and that the next step in the advance of knowledge will lead to the discovery of theory X, connecting Z with the as yet unknown set of phenomena a.

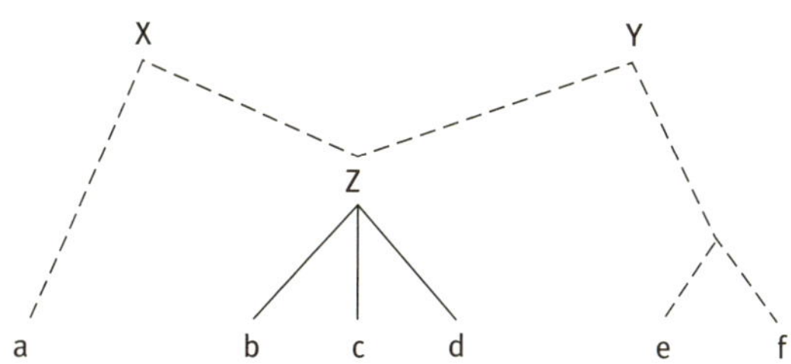

Getting to Y, then, involves a "logical jump." It is not possible by use of deductive logic, but if we do not use deductive logic to obtain our theories, how do we obtain them? The simple reiteration of the term "inductive logic" obviously does little to solve this problem without some explanation of how "inductive logic" works. The rest of this chapter therefore will be a sort of theory of theories. It must, however, again be emphasized that no matter how we get our hypotheses, what counts is how well they stand up to tests, and this is a matter of deductive logic and experience rather than induction.

Let us consider a schoolboy trying to solve a problem set by his math teacher. Some such problems may be solved by simple routine carrying out of prescribed rules. Multiplying 138,975,017 by 2,386,945 is tedious, but it involves no "insight." Most mathematical problems, however, require that the student make certain choices in his operations. The process to be followed in reaching the answer is not fully prescribed by the problem, but must be worked out by the student. $X^2 - 3x + 2 = 0$, for example, can be solved only by first deciding whether to use the formula or to try factoring. If factoring is tried, then it will be necessary to try several sets of factors in most cases. It might be possible to make a list of all procedures which can be followed in reaching the solution of the problem and then to apply them in turn. This would constitute a fixed procedure like that used in multiplying, and we could still use straight deductive reasoning in reaching our result. This requires two things, a finite number of possible procedures and a method of recognizing a correct answer when we reach it.

The problem, of course, concerns the requirement that the list of possible methods of solution be finite.[7] In the examples normally given in textbooks, the list is finite because the student knows that all problems have been selected to be at a given level of difficulty and therefore knows that the more difficult procedures have been ruled out. In an algebra problem the student would know that if it was factorable, the factors would be small whole numbers and, thus, that they must be contained in quite a small list of possible solutions. This, however, is because of the kindness of the authors of texts; we cannot expect nature to be so co-operative. In practice, however, the better students do not simply exhaust the possible procedures in solving equations.

7. This is the basic problem in the work of Herbert A. Simon in attempting to program machines to "think." His programs do appear to produce original solutions to problems, but normally out of a finite set. For an introduction to his work, see A. Newell, J. C. Shaw, and H. A. Simon, *Self-Organizing Systems* (New York: Pergamon Press, 1960).

They "see"[8] the solution and proceed directly to it, albeit after a few false starts. Now it might be argued that what really happens is that all possible procedures are tested by the subconscious mind, and the "illumination" occurs when one works, but considerations of time taken and introspective examination of my own procedure in such cases convinces me that this is not so. Somehow a pattern of the whole problem appears in the mind and is then tested by working it out. The process of producing the pattern is the process of induction.[9]

Scientists, of course, are normally not presented with such neat problems as mathematics students are. Typically they have a mass of data, accumulated by the methods which we have already discussed, and they are searching for a pattern in that data which will permit its theoretical elucidation. The formulation of all possible patterns and the systematic testing of them one by one is the only method deductive logic can offer for this problem. A statistician can provide convenient and efficient tests for the hypothesis and possibly assist in the ordering of the hypothesis, but normally no more. In fact, it is usually impossible to specify a procedure which would, even if applied infinitely, produce all possible explanatory hypotheses. The infinity of possible hypotheses will thus be one of Cantor's higher-order infinites.

Logically the problem would appear insoluble, yet experience indicates that such problems are solved daily. Before turning to my attempt to explain how it is done, let us consider one possible procedure for somewhat simplifying the search. Let us assume that we have a quantity of data on some subject which we suspect to be logically interrelated, but for which we do not know the interrelationships. Making a comprehensive list of all possible interrelations and then testing each one is clearly an infinite process. As a simplification, suppose we follow the following procedure: From the main mass of data, we select random or non-random subsamples of fairly small size. These small samples are then tested for a list of possible hypotheses more limited than the total number available for the larger sample. This would in part be necessary since some possible patterns for the whole body of data would

8. "Illumination" in the vocabulary of Poincaré.

9. N. R. Hanson, *Patterns of Discovery* (Cambridge: Cambridge University Press, 1958), emphasizes the importance of "seeing" patterns. If I understand Professor Hanson, however, he either thinks of these patterns as creations of the mind or believes that there are a number of equally valid patterns and that the mind selects one or more of them. This differs considerably from my position.

not be testable in the smaller sample, but let us suppose that we test only the stronger patterns among those which could be tested in the smaller sample. If we get no results with our first set, we select larger subsamples and try out more hypotheses, including some that are more complicated than those included in the first run.

This process, of course, is also an infinite one, but it has one very great advantage. If any reasonably likely pattern is strongly present in the data, it will be detected toward the beginning of the process of search. This process organizes the hypotheses to be tested in order of simplicity and strength and thus is much more likely to find a simple, strong pattern in the data than would almost any other system. I shall later argue that the human mind does, in fact, do something very like this, although I shall also argue that the human mind has a special tool to use in the search which is not available in mathematics.

Turning now to induction proper, in order to explain my theory, I must begin with a discussion of a very common phenomenon, the recognition of another person. Suppose you are walking down the street when you recognize someone coming toward you. It may be a close friend or relation or a very slight acquaintance; it makes no difference. As he comes closer, suddenly you realize that you are mistaken; he is not the person you thought he was. Continuing to observe him as the two of you approach each other, you will normally be surprised at your initial recognition. At closer hand, he not only does not look like the man you thought him to be, he appears to have practically no characteristics in common with him. How, then, did it happen that you mistook him for an acquaintance?

The whole phenomenon of recognition of other people is mysterious. A man who has not seen a childhood acquaintance for years *may* instantly recognize him in spite of apparent great physical changes. Recognition of a person whom you have known as an adult, even after many years' absence, is usually easier. The regularity with which our papers report the accidental recognition and capture of fugitives who have disguised themselves and lived peacefully for a number of years and are then noticed by someone who "knew them when" is evidence of the efficiency of the recognition process. At the same time, it points up the difficulty of explaining it. Of course recent research has indicated that almost all forms of perception are much more complicated than was formerly believed. The sense impressions transmitted to the brain are apparently subjected to quite elaborate manipulation.

It seems probable that what we recognize in others is a "pattern" of characteristics, not any given characteristic. What we see in the distant passer-by is a collection of attributes which fits the pattern held by our mind for some acquaintance. As he comes closer and the senses absorb more attributes, the additional attributes do not fit the pattern, and we therefore no longer recognize him. We know people, if this theory is true, not by individual characteristics, but as a pattern of attributes. The sense data are compared with memorized patterns of data and recognition or non-recognition follows. If we have less data, which would be true if the man were some distance off, these data are more likely to fit one of the patterns in the mind than if we have more data.

Similar patterns can be seen in much identification work. The art expert has no difficulty in telling us who painted a picture which he has never before seen. If he cannot tell us the painter, he can at least tell us a good deal about him. Normally he will know the nationality, probable date, and school. Now, he cannot really explain how he knows this. Art experts, it is true, write books "explaining," but no one tries to learn how from the books, and the books do not even advise this. The prospective art expert simply studies a large number of attributed paintings. Eventually, a pattern for the work of given painters, schools, and nations will emerge in the budding expert's brain. This pattern he will not be able to explain to others (although he may mistakenly think he can and write a book on the subject), but it will serve his purpose. He has learned this pattern by examining the paintings, not by reading what his predecessors have written (he may or may not have read a good deal in the literature). No one even pretends that the explanations of how this is done contained in the literature in themselves will teach the art. Further, careful examination of the work of various experts will reveal that their explanations of their abilities are inconsistent.

In each of these cases, then, I contend that the mind, in fact, perceives patterns in the sense data it receives from the sensory organs. The patterns must be directly perceived by the mind, since no "intellectual" explanation is available. No one can explain the pattern by means of which he recognizes a given person. Nevertheless, we have no difficulty recognizing people; the type of skill possessed by the art experts is also widely available. The efficient mechanic normally has it in a great degree. What seems to be clear is that there is some pattern to the data and that the mind perceives this pattern directly, without having it explained by someone else. The pattern must exist, at least approximately, since we can and do use it to recognize things, and we must have some method of detecting it, since it is manifest that we do. The mathematical argument at the beginning of this chapter proves that we cannot obtain this recognition of the pattern by successively testing all possible patterns, because that would take an infinitely long time. The only remaining possibility is that the human mind has some direct method of discerning a pattern in received data, if a pattern is there.

How this process works, I cannot imagine. All of our formal knowledge of the reasoning powers of the human mind turns on the use of deductive reasoning and thus can give us little assistance in talking about another, non-deductive power of the mind. To demonstrate the existence of another power of the mind is not to explain it, but we also do not really understand how we deduce. We have good step-by-step descriptions of the process, and it is possible to deduce general rules from given assumptions which seem reasonable, but we have no explanation as to why the human mind reasons this way. Just as there are non-Euclidian geometries, there may well be non-Aristotelian logics. Thus pattern detection, as an attribute of the human mind, is really no more mysterious than deductive reasoning. It is simply a somewhat newer idea, and hence a little harder to accept.

If the human mind is capable of directly detecting patterns in data, then this would explain "induction," which could then be taken as simply the perception of a pattern in the data. This pattern, in some cases, would be a logical pattern, i.e., a pattern of deduction, and, in some cases, like the recognition of another human being, not. In any event, the perceived pattern might be incorrect.[10] As we obtained more data, we might realize that this new data did not fit the pattern achieved on the basis of the less refined information. It is also quite possible that the pattern-perceiving process is less dependable than the deductive reasoning system. If this is so, then our tendency to put greater weight on deductive reasoning would be justified. That we do put at least some reliance on directly perceived patterns in the absence of contrary

10. Dr. James Buchanan has pointed out to me that the pattern-perceiving process may well be the explanation for the phenomena of religious conversion. It seems likely that the human being is not only equipped to perceive patterns; he is strongly motivated to find them. The "ordering" of his universe is necessary for the mental equilibrium of the individual. Thus the sudden "perception" of a religious pattern which orders a large part of reality might well be as impressive an experience as the descriptions of "conversion." This would also explain both the extreme reluctance of most religious believers to accept simple disproofs of their religion, and their relative willingness to switch to another. See also Charles Joseph Singer, *A Short History of Scientific Ideas to 1900*, p. 239.

evidence is obvious to anyone who takes the trouble to examine carefully his own thought patterns.

The part played by pattern detection in science can best be understood if we start by examining some examples of pure "pattern" theories. The Greeks, particularly the Pythagoreans, put great emphasis on discovering patterns in nature. Although we now tend to consider this work largely number magic, it cannot be doubted that it had a great part to play in the early development of science. The general importance of such patterns may be illustrated by the gloomy speculations of physicists immediately after the discoveries of Li and Wang which destroyed one axis of symmetry around which the nuclear particles had previously been tentatively grouped.[11]

Better examples of pure pattern thinking, however, can be drawn from the history of chemistry in the nineteenth century. Early in the century it was noticed that the atomic weights of the various elements approximated a series of whole-number multiples of the weight of the lightest of them, hydrogen. This was a pattern and gave a logical way of listing the elements, and it could also be considered a hypothesis, or more exactly, a part of a hypothesis concerning the atoms. Insofar as it was hypothetical, it could be tested by two methods. There were gaps in the series, and it could be guessed that new elements would be discovered to fill these gaps; and this gradually happened. The other test, however, was much more precise. If the weights of the atoms were really simple multiples of the weight of hydrogen, then the irregularities shown in the existing data would be progressively reduced as the methods of measuring improved. Great progress in such measurements was, in fact, made. In 1912 the Nobel Prize for physics went to a scientist who had made extraordinarily precise determinations of the weights. There was, however, not the slightest tendency for the more precise measurements to approach simple multiples of the weight of hydrogen. Chlorine, in fact, persisted in approaching with greater and greater accuracy a figure about half way between thirty-five and thirty-six times the weight of hydrogen.

All of this made no difference to the chemists. The pattern was still there,

11. For an extreme example of the domination of pattern thinking before Li and Wang's work, see Murray Gell-Mann and E. P. Rosenbaum, "Elementary Particles," *Scientific American,* 197, No. 34 (July, 1957), 72. In spite of the blow dealt by Li and Wang, Gell-Mann, this time with Geoffrey Chew and Arthur H. Rosenfeld, has another article, in the February, 1964, issue of the same magazine, which is once again dominated by two elaborate charts showing a strong pattern ("Strongly Interacting Particles," 74–93).

even if it was rather fuzzy, and they continued to think it significant. Eventually, of course, it was discovered that elements, in the state of nature, are composed of mixtures of various isotopes and that the weights are consequently little more than coincidences. The pattern is still there, however, and is still considered important by chemists.

A more elaborate development of the pattern of the elements was developed by Mendeleev, who noticed that certain chemical characteristics seemed to recur at regular intervals if the elements were considered in order of their weight. This regular pattern was expressed in the form of the periodic table, which ordered all elements on two axes. Again, the system was both a pattern and a hypothesis, but the hypothesis was rather quickly disposed of. It was hypothesized that newly discovered elements would fill the blank spots on the table. Some of them did, but the rare earths resolutely refused to fit in, and the majority of elements discovered since Mendeleev's time are rare earths. This has never bothered the chemists very much. They simply print up the periodic table in a form which gives the rare earths special status and go on with it. Eventually, in this case, atomic physics produced explanations for the regularity and the irregularity of the chemical characteristics of the elements, but even the nuclear physicists have standard periodic tables in their offices because they find the pattern important in itself.

The pure pattern type, although important to my theory of theories, is a rather rare type of theory in the present age. Most modern theories are logical and deductive. Certain premises to certain conclusions is the normal form of a modern theory. This is, from my standpoint, simply a particular type of pattern. The ordering which the mind perceives in nature is a logical ordering, not some type of symmetry as in the periodic table of elements or in the organic ordering which is involved in recognizing the pattern of an individual. The logical pattern, however, has a very important special characteristic. It is frequently testable. It is possible to deduce from such a theory at least one testable hypothesis, and the theories which survive such tests are much more reliable than those that do not. Even among such logical theories, however, there are some which cannot be tested. The theory of evolution has so far been untestable.

The testable characteristic of logical patterns, in general, accounts for their predominance among present scientific theories. We prefer to depend on theories which are subject to deduction and experimental testing rather than on those which are "verified" solely by our perception of a pattern. In the case of the former there is further evidence in addition to the existence of the pattern, and we therefore feel more confident. A good many theories, as was demonstrated earlier, are the product of deduction, rather than induction, in their original form. These constitute logical patterns, but the logical pattern is the result of deductive operations, not a previously discovered pattern.

We are now in a position to describe the process of forming a hypothesis by induction. In practice, of course, a great many hypotheses are obtained by deduction. Further, the hypotheses are tested on being discovered, and the information obtained from the tests of unsuccessful hypotheses is then available for the formation of new theories. The interrelation between data collection, hypothesis formation (both deductive and inductive), and testing is complex. Each hypothesis is formed on the basis of available information, much of which may have been obtained in the testing of previous hypotheses, and the remainder of which presumably was obtained as a result of a hypothesis on the desirability of collecting some sort of data. The hypothesis is then checked, which normally involves further data collection, and either accepted or rejected. If rejected, the data collected (and the failure of the hypothesis is part of the obtained data) will then be used in attempts to form further hypotheses.

We can, however, analytically confine ourselves to the history of one hypothesis. This will involve considering the collection of data preceding the formulation of the hypothesis in relation only to that hypothesis and ignoring the other hypotheses which were actually involved. We can, also, for purposes of study, consider only inductive hypotheses, since the deductive hypotheses raise rather different issues. As a final simplification, we shall temporarily ignore the process of checking on the hypothesis once formed and stop our analysis at the point when we have a hypothesis. We have, then, a man whose information on some problem is increasing as a result of data accumulation. He will continue to increase his data and search for a hypothesis until he either formulates a theory or grows tired of the problem. Even after he has tired of the problem, his mind may continue to work, and he may produce a hypothesis long after he stops specific data accumulation.

The process of "induction," in my opinion, consists of examining the data for patterns, using the mind's ability to perceive such patterns directly.[12] The

12. Although I have no idea of the process by which the human mind finds "patterns," it is possible that we may be about to learn. Computers that can be trained to recognize patterns now exist. They have been developed to the point where at least one company, Bendix, is advertising its product in full pages of the *Scientific American,* 213, No. 1 (July, 1965), 12. Although

human mind is limited, however, in the number of facts which it can hold and even more limited in the number which it can hold at the front of the mind for the purposes of such a search. Analogously, we can assume that a scientist who has ten thousand "bits" of knowledge about a given problem can at any one time consider a group of one hundred of them while relegating the rest to the back of his mind. He then searches this group for a pattern, and if he fails to find one, he selects another group of one hundred "bits" (which may or may not include members of the first group). This description sounds rather mechanical, but I think it is what actually happens. The mind considers a selected group of facts. If no pattern is perceived, a new group is considered. Apparently, the process can be carried on by the subconscious mind while the conscious mind is otherwise engaged, since discoveries sometimes "come" to people who are consciously thinking of something else.

Earlier in this chapter, I pointed out that considering small samples of data selected out of a larger mass was a method of ordering the potential patterns in the mass so that the stronger patterns would be perceived first. This procedure of the human mind, therefore, is a good one for finding the strongest patterns, but almost insures that less conspicuous patterns will be overlooked. This is unfortunate, but patterns which are so feeble that they can be detected only by considering more data than the mind can hold at one time cannot be discovered except by accident. Only if such a pattern was deducible from other theories or if it was one of a finite universe of possible patterns for a given area would it be possible for the human race to become aware of it.

The mind, in considering a small part of all the data available to it, does not follow a truly random process. Since the theory sought is not known at the beginning of the procedure, and, indeed, since it is not even known that there is a theory, the initial selection, however, may as well be called random. Normally the procedure from this point forward, however, is to consider the given group of "bits" of information. If no hypothesis appears, a few more bits of information will be brought into consideration, and this shifts a few others out. This process of gradual shift in the information under consideration continues until the problem is solved or abandoned, or until it is decided to undertake a radical change in the approach to the problem. In the latter case, the investigator tries a new starting point using a radically differ-

---

I have no very clear idea of exactly how these machines make their decisions, their operations do not appear very much like human pattern perception. They are, however, a first step toward understanding the phenomenon.

ent selection of information and then goes through the same process of gradual change.

As time goes on, two processes somewhat improve the "span" of information which the investigator can consider at one time. In the first place, as he becomes more bound up with the problem, the amount of extrinsic information kept in the forefront of the mind declines. He devotes more of his mind to the problem and less to other matters, and this permits him to keep somewhat more knowledge under consideration at a time. Thus a pattern too faint to detect at the beginning of the study may now become visible.

More importantly, the investigator begins to group the information in clusters and then to think of the clusters as "bits." In the ideal case, these clusters of information themselves are genuine theories, which have been well tested. The simplification of the whole mass of data and the increase in the amount which can be brought under active consideration at any given moment by the development of such theories are of the very greatest importance. If a whole range of data, comprising thousands of "bits," can be compressed into a theory which itself can be treated as one or a few bits, then the real capacity of the mind is vastly increased. The greater the generality of the theory, the more useful it is in promoting thought by this process.

Unfortunately, most of the "clusters" which the mind will construct out of individual "bits" of information, if it considers a given problem for a long time, are not highly validated theories, but rather vague associations. The clusters, even if much less than genuine theories, are still of great value in permitting the mind to carry on active consideration of a larger range of information than would be possible without this labor-saving device. This is the reason why an expert in a given line is so greatly superior to others in solving completely new problems in his specialty. Familiarity and the ability to carry a good many more bits of information in the forefront of his mind (in the form of "clusters") give him the ability to reach almost immediate solutions to problems which are completely beyond the capacity of less well-trained minds.

This phenomenon, at the same time, explains why sometimes an outsider, or a man just learning a new field, will discover things which have escaped all the experts. The expert thinks in terms of the "clusters" of information which he has developed over the period of his experience. It may happen, however, that these clusters will be inappropriate for a new problem. In this case they actually handicap the search for a new solution, and a fresh approach will more probably be successful. A new mind will, of necessity, have a fresh approach and is unlikely to develop exactly the same clustering of ideas as the older experts have. Thus the procedure, often used by administrators attempting to expedite the solution of some problem, of bringing in a new man with a "fresh" viewpoint or of "going back to first principles" is rational. If the problem resists solution by the regular experts, either bringing in people who do not have the same mental clusters or trying to rearrange the clusters in the heads of the existing experts is a rational step.

It should not, however, be forgotten that the reason that the problem resists solution may be that it is insolvable, either in the present state of knowledge or permanently. Probably no problem has attracted as much intellectual effort as the trisection of an angle with ruler and compass. The eventual outcome was a proof that it was impossible, but only after almost two millennia of efforts for a solution. Any new problem we try to solve may be just as insolvable. We cannot tell an insolvable problem from a solvable one by examining the problem (unless, as in the trisection problem, we happen to have a proof of insolvability), nor does the fact that we have so far failed to solve a problem prove it insolvable. We may simply not yet have tried the right method. Problems may be divided into three classes, a small group that we have solved, another small group that we can prove to be insolvable, and the vast majority of problems about which all we know is that we cannot now solve them.

Any effort to solve a given problem, therefore, may be simply wasted. We cannot be certain that the problem is solvable at all. Even more, we cannot be certain that it is solvable with present knowledge and techniques. Many problems which bothered the Greeks were insolvable with their equipment but are very simple to our scientists. Similarly, we must expect that many problems which are not really insolvable are insolvable in the present state of knowledge. We may hope for the solution to a given problem and direct resources into the area, but we cannot really plan on its solution. A tendency to ignore this fact has characterized much recent writing about science. Doubtless we must make some anticipations of future developments in science as in other fields if we wish to invest our resources wisely, but it should not be forgotten that they are guesses. Somehow the fact that these guesses are guesses about science seems to carry the implication that they themselves are scientific. In fact, the one area of human activity in which we have a good logical proof that it is not possible to foresee developments is science. We cannot know today what we will discover tomorrow.

This principle has, however, certain encouraging aspects. If we cannot plan today on what we will discover tomorrow, we also cannot say what we will not discover. The process of induction which we have been discussing in this chapter is essentially unplannable. Discoveries by this method may occur in the most surprising ways. A man investigating one problem may suddenly see a pattern completely outside his field. It may, in fact, be argued that most important developments have occurred through this process. Certainly, it is common and important. In our earlier explanation of the process of investigation leading to the perception of a pattern, we spoke of the accumulation of data and the successive consideration of samples of that data. We said this process continued until a hypothesis was achieved, but we did not specify that the hypothesis would concern the original problem. In practice, it frequently does, but in a surprising number of cases it does not. The scientist, if he is a pure scientist, is motivated both by his particular curiosity about this specific problem and by a more general curiosity. The general curiosity is likely to remain with him while he investigates the specific problem, and the "induction" may well concern some problem other than the one he is specifically investigating. The same line of reasoning may be applied to practical investigations. The man who started out to find a substitute for ivory in billiard balls and made a whole vast series of important discoveries in the field of plastics en route is legendary, but not even slightly improbable.

Here we have another reason for not trying too hard to plan science. The solution of problem A may most easily be reached through investigation aimed at a solution of the apparently unrelated problem B. If this is so, then resources put into attempts to solve A would, from the standpoint of their own objective, be simply misdirected. Obviously, since we have no way of telling which non-A line of research is the most likely one, we will concentrate on direct approaches if we wish to solve A. Nevertheless, we should not consider our "plan" as more than a rather poor guess, relied on only because we have no better guesses. When we begin a given line of research, we cannot know whether the problem is solvable, solvable with our present knowledge, or best approached by the methods we have chosen. On the other side of the coin, it is quite possible that our investigation will lead to the solution of another problem which is more important.

As a final reason for not trying too hard to plan research, we must return to our discussion of the methods used by the mind in searching for a pattern. It is my theory, as will be recalled, that successive samples of data are examined for patterns by the mind. Now, planning of research must involve deciding on areas to be given priority, and priority will normally involve the assignment of more personnel. The number of samples scanned will, by this method, be increased, but not proportionally. There will be at least some duplication between individuals. The same samples will be scanned by each of two scientists working on the same problem at least occasionally. Further, the amount of such overlapping will increase exponentially with the number of men in the field. The marginal return on increased personnel is thus a declining function of their number, and it is therefore wise to keep scientific investigators dispersed in their interests. Concentrating them in one or a few fields will only marginally increase the rate of discoveries in that field, but will greatly reduce the rate of discoveries in the fields from which they have been drawn.

Thus, I finish my digression on the operation of the mind of the individual investigator and will return to the social organization of science. The possibility that I am completely wrong here is high enough that I feel an apology for including it is in order. I take comfort, however, in Hume's observation that "the errors of philosophy are only ridiculous and its extravagances do not influence our lives."[13]

13. *A Treatise on Human Nature,* Part IV, Section VII.

CHAPTER VI

VERIFICATION AND DISSEMINATION

It is sometimes alleged, particularly by scientists, that scientists are exceptionally honest and truthful and that their success in research is largely a reflection of these virtues. In fact, there is no reason to believe that scientists are much more truthful and honest than other men. The obvious high degree of truthfulness in scientific research comes not from the superior moral probity of the individual scientists, but from the social environment in which they operate. This environment combines a relative lack of temptation to be dishonest with extraordinarily strong "auditing" procedures to catch the occasional deviant. The scientific community, not normally having state power, cannot punish a man who is caught cheating by killing or imprisoning him, but the sanctions it does control are unsparingly used against the man who fakes an experiment or otherwise tries to fool his peers.

In the 1920's Paul Kammerer committed suicide in Vienna because he was "unable to survive the scandal" of being associated with a faked experiment.[1] He was a most prominent biologist, but one slip ruined him. He suddenly changed in the eyes of his peers from a respected figure into a man whose work was always suspect. His experimental results were no longer trusted, and his lines of reasoning could no longer be considered to be honestly derived.[2]

The man caught faking can expect to lose his position (even if he holds a tenure post in a university), to be unable to get any other decent job in his field, and to find that the learned journals are not interested in any further work he may produce. He is almost formally excommunicated from the professional world in which he lives.[3] It means the end of his career. The strength of the sanction, together with the certainty that it will be imposed, makes faking experiments a most unlikely course of action for the average scientist. The

1. David Joravsky, "Soviet Marxism and Biology before Lysenko," *Journal of the History of Ideas* (January, 1959), 85–104, esp. 92.

2. Kammerer was an indirect victim of "Lysenkoism." For a complete account of this remarkable subversion of a respected science, see Conway Zirkle, *Death of a Science in Russia* (Philadelphia: University of Pennsylvania Press, 1949). With the death of Stalin, "Lysenkoism" began a slow retreat and seems now to be on its last legs.

3. For a recent example, see "An Unfortunate Event," *Science,* 134 (September 29, 1961), 945–46. See also D. N. Misra's letter on page 199 of the April 13, 1962, issue (136).

absence of any formal "trial" system and the impossibility of the "defendant's" presenting a formal defense against formal charges means that injustices do occur. The scientist lives, in essence, under the law of the suspected. Like Caesar's wife, he must be free even of suspicion of wrongdoing.[4] As we shall see, although this system has no doubt blasted the career of innocent men, it is not irrational from the standpoint of the whole scientific community.

The influence of these extremely high standards on scientific work, and the lack of any particular moral distinction in scientists when they operate outside the area they cover, can be most readily illustrated from the history of the "atomic" debate. Since Hiroshima the political world has been violently divided on a number of issues concerning atomic energy. The physicists, being very directly involved in the whole thing, have always taken a leading part in these debates.[5] As anyone who has kept up with this discussion can testify, their contribution has not been distinguished by love of truth or impartiality. They have oversimplified, distorted, misunderstood opposing arguments, used unfair arguments themselves, gotten involved emotionally, occasionally engaged in direct lying, and in general acted just like people engaged in any other political dispute.[6]

In the normal practice of their profession, however, the scientists are re-

4. In C. P. Snow's *The Affair* (New York: Scribners, 1960), the plot turns on efforts to "clear" a scientist of a charge of faking which is not certainly true. Emphasis is put on the "desirability" of preventing "injustice" if there is any doubt of guilt. *The Affair,* of course, was written long after Snow had ceased to be a scientist and can be taken as a presentation of the non-scientific attitude. Compare it with his attitude toward much the same problem in *The Search* (New York: Bobbs-Merrill, 1935), written almost immediately after he ceased scientific activity, to see the difference between a scientist and a civil-servant–novelist.

5. In the early days of the new era they not infrequently took the view that they were the only people legitimately involved. I remember being told by a physicist at the University of Chicago in 1946 that my opinion on whether we should immediately publish all we knew was worthless because I did not know the mathematical equations for uranium fission. I inquired whether he felt that he fully understood either the Russians or international affairs in general, but he assured me that this was quite a different matter. He also seemed to think that the fact that distinguished physicists were to be found on all sides of the issue had nothing to do with the matter.

6. In considering this matter, it is best to examine the position of physicists whose political views on the matter are the opposite of your own. As in other political disputes, there is quite a range of positions within each camp. There are people who have pretty much succeeded in avoiding distorting facts to meet their political opinions, people who apparently see facts only if they coincide with their political positions, and all the points between.

markably free from these defects. Why is this? No doubt the scientists do, to some extent, feel that they have an obligation to be especially truthful in their scientific work. But the fact that they make misstatements about scientific matters when engaged in political debate seems to indicate that this "vocation" has no very deep effect. Apparently the basic reason for scientists' strict adherence to scientific standards arises not from any moral superiority, but from the social situation in which they find themselves.[7] It is not that scientists are more honest than other men; it is that they are more carefully watched.

In addition to a system of inspection which makes fakery unlikely to be successful, scientists do spend a lot of time indoctrinating other scientists (and themselves) with the "moral principles of science." I should not like to imply that I think this process has no results at all.[8] Probably there is some improvement of moral standards. The belief in the moral superiority of scientists which most of them hold in itself probably strengthens their antipathy to violations of the standards of scientific work. The main reliance, however, is not on indoctrination of moral principles, but on an apparatus which makes violation of the principal tenets of scientific probity unprofitable.

If we turn temporarily to motives, the scientist inspired by curiosity or by the desire to make some practical application of his discoveries is not much tempted to produce fake results. There are no practical applications of false scientific discoveries. If they are false, then practical devices based on them would not work. The applied scientist is forced, by his objectives, to confine himself to a scrupulous pursuit of truth. This, however, refers to applied science as we have defined it. There are some people in industrial laboratories who are motivated to cheat on their experiments. The situation arises generally in areas where the problem is not to develop something new, but to develop sales arguments for an existing, possibly slightly modified, product or process.[9] Science having prestige, scientific reports proving the superior-

7. Hans Ertel, vice president of East Germany's Academy of Science and a leading theoretical meteorologist, was convicted on a fraud charge in a West Berlin court. In pleading for mercy he said, "Thirty years of life in the abstract sphere of natural science made me lose the grips of reality." *New York Times,* April 25, 1965, p. 18.

8. See Meg Greenfield, "Science Goes to Washington," *The Reporter,* 29 (September 26, 1963), 20–26, for a discussion of the behavior of scientists in situations where moral judgments are difficult.

9. The development of research as a major economic activity has opened another avenue for dishonesty. Under some circumstances an individual or organization may be able to im-

ity of Brand X or possibly proving that a battery additive will do anything at all may be of use to men with money to hire scientists. True laboratory results would normally be more helpful than false, but false reports may be better than none, and a good deal of minor faking on these lines goes on. Generally, it is regarded by everyone concerned as less important than trying to develop real improvements. From our standpoint, this simply is not science.[10] This appears to be also the opinion of the scientists themselves. The people who do this sort of work are normally considered as being outside the profession, regardless of the number of degrees they hold.

The pure scientist is equally bound by his own motivation system to avoid false discoveries. His curiosity is a desire to find the truth, not to invent falsities, and can be satisfied only by scrupulous adherence to the facts. Here again, however, this is a product of our definition, and some people who work in university laboratories have other motives. The most important of these other motives is vanity. A man who has made what he thinks is an important discovery may feel injured by further information tending to disprove it and may be led by his injured vanity into various deviations from the straight and narrow path. That this has occurred in the history of science cannot be denied, but I doubt if it is of great importance. The man inspired by curiosity may be temporarily misled by a devotion to his own ideas, but eventually he will usually come around. In any event, the verification process of science will normally result in other people's correcting his errors.[11] Scientists are fairly tolerant of this type of human failing, and a man who gets results in experiments which support a position which he has taken but which cannot be repeated by others will normally be forgiven if he does not do it too often.

The man motivated by induced curiosity presents a more difficult problem. His concern is not with reality, but with making an income by investigating reality. Since the size of his income will normally correlate with the importance of his results, he is motivated to get "significant" results even by fakery. However, as will be demonstrated below, in the environment of the

---

prove its income by falsifying its results so as to stimulate further research in an area which should be abandoned. How important this is I have no way of saying. Surely scientific administrators who wish to maximize the results to be obtained from a given appropriation should keep the possibility in mind.

10. A genuinely scientific investigation might be undertaken to determine which particular type of fake laboratory results were most convincing.

11. W. C. Allee, *The Social Life of Animals* (New York: Norton, 1938), p. 90.

natural sciences, fakery is almost certain to be detected, and the probability of detection is highly correlated with the importance of the result reported. As a result, the induced-curiosity researcher normally makes no effort to fake his results despite his motivation to do so, because he knows the probable long-run effect of such fakery would be detrimental to his career.

Possibly I should take this opportunity to repeat that the three motives we have distinguished for the purposes of analysis do not normally appear in their pure form in individual scientists. Normally a scientist will be motivated to at least some extent by each of the three considerations; our separate treatment is justified by analytical considerations. I do, however, rule out certain other motives which may be present in human minds. As will be explained in the next chapter, investigators in the "social sciences" are not infrequently motivated by drives other than the three which we have been considering, and this fact is one of the more important reasons for the backwardness of these fields.

Turning now to the actual procedure of verification and dissemination of new discoveries, we must start by pointing out that, in a sense, this chapter runs over the same ground as does Chapter IV. The dissemination of data and the collection of data are in part simply different ways of describing the same process. The process of looking something up is data collection from the standpoint of the man doing the looking, but data dissemination from the standpoint of the man who originally discovered it. This fact will result in this chapter's duplicating to some degree the material in Chapter IV, but I have tried to examine it from a new viewpoint and to emphasize those aspects of special importance to the investigator who has completed a given line of investigation. Nevertheless, the division of material between Chapters IV and VI is essentially arbitrary; it would not be possible to prove that any given paragraph is in the right chapter.

Having formed a hypothesis—and this is the point at which we left our scientist at the end of Chapter V—the investigator will try to verify it. As pointed out by Dr. Popper, this really means attempting to find evidence which will contradict the hypothesis, not evidence which will bear it out. For linguistic convenience, I will use "verify" as a handy term for the results of investigations which fail to falsify a given hypothesis. The first step in verification, then, usually consists of simply giving the hypothesis more thought. In the vast majority of all cases, this leads to immediate falsification. Most of our initial guesses are wrong, so wrong that they are given up after only a little further consideration. With those which survive this initial screening, the investigator proceeds to further checks.

Basically, the process of checking a hypothesis consists of data collection, just like the data collection which preceded the formation of the hypothesis. The procedure is to reason from the hypothesis to some conclusion which is subject to factual checking and then to find out whether the facts are as hypothesized. For any given set of facts, there are, theoretically, an infinite set of possible theories. Choosing one rather than another is inherently arbitrary. If, however, a man formulates a theory from a given set of data, and it then turns out to fit other information, we have better grounds for believing it to be generally valid than if it were originally formulated as the result of consideration of the whole body of information.

The data collection involved in verification of theories does not differ from that involved in the preliminary stage of the investigation. In fact, if the hypothesis is disproved, the new data collected in the process of disproof will form part of the data on which new hypotheses are built. It will be recalled that the process of data collection largely runs by formation of hypotheses and that the disproof of substantive theories is a major source of new data. Thus, the scientist checking on a new hypothesis will normally first turn to the literature to find out whether certain "predictions" of the theory are true and, if this fails, will turn to direct investigation of nature. Eventually, he decides either that the theory is false, which puts him back in Chapter IV, or that it is true, and, for the purpose of this chapter, we will assume that he has reached the latter conclusion.

Being himself assured of the accuracy of his discovery, the scientist has now reached the stage of dissemination of the discovery. The procedure differs in applied research and pure, however, and we must discuss the two fields independently. We shall start with a discussion of the process of dissemination in applied research and then turn to that in the pure field. In some cases the successful investigator may make strenuous efforts to prevent the dissemination of his discoveries. The geology department of an oil company, for example, will normally do its best to keep its discoveries strictly secret. The reason, of course, is obvious. Obtaining scientific information normally costs money, and if it is freely available to all, then the enterprises which have not spent money on research will make more profits than those that do. Without the patent system, there would be little research except in fields where it was possible to keep the results secret. In fields where patents are not available, like subterranean geology, secrecy is the rule. Little research is undertaken except where it can be kept secret, at least for long enough to pay for itself.[12]

The result of this system is the development of "industrial espionage," which functions much like regular espionage. The hiring of an engineer away from a company is the commonest way of getting its secrets, but there are others. Recently there has been a good deal of litigation on the problem. The end result is that secret processes are normally not kept secret very long (though there is a man in California who has been making artificial emeralds by a secret process for twenty years).

In any event, however, there is no point in keeping false research results secret. Only correct discoveries will assist a man to make money by applying them.[13] This same consideration applies also to applied research which is not kept secret. A chemist, say, in DuPont's laboratories will normally find that his superiors consider his discoveries solely in terms of whether they will sell, and the ultimate customers will buy only if the product lives up to expectations. Normally, then, the applied scientist simply cannot fake his research results, because no one is interested in his experiment qua experiment; the only concern anyone has with his result is to apply it somewhere else. Since the application will occur outside his control, any dishonesty in reporting results will be readily and immediately detected.

The method of dissemination of discoveries in the applied sciences is simply a special application of the general system of advertising used to sell any other product. A glance at the advertising pages of *Science* or the *Scientific American* will show that advertising of new scientific advances, even if they are in the field of experimental aids and laboratory devices and sold solely to scientists, is no different from the advertising of anything else. The same principles, the same advertising personnel, and the same testing techniques to check on the efficiency of the advertising are used in both fields. This is, of course, no criticism. There is every reason to believe that advertising men are

12. In the case of geology, a law requiring all mineral prospectors to deposit the records of their investigations in open files within five years of their completion would result in a vast economization of research expenditures without more than marginally disadvantaging the individual investigators.

13. There are some areas where it is very difficult to tell whether the results are correct or not; weather modification will serve as an example. Here the applied scientist may not be able to tell for certain whether his results are correct, and neither he nor his customers will know for certain whether he is really selling something.

as skilled in disseminating ideas as any group in the world today. Certainly the scientists in the non-psychological fields have no grounds for thinking that they could do better.

Nevertheless, the fact that applied scientific advances are disseminated through the same channels of advertising, salesmanship, and public relations as other commercial products does have some effect on the development of science. These channels, of course, are much faster than the system of scientific publication used for "pure" discoveries, but they leave fewer permanent records. A scientist is much more likely to have a new discovery in the applied field brought forcibly to his attention by various people than he would if it were a pure development. On the other hand, it is usually harder to find out about older developments in the applied field than in the pure. The advertisements in the *Scientific American* are not indexed according to the device advertised. If something is developed, promoted, and then abandoned for any one of a large number of reasons, it is unlikely that a scientist in the future who needs this exact device will ever find out that it has already been invented.

In part, of course, this problem is met by the publication of articles describing new devices and processes in scientific journals. These articles, inspired partly by public relations men and partly by the desire of the designers to spread their ideas, do appear in large numbers in respectable journals and are indexed and available to future investigators. The limitations on this method, however, can be most serious. Many applied investigators have backgrounds different from those of the pure scientists and "speak another language," with the result that their research results may not appear relevant to the university man. This is particularly likely if the applied scientist has, without realizing it, solved a problem of great theoretical interest. An engineer who has discovered, by simple trial and error, that a certain internal geometry is particularly effective in preventing cavitation in high-speed-liquid flows through a valve may not realize that his discovery would be of great importance to some pure scientist. The pure scientist, on the other hand, is not likely to suspect that the most fruitful line of investigation open to him would be to disassemble one of the valves in his laboratory and make a careful study of its geometry.

There does not, however, appear to be much which can be done to solve this problem. Certainly, few improvements in the dissemination of applied ideas can be suggested. The existence of strong monetary incentives for wide dissemination, combined with almost equally strong incentives to avoid producing devices which will not work, insures that developments in the applied lines will be widely advertised. Although the methods of dissemination and verification in the pure sciences are different, we shall see that they are also efficient. Unfortunately, they are much more complicated.

A scientist motivated by curiosity or induced curiosity, who is assured in his own mind that he has made a significant discovery, normally proceeds to write it up for publication in a journal or, more rarely, as a paper to be read at a meeting. He then has the problem of getting it accepted.[14] If he is well known and widely respected, this is usually not very difficult. Editors and organizers of meetings will tend to assume that he is right in his own judgment.[15] This, of course, amounts to a prejudice against the man who is not yet "established." If some way could be developed of eliminating this prejudice, so that all papers were judged strictly on their merits, it would obviously somewhat increase the likelihood that new and original minds would be given a chance, but this seems impossible. Further, as will be demonstrated below, it would be inefficient. Submitting all papers with the name of the author concealed until acceptance or rejection was decided on would, in the first place, be objected to by the editors, who would have to work harder, and, secondly, be ineffective anyway, since any competent judge of the work in a given field would frequently be able to recognize papers by the leading authorities.

We have already discussed the necessity of a "threshold" which the article must pass to be published. A certain degree of importance is a minimum requirement for publication. There is, unfortunately, a converse problem; some articles may be too important. The careful study which makes some minor, but respectable, improvement in knowledge in a given field poses few

14. For two discussions of the problem of dissemination, see Dwight E. Gray, "Information and Research, Blood Relatives or In-Laws," *Science,* 137 (July 27, 1962), 263–66, and Jack MacWatt, "Improving Scientific Communication," *Science,* 134 (August 4, 1961), 313–16.

15. In some cases the practice of judgment by reputation may lead to serious errors. See Joseph Roucek, "Some Academic 'Rackets' in the Social Sciences," *American Behavioral Scientist,* 6, No. 5 (January, 1963), 9–10. Sometimes completely irrelevant matters may have a serious effect on the "reputation" of a scholar. Professor Roucek is not a native-born American and, when excited, tends to fall into the grammar and controversial standards of his upbringing. This permitted *Problems of Communism* to "answer" a letter he sent in criticizing a couple of articles by simply printing it as received. May–June, 1965, 56.

problems for the editor. An article proposing a drastic revision of existing theory or reporting dramatically unexpected research results is a much more difficult problem. Obviously, such articles are much more important, but they are also much more risky. The probability of error on the part of the original investigator is greater, the possibility of error by the editor in misjudging the article is also great, and it is certain that the article, if published, will be very carefully examined by a large number of specialists. Under the circumstances, the possibility that the editor's own reputation will suffer from publication of such articles is a real one. It is not surprising, therefore, that these articles are sometimes hard to place.

The basic problem, of course, is the quality of the editorial work in the journals. At present, this is fairly good, but it could be greatly improved. In the first place, the job of journal editor, although respectable, is not one of sufficient attraction to get the very best personnel. An editor should have a grasp of his field firm enough to recognize new work which is important, time to read carefully everything he receives, and motives leading him to be most careful in selecting the articles which he will publish. This may seem like a utopian listing of desirable characteristics, but much can be done. We shall discuss these three desirable characteristics in turn.

Present-day editors of journals vary greatly. While the editor of a journal is seldom the leading figure in a given field, he may come close to that level. At the opposite extreme, and more commonly, the editor may be simply a respected but ordinary worker in the field covered by his journal. If all journal editors were leading specialists in their fields, the change would obviously improve the level of the editing of journals. The problem of work that is "over the head" of the editor should never arise, but under present circumstances it does. The reasons for the less than exalted level of ability among journal editors is simple. Such jobs are, in both prestige and monetary compensation, less attractive than certain types of "administrative work." Even the greatest scientists, as they get older, tend to lose their ability to do original work of great importance.[16] Currently, this normally leads them into "administrative" positions. In the last chapter, I shall argue that such work, in the present organization of science, constitutes almost pure social waste. The type of "administration of science" which determines what research shall be pub-

16. There are exceptions to this rule, but it does represent the general trend. In any event, the line of reasoning presented does not depend on this assumption, but can be supported from the much weaker position that some great scientists lose their creativity as they get older.

lished, on the other hand, is of the utmost importance, and it is highly desirable that the best personnel be brought into this field.

The problem of improving the quality of editors is largely a problem of incentives; higher pay and improved prestige for these strategic members of the scientific community would be desirable. The higher pay could be easily taken care of by the foundations, which now put much money into less important aspects of science. From their standpoint, it would be both cheap and easy to administer. They would only have to make the money available. The selection of editors could be left to the people who now do it, but there would be more and better candidates for the job, and the results would normally be better. The improved salaries would have some effect in improving the prestige of the jobs, the better personnel attracted would further this improvement, and I would hope that an information campaign would have a still greater effect.

If this program did, in fact, attract into editing leading investigators who had lost some of their creativity, the improvement in the quality of the journals would obviously follow. It is not certain, however, that the editors would have a grasp of their fields firm enough to recognize new work which is important. In many cases the fields covered by journals are so wide that no one man can hope to have a firm grasp of the whole. We can first inquire whether this fact does not in itself constitute a defect in scientific publication procedures. All journals are specialized; is it not possible that the measure of desirable specialization might coincide with the field which one man can hope to understand? If the answer to this question is yes, then the editor who simply rejected articles which he felt were outside his competence would be performing his duty.

This question, however, is one which we do not have to answer. If the scope of the magazine is too wide for one man to cover, then obviously it will be necessary to provide more than one man. Currently, there are two different ways of dealing with this problem.[17] The first, and most desirable, is to maintain a board of editors, each of whom is competent in some part of the general field covered by the journal. Articles are simply sent to the appropriate editor for examination. This seems to me rational, and I would only suggest that the pressure on members of the board to review contributions carefully would be increased if the responsibility of each member for a given substantive category were specifically and publicly spelled out, and if the ac-

17. For some brief, and rather lighthearted, discussion of the problem of referees, see the letters under "Referees: Credits and Demerits," *Science,* 148 (May 8, 1965), 1174.

ceptance or rejection of any given article were clearly allocated to the specialist responsible rather than to the chief editor.[18]

The other process now in use, which works much less efficiently, is to send contributions to anonymous readers. There is, of course, no reason why the editor should not ask for advice from anyone he feels like, but substituting the judgment of the reader for his own is another matter. If the reader is really more competent, then he should be editor; if he is less competent, he should not be given the deciding voice. There is some tendency for editors to submit manuscripts to relatively junior scientists, since such men are rather flattered at the honor and are unlikely to delay and delay. The anonymity of the process is also objectionable. The editor turns an article down (or accepts it) because he agrees with his reader and normally does not feel particularly strong personal responsibility for his action. On the other hand, the reader, under the shield of anonymity, is also not under any great pressure to reach the correct decision.

The recommended changes in policy, the use as editors of prominent members of the profession who are in a non-creative stage of their lives and the elimination of anonymous readers, would, I think, greatly improve the scientific journals. Unfortunately, the next problem, providing enough time for adequate consideration of each article, is much more difficult. The problem is intensified by the practice of sending rejected articles to other journals. This means that multiplying the journals does not reduce the number of manuscripts received by anyone. (Except marginally, insofar as the articles already accepted by other journals are not sent out. For the leading journals, not even this reduction would result.) It simply means that a rejected paper can be sent out to more journals. Sending an article to five journals before either getting it accepted or giving up is by no means unusual. Restrictions on the resubmission of articles should not be considered as a solution to this problem, since the possibility of trying an article out with several editors is one of the major advantages of the present system. As explained in Chapter III, this functions as a necessary safeguard for original ideas. Any editor can decide that a given article will be published, but no editor has, or should have, the power to decide that it will not.

The problem, then, is not subject to any simple and straightforward solution. A journal which normally receives a number of articles which is too

18. This would require some mechanical process for deciding how many articles in a given period of time could be accepted by each editor.

large for careful reading by one man can, it is true, maintain several editors. This solution, in moderation, offers some assistance, but is subject to a severe drawback. The more editors obtained with a given quantity of resources (whether money or prestige), the lower the average quality. Thus this larger number of editors, although they have more time to appraise each contribution individually, probably have fewer mental qualifications to do a good job. Obviously, the two considerations must be balanced against each other, and the final decision in any given case will largely turn on the personnel available. Still, it seems fairly certain that the editor(s) will be pressed for time. This means that he (or they) will have to economize on time, and certain rules of thumb are likely to be used to that end.

The first scheme, already discussed, is to take into account the reputation of the writer of a paper. In some cases this takes the extreme form of simply automatically publishing anything which comes from a prominent authority. More commonly, the editor will read over the contributions of prominent men and reject those he considers substandard, but he does give them special treatment. In the first place, he is likely to give them priority in his reading. A contribution by a famous scientist will be read almost as soon as received, regardless of the number of unread manuscripts from less well-known men on the editor's desk. It will also be given more consideration. This last may be contested by some editors, but a little reflection will convince them of its truth. If an editor receives a manuscript from an unknown man which seems wrong, obscure, or absurd, he will normally simply reject it after one reading. The same manuscript from a prominent man would be reread a number of times before the editor decided that it was really wrong, obscure, or absurd. The reputation of the author may not convince the editor that the article is a good one, but it does cause him to be very careful about deciding that it is bad.

The reverse of this rule is also used. There are some well-known crackpots in every field, and their contributions are normally rejected with little or no consideration. The man who has been caught faking experiments is likely to get the same treatment. These are extreme cases, but somewhat the same principle applies in less obvious situations. An editor receiving an article from a man about whom he feels a little suspicious will normally discriminate against it. He will realize that he must read it carefully and check the factual information before he publishes it, and it may simply not be worth it. He has many other contributions on his desk, and the giving of disproportionate time to one may seem unjust to the others. This is, of course, one of the reasons why a scientist's reputation for complete honesty is so important to him.

Another rule of thumb concerns the nature of the research. Routine reports are both easier to evaluate and less likely to be spectacularly wrong than "bold pioneering efforts." Thus, although the editor will normally fully realize that the "bold pioneering efforts" are most important, he will also realize that he should give them much more consideration before publishing than is necessary with the routine papers.[19] Since the editor is usually pressed for time, this may well result in implicit discrimination against the new and original. This problem is, I think, well known to most editors, and they usually make considerable effort to balance properly the time spent on such articles with that spent on the humdrum type, but some restriction on the publication of the type of paper which might represent a major advance is inevitable.

These rules of thumb, I should like to emphasize, are rational. Although they result in some misjudgments, they do perform the function of economizing on the editor's time and, consequently, result in his whole task being more efficiently performed. It is true that the average article submitted by a prominent authority is more worthy of careful consideration than that of an unknown. It is true that articles by crackpots and suspected fakers are, on the average, less worthwhile than those of ordinary scientists, and last, but not least, although the "bold pioneering efforts" are more important than the routine reports of experiments, the time needed to evaluate them adequately is so great that the editor behaves rationally in discriminating, to some extent, against them.

The motivation of the editors of learned journals is rather complex. In the first place, they are normally really interested in their subjects and eager to increase knowledge in their spheres. The importance of this motive to their work can hardly be overestimated, but it is hard to say anything in detail about it. Secondly, they are motivated by the same monetary and prestige motives as the induced pure scientist. The primary motive, interest in the subject, is not controllable by the sponsors of the journal or magazine, except insofar as they attempt to choose someone with a strong drive as editor. The monetary and prestige items are, in part, under their control. Certainly they can arrange a salary large enough to give the editor a strong motive to do his work well enough to avoid removal.

As we have pointed out before, the prestige of a journal is largely determined by the opinion of the profession in general and turns mostly on its ap-

19. J. R. Porter, "Challenges to Editors of Scientific Journals," *Science,* 141 (September 13, 1963), 1014–17.

praisal of the contents. The editor's prestige is, to a large extent, dependent on the prestige of the journal, and he therefore has a strong motive to improve the magazine. It should be noted, in this connection, that the number of subscribers above a certain point is more or less irrelevant to the prestige of a given journal. Most journals (except those that come automatically with membership in sizable professional organizations) have few subscribers aside from university libraries, research organizations, and other institutions. This lack of concern with mass sales is particularly noticeable when pure-science magazines are compared with applied-science magazines. The engineering journals are clearly organized to make money, and they try to get as large a readership as possible. The pure-science journals, on the other hand, try to maintain such a high standard of scholarship as to frighten off the bulk of potential readers. They depend on endowments or subsidies of some sort for their operating expenses and aim to please the very restricted group of people at the top of their particular specialties.

This scheme, as we have pointed out in Chapter III, leads to a most efficient system of transmission of information of real importance. It does, however, have one serious flaw. The prestige of a journal is affected by the articles it prints; it is not affected by those it turns down. This probably leads the editors to some degree, at any rate, to play safe. They are unlikely to publish an article which looks as if it might start a violent controversy and eventually result in criticism of the magazine. This means that very important articles are sometimes hard to publish. As a method of adjusting the motivational scheme of editors, a system should be devised for giving publicity to their rejection policies. Two methods suggest themselves. If scientists who publish collections of their articles would indicate who had turned them down, particularly the ones written when they were not well known, considerable pressure on editors to be careful in reading revolutionary articles from unknown scholars would result. This procedure has the disadvantage that most scientists are loath to annoy the various editors who are people of great power in the scientific community.

A second method would involve a more formal approach to the problem. If, after a period, say five years, the best articles from a given year in some specialty were selected (this would show which ones had stood the test of at least a little time) and an investigation of how many times they had been rejected and who had rejected them were undertaken, we would get a good deal of information on an important point. If this process were a yearly routine, it would, again, put pressure of a desirable sort on the editors. It would also probably somewhat undermine the prestige of editing in general, since most editors would have at least one bad error show up. It might be necessary to pay somewhat higher wages to editors to compensate for this loss.

A most useful general research project could be performed here. A careful study of the history of rejected articles would show how accurate the judgment of editors is, how often articles are normally submitted before the author becomes discouraged, and many other interesting things. The *American Economic Review* rejects 91 per cent of all articles submitted to it.[20] How many of these are never published? How many are published in the two or three other leading economic journals? And how many get into the secondary journals? How accurate is the selection process? Presumably the editors reject all of the really worthless articles submitted, but are the articles accepted actually better than the top 10 per cent of the rejects? It is easy to extend the list of significant questions almost indefinitely. Given the importance of these editorial decisions to science, the absence of research into them is surprising.

Once an article has been published, the first and most important step in its dissemination has been taken. The verification process, however, has just begun.[21] Further dissemination and verification processes now proceed together, but we can confine ourselves temporarily to the verification system and then return to discuss the dissemination of the new discovery. The verification process involves two different techniques, repetition and discussion. Again, we shall, for convenience, consider these two simultaneous processes separately, beginning with repetition.

The repetition of scientific work is one of the most conspicuous features of the system of investigation. The absence of such repetition in such "social sciences" as sociology is one of the strongest evidences of their non-scientific character. Sociology, oddly enough, involves a lot of repetitive research without real repetition. The conundrum results from the fact that sociologists apparently do not have very original minds and tend to partially copy each other's research. They almost never, however, copy the previous research completely, with the consequence that their work never constitutes a real repetition.

20. *American Economic Review* (May, 1965), 610.

21. Although scientists are remarkably open-minded, they still tend to cling to old ideas to some extent, which makes the verification process particularly painstaking. See Bernard Barber, "Resistance by Scientists to Scientific Discovery," *Science,* 134 (September 1, 1961), 596–602, and Michael Polanyi, "The Potential Theory of Adsorption," *Science,* 141 (September 13, 1963), 1010–13.

Repetition occurs in three types of cases—theory, observation, and experiment. The repetition of theoretical work is not obvious, but it is a necessary part of science. An article which simply presents a theoretical argument may, like other types of research, be wrong. Some method of checking on such articles is necessary and is provided by normal practice, but the method is largely unconscious. A scientist who sees a theoretical article in a journal may do two things (other than skipping it, of course). He can simply examine it closely enough to determine what the result of the investigation was and then utilize that result, or he can read it carefully in an effort to understand its reasoning. Given the volume of material turned out, we can hardly criticize investigators who take the first alternative for a given article, but this obviously presents no guard against errors. The man who reads in search of understanding, on the other hand, must mentally go through all the steps of the proof, and this repetition of the line of reasoning provides a check on the accuracy of the article. Since at least some of the readers will repeat the reasoning and may notice errors, we are provided with some assurance that any article which was published some time ago and has not yet been demolished is correct.

The difference between observation and experiment turns on whether the investigator does or does not have control of the repetition of the reported events. Recently, for example, a Russian astronomer reported observing what he took to be volcanic activity on the moon. Obviously, this is not something we can check in the laboratory. Repetition in this case takes the form of simply looking more frequently at the moon in hopes of repeating the observation. Eventually, some American astronomers also saw the phenomena. Logically, of course, the failure to see a repetition does not disprove the original observation, but the number of hypotheses which cannot be logically disproved is infinite, and a scientist can consider only a finite number of ideas.

These problems fortunately do not arise in the case of experiments, which can normally be repeated at will. The reasons for repeating scientific work can be summed up in a word: "verification." Scientists naturally feel much more confidence in working with results that have been repeatedly tested. Further, the repetition process puts pressure on investigators, the end result of which is a greater degree of reliability even among those experiments which are not repeated. The principal potential causes of erroneous "discoveries" in science are conscious fraud, subconscious bias, and accident. Obviously, a system of automatic checking makes fraud unlikely and puts pressure on investigators to avoid bias. Although it cannot prevent accidental errors, it does put pressure on investigators to be careful and will detect such errors if they are committed.

The elimination of conscious fraud is seldom mentioned in formal discussions of the reasons for repetition in science. The quasi-mythological view that scientists are uniformly of higher moral standards than ordinary mortals is maintained, and subconscious bias is usually depended upon to explain the importance of independent repetition.[22] To repeat, scientists are not much better than other men, and there certainly are at least a few among them who would fake experiments if there was something to be gained therefrom. The induced researcher has something to gain if he can get away with such a fraud. His income depends largely on the reputation he can develop, and this, in turn, depends on his "discoveries." It is obviously easier to produce an important and exciting article if one simply invents the facts reported than if one is confined to reality. This being so, the prevention of fraud depends on a detection apparatus. Part of the detection apparatus involves repetition.

Not all reported experiments are repeated, but the potential faker must realize that he runs a real risk. Further, his risk is the greater if his "discoveries" are of any great significance. In most fields, routine research leading to routine and unexciting results is fairly easy for a qualified investigator. Thus, a modest reputation can be built up by solid work, and faking results on this level would not improve that reputation.[23] The important results, on the other hand, are almost certain to be repeated. Thus the risk of detection in fraud is highly correlated with the gain from success. At all levels, the combination of risk of detection and probable sanction is enough to counterbalance the gain from successful fraud for any even modestly rational "wicked man."[24]

Subconscious bias is the normal explanation used by scientists in explaining the use of repetition. No doubt, it is in fact an important reason. Pure detachment is a myth. Even the best investigator may have his judgment clouded and his ability to read instruments affected by strongly held opinions. The man who has discovered and promulgated a theory is more likely to find evidence supporting that theory in a given experimental design than

22. Jean Rostand, *Error and Deception in Science* (New York: Basic Books, 1960), title essay.

23. Faking results is, of course, easier than actually doing the experiments. The lazy investigator might therefore be motivated to fakery even in this sphere. Dishonesty seldom arises from laziness, however; it is much more likely to come out of ambition.

24. Oliver Wendell Holmes, *The Common Law* (Boston: Little, Brown, 1881).

is another man who has opposite personal biases and interests. Nevertheless, scientists are remarkably good at keeping the influence of these factors to a minimum in their work. One of the reasons for their success in this regard is their knowledge that their work will eventually be checked by others and, in particular, that their experiments are likely to be repeated by unfriendly critics.

Although scientists tend to be tolerant of the type of mistake which arises from too great concern with the results of an experiment, there can be no doubt that at least some penalties are imposed on a man who makes this kind of mistake. He can expect to have his future articles subjected to a rather closer scrutiny and his discoveries greeted with somewhat more skepticism than if he has never been misled by enthusiasm. There is, therefore, a sound material motive for great care on the part of the scientist. Most scientists, if observed in operation, take the most extreme precautions to avoid observational errors due to their own biases and interests. Although this sometimes leads to leaning over backward, it still does not completely eliminate errors from this source. Such errors are generally caught by repetitions, and the process of repetition also provides a strong material motive for the precautions of the scientist.

These two functions of the repetition process effectively motivate the scientist to avoid certain types of "error" which are within his control. The last function deals with a "fact of nature," not with human errors. It is unfortunately true that accidents happen in laboratories as well as everywhere else. The favorable result obtained in an experiment may result not from the phenomena under investigation, but from the accidental effect of something else. Possibly the experimental setup involves some as yet undiscovered natural phenomenon which was completely unexpected. It is a common story that the discovery of radioactivity resulted from the accidental simultaneous presence in Becquerel's desk of a pack of film, a key, and a lump of pitchblende. Becquerel performed an experiment using the film and was astonished to see the image of the key on the developed sheet as well as the expected result. He was then able to trace the phenomenon back and to announce the revolutionary discovery of radioactivity. Suppose, however, that his experiment had been an effort to test a hypothesis which was, in fact, false, but which would be verified under his experimental setup by the appearance of a key on the film. He would have received a particularly clear "verification" and the experiment would have been easily "repeatable" until he had used up all of the films in that particular pack. Repetition by somebody else, on the other hand, would have quickly shown the falsity of the results.[25]

This spectacular type of error may be rare, but a less obvious and no less important type of error is quite probably due to the use of statistical methods in verification of hypotheses. Modern statistics is a very powerful tool, but, like other things, it does have drawbacks. One of these drawbacks is the existence of erroneous "confirmations." It can easily be argued that these erroneous results are no more common than if we used "verifying" evidence of some other sort, but the fact is that we do use statistics. The elegance of the method is such that we may accept rather less evidence if it is statistical than if it is "merely" qualitative.

In order briefly to explain the problem, let us consider the example which has introduced innumerable people to statistics: the tea-tasting test in the second chapter of R. A. Fisher's *The Design of Experiments.* "A lady declares that by tasting a cup of tea made with milk she can discriminate whether the milk or the tea infusion was first added to the cup."[26] The experiment to test this rather unimportant hypothesis consists of allowing her to make four choices out of eight cups arranged in pairs, in one of which the milk was first added and in one the tea. By chance she would be right two times, and being right three out of four times would also not be particularly improbable, so the hypothesis would be considered confirmed only if she was correct on all four. The method consists, essentially, in computing the probability of obtaining a given experimental result by chance and, if the probability is small enough, accepting the hypothesis that the result was obtained through some causal factor other than chance.

Now, by simple definitional reasoning, it is obvious that this system of verification will result in errors. Out of a hundred ladies about six would pass the test even if none of them had any ability to discriminate between the two types of tea. The same can be said about any statistical test of a scientific hypothesis. Since a great number of experiments, in fact, lead to rejections of the hypothesis, it is clear that there must be occasions on which false hypotheses are accepted.[27] There are no statistics available on the subject, but

25. Unless, of course, the second investigator obtained his film from Becquerel.

26. London, 1935, p. 13.

27. See Theodore D. Sterling, "Publication Decisions and Their Possible Effects on Inferences Drawn from Tests of Significance—or Vice Versa," *Journal of the American Statistical Association,* 54 (March, 1959), 30–34, and my own comment on this article, page 593 of the September, 1959, issue of the same journal.

my guess would be that there are about four experiments performed in which the hypothesis is rejected for each one in which it is accepted. Generally, these experiments in which the hypothesis is rejected are less likely to be published.

It should not, however, be deduced that we could determine the number of false results in the published literature by counting all of the rejected hypotheses and dividing the total by the appropriate number. There are two difficulties which make this impossible. In the first case, we may be wrong in our view of what the results of chance would be. In the teacup experiment, there is little possibility that this problem will arise, but in the most difficult parts of science, it is an important problem. Normally, in biological experiments, the chance variations are tested by some variant on the control-group system, while in the physical sciences they are simply computed. Both methods may lead to errors, and there is nothing in statistical methods which tells us when we have made an error of this sort.

The second problem, which is probably much more important, concerns the possibility of the hypothesis being partly true. To continue with the tea-tasting experiment, it might be that the lady, although not always able to detect the difference between tea brewed by the two methods, was generally able to do so, being successful, let us say, in three out of four cases. In this case, the test is simply inappropriate. If she hits squarely on her average performance, guessing correctly in three cases and incorrectly on one, the hypothesis that she can tell the difference will be rejected by this test. On the other hand, it is fairly obvious that a person able to detect the difference three times out of four on the average might quite commonly (about one time out of three) hit four out of four on any given test. About all that can be said about this kind of a situation is that the statistical test is the more likely to "confirm" the hypothesis the closer the hypothesis is to the real situation.[28] In such cases, of course, increasing the sensitivity of the experiment by increasing the sample size (or by some other method) will help, but this, in effect, requires changing the hypothesis. Further, the statistical method gives us no instructions on the degree of sensitiveness of the test. If we apply the test and get a given result, it will always, regardless of what the result is, be possible to improve it by using a larger sample. There is nothing in the nature of the test or the outcome which would indicate that any given test should be expanded.

It is thus impossible to tell how many false results are accepted as a result

28. Ronald A. Fisher, *The Design of Experiments* (London: Oliver & Boyd, 1935).

of statistical tests, but it is certain that some are. Since most hypotheses are supported by evidence other than the statistical, it is likely that the number is fairly small, but even a small number of errors, if widely accepted and used as the basis for further reasoning, can lead to major retardation in the advance of science. It is here that repetition plays its third role. The repetition of an experiment is equivalent to a vast increase in its sensitiveness. If the possibility of getting some certain result is one in forty, then the chance of getting it twice in a row is one in sixteen hundred; three times, one in sixty-four thousand.[29] Thus the odds against a false result rapidly grow as the experiment is repeated. Since the more important experiments may be repeated hundreds of times (they are used in teaching), the odds become astronomical.

If the importance of repetition to the development of science is now clear, we still must ask why the individual scientist goes in for it. Again the social organization explains it easily. In the first place, most scientists are highly curious about their fields and simply would like to see some new important effect. This may take the form of a visit to the original discoverer's laboratory, but is more likely to involve running through the experiment themselves. There is also, often enough to be significant, somebody whose pet scientific theory is contradicted by the new experiment, and repeating it is an obvious thing for such a man to do. Last, but by no means least, scientists already know everything we have been discussing in the last few pages and are, therefore, skeptical of non-repeated experiments. Thus the repetition of an experiment seems worthwhile. A scientist who is temporarily out of hypotheses of his own (and all scientists must be in this state pretty frequently; the spring of invention is notoriously uneven in its flow) may decide to use his facilities to repeat somebody else's experiment. This is a perfectly respectable thing to do, and even a scientist whose motives for research are entirely induced may well devote time to such work.

Of course, not all experiments are repeated. Statistical theory would indicate that we can maximize our gains from a given amount of research activity by repeating only a sample of the experiments.[30] This sample should be larger from the more important experiments than from the less important.

29. Actually the odds are even greater. The system amounts to a crude sequential sample and gives a somewhat higher degree of reliability than the product of the individual results.

30. Strictly speaking, since the game is one against the potential cheater, not entirely against nature, strategy rather than pure probability is required. The difference, however, is slight. See John von Neumann and Oskar Morgenstern, *The Theory of Games and Economic Behavior*

This is precisely what the present practice provides. If the gradient of intensity of sampling cannot be proved to fit any given function, still it is clearly in the right direction, and there is every reason to believe that the estimate of importance made by individual scientists in deciding whether or not to repeat experiments is a reasonably good measure.

In addition to repetition of research, the discussion of various purported discoveries also serves as a check on their accuracy. This is particularly important in the case of observations which cannot be readily repeated, but it performs a function in verifying the results obtained in any type of investigation. It is sometimes thought that the results obtained by scientific work are precise and exact and that no legitimate difference of opinion can exist between scientists. This is only occasionally true with new discoveries. Even apparently well-established scientific "facts" and theories may be the subject of legitimate differences of opinion. Under these circumstances, wide discussion of the issue may have considerable clarifying and stimulating effect.[31] Science is essentially a social process, and the interaction of different independent minds is an important part of it.

Another widely held illusion about science is that such discussions as do take place are calm and dispassionate. The public image is of a number of men who are engaged in a search for the truth without bias or preconception and whose emotions are involved only to the extent that they are devoted to truth. This is simply not true. Scientists are human and tend to get as emotionally involved with their work as anyone else. They may develop an emotional attachment to some given theory, or they may prefer some given theory because it fits into their own general philosophy well. Either of these "biases" may lead them to highly emotional attacks on new experimental results or theoretical developments. In addition, they tend to be heavily prejudiced in favor of their own work.[32]

(Princeton: Princeton University Press, 1944), and R. Duncan Luce and Howard Raiffa, *Games and Decisions* (New York: Wiley, 1958).

31. "Superconductivity: A Theoretical Approach" in the April 24, 1964, issue of *Science* (149: 373–80) is a good sample of scientific discussion. P. W. Anderson and B. T. Matthias, the two authors, obviously disagree quite strenuously on this highly technical problem.

32. The treatment of Velikovsky's *Worlds in Collision* shows how emotional scientists can become. The book, which in my opinion can be fairly classified as crackpot, was reviewed in scientific journals by people who apparently had not bothered to read it carefully and who hence made mistakes. A general attack on the book by prominent scientists was then launched,

Scientists arguing about which of two theories, each invented by one of them, is correct may show all the signs of violent emotion and extreme prejudice which we would expect from mothers arguing over which child should be thrown into the fiery furnace. This emotion will show up mostly in oral discussions, not in the literature, but the disagreement between a minority of physicists led by Einstein and the majority led by Heisenberg and Bohr over the interpretation of the quantum theory was carried on in print. Einstein, in particular, was attacked as a reactionary and "retrogressive thinker." This very human tendency to become attached to one's own creations is an important factor in any scientific discussion. Sometimes it is extended to whole schools of thought, each member of which tends to identify with the work of the others. The "Copenhagen orthodoxy" in the interpretation of quantum theory is a recent example of the phenomenon.

This attachment is by no means entirely irrational. The failure of a man's theories may well have a pronounced effect on his future career. The discovery of an important phenomenon or the performance of an exceptionally significant experiment will normally greatly improve his prospects, in the sense both of physical well being and access to research facilities. The disproof of his work has the opposite effect. Imagine, for example, a physicist who succeeded in getting $750,000 to build a complex device which was intended to measure some phenomenon. After he builds the gadget and presents his data, some other scientist alleges that the design was defective and that the resulting data are therefore useless. Obviously, the original physicist has the strongest material motives to defend his results.

There is, thus, a good deal of emotion and bias in scientific discussions. Whether this is a good thing or a bad thing is an open question. It is analogous to the debate as to whether the adversary system of judicial proceedings used in Anglo-American law is better or worse than the "inquisito" form used on the Continent. Without making any final judgment on the question, clearly there are both advantages and disadvantages. A man who is motivated to support some given position by external drives is not as likely to be discouraged by superficial evidence against him as the disinterested student. If an apparently conclusive case is made against his position, this will frequently merely stimulate him to deeper research in hopes of demolishing his critic.

---

which in part took the form of an attempt to institute a sort of censorship over a number of leading publishers. The *American Behavioural Scientist* devoted its entire September, 1963, issue to a discussion of the matter, and further comments appear in succeeding issues.

Sometimes this leads to discoveries which would not be made by any other method. Sometimes, on the other hand, it leads to waste.

Controversy in the sciences quite frequently takes the form of experimentation. Not only are experiments repeated; somewhat different experiments are performed in an effort to provide a different explanation of some given phenomenon. New theories are tested by new experiments, and experimental results are incorporated in old theories to develop new, experimentally testable, forms of experiments. These new experiments are then themselves repeated, and the discussion goes on. In the case of strictly theoretical discoveries, discussion is likely to take a non-experimental turn, but even here experiments may be relied on.

The amount of misunderstanding and error in scientific discussion does not differ by very much from that in any other discussion between technically competent personnel. Stupid mistakes are made, new theories are frequently simply not understood by their opponents, and erroneous arguments are offered. Scientific publication is usually a leisurely business, however, and by the time an article gets in print many of the more ignorant errors have been removed. The literature therefore gives a much more "rational" picture of scientific discussion than is really justified. Even in the journals, however, errors and misunderstandings are far from uncommon. In oral discussion and in informal correspondence, mistakes are much more common. All of this should be taken not as an attack on scientists, but as simply pointing out that they are human, make mistakes, have difficulty with new ideas, and are sometimes prejudiced. The subject of this book is the organizational system which takes these rather normal human beings and uses them to produce knowledge of a very high degree of reliability.

It is the organization and the pressure it brings to bear on the individuals, then, which account for the result. The organization, however, is a purely voluntary one, composed of the very individuals it controls. The system works because of the interrelations between these individuals. First, a large part of any scientific community, as we have remarked, are applied scientists. While we are now discussing the system used in pure science, the applied workers have a great importance for pure science. They are interested in developing their devices with the minimum of wasted time. The discoveries of the pure scientists are frequently of great use to them, but only if they are true. If they find themselves wasting time (which is money) in their laboratories because some theory or discovery which appeared in the "pure" literature is wrong, they may complain. Since the applied workers "have their feet firmly on the ground," they are less likely to be affected by emotional considerations or questions of pride or even aesthetics than are the pure scientists. In consequence, they are particularly likely to emphasize truth. They are subject to very strong economic pressures to stick rigidly to the truth and, in fact, can succeed in their personal lives only by doing so. The consequence is that a large part of the scientific community is likely to be highly impatient with errors.

The pure scientists themselves, although normally less interested than the applied scientists in practical applications of someone else's work, are nevertheless still interested in its truth. We have hypothesized that pure scientists are motivated by curiosity, and only a true report can satisfy this curiosity. Thus, although the discoverer of some alleged experimental effect and the people who engage in public controversy with him have a number of personal motives which may lead them to erroneous conclusions, they carry on the controversy before a large and highly qualified audience with an almost exclusive interest in the truth. Since the reputation of a scientist is of the greatest importance to him, he must act in such a way as to avoid annoying this audience. Further, it is this audience which will finally judge who is right. Certainly, the consensus of qualified scientists is not always right, but no better mechanism for allocating praise and blame is known.

Thus the eventual result of any controversy will be determined, not by the participants, but by a sort of jury. This jury will not only decide which side is right, it will decide whether any credit or discredit reflects on either side, and the decision will markedly affect the future careers of the participants. Under the circumstances, it is not surprising that most scientists try to avoid the types of errors which we have been discussing—those which arise from bias, emotion, and interest. They try, but, of course, they are not completely successful. The result of their efforts is simply to reduce the effect of such factors, not to eliminate them. Sometimes the effort has the reverse effect, as when a scientist will lean over backward so far to avoid what he thinks are his own prejudices as to miss a real discovery.

The impartiality and coolness of scientific investigation inheres not to the individual investigator, but to the environment in which he works. It is not that scientists are better than other men, it is only that their environment is so organized that they are not often tempted. It must, however, also be recognized that the scientists themselves are in fact motivated by curiosity. Other motives may get in the way with respect to some particular experiment, but they are interested in reaching the truth. This also leads them to try to suppress their own emotions and biases. The abandonment of a basic position by a major scientist is a fairly common occurrence; in fact, this is one way of recognizing the really great scientist. The man who rigidly clings to his own ideas is less likely to be truly great than the man who will freely accept someone else's work as better than his own.

The final subject of this chapter is the dissemination of new knowledge. Of course, the repetition and discussion processes are integrated with the dissemination of knowledge. It must be disseminated to other scientists before they can either repeat or discuss it. Further, the repetition and discussion lead to further dissemination as they bring knowledge of the discovery to other people. It will be remembered that we devoted a large part of Chapter IV to a discussion of the process of obtaining information about other scientists' discoveries. The process of dissemination is simply the other side of the coin. The first step is usually publication and the reading of the published article. This has already been adequately discussed. The second step consists in "filing" the information so that it can be found by researchers who need that specific bit of information.[33] Again, we have covered this subject adequately. What remains to be discussed is the relationship between the dissemination and verification processes.

The process by which a scientist looks up some work which he thinks is relevant to his own investigation obviously results in the original finding's being more widely disseminated. Further, if the idea contained in the original article fits into the new project, it will be further disseminated by the new research. In this sense, each research project can be seen as the focus of a gradually spreading network of other projects which will continue to grow until someone disproves the original work. (This may never happen. Archimedes' theory of displacement is still generally accepted.)

This dissemination process, however, also plays a major part in the verification process. Each new researcher who hears of a given discovery may think of a way of disproving it or find a flaw in the reasoning. Further, each application of the new discovery in new research is, whether intended or not, a test of the original discovery. Thus the practical and pure applications of a given

33. There is now a gigantic literature on information retrieval. I had originally intended to put in an equally gigantic bibliographical footnote at this point, but I noticed that almost half of the items in my list had been published in *Science* and the remainder were footnoted in the *Science* articles. Under the circumstances it seemed best to simply refer the reader to the indexes of this journal. See notes 25 and 26 to chap. IV.

discovery present an almost infinite series of tests to which it will be submitted. The scientist considering some problem knows not only that his conclusions will be formally tested by repetition and discussion, but also that other scientists will make use of them in completely unpredictable ways, and that the failure of his results under these conditions will reflect on him. It is hard to think of a stronger disciplinary system.

Certain of the sciences have not yet reached the stage where the discoveries of one man are tested by being incorporated in the work of another. In these circumstances, much less reliance can be put upon announced results because the check which such applications provide is not present. The development of a science to the point where it is a web of continuously growing, but closely interconnected, knowledge is thus important because the interconnections present an automatic device for continuously reconsidering the truth or falsity of earlier discoveries without wasting resources in doing so directly.

With this chapter the basic task set in the introduction is completed. I have presented my analysis of the social system which governs science, which permits a group of people without any central guidance to behave in a highly coordinated manner. Whether my analysis is correct must, of course, be left up to the reader. I would hope that, with time, my theory may be subjected to the careful examination and testing with which this chapter has been concerned. It is by no means sure, however, that it will. This book, unfortunately, falls in that portion of the sciences called "social," and this is clearly an underdeveloped area. The next chapter will apply the analysis to the question of why the development of the social sciences has been retarded. Finally, in the last chapter, I will adopt the meliorative attitude of the Enlightenment and suggest some minor improvements in the organization of science.

CHAPTER VII

THE BACKWARDNESS OF THE SOCIAL SCIENCES

One of the more popular superstitions in the social sciences holds that we can say nothing about anything until we can measure it. People holding this belief, of course, cannot believe that the social sciences are less advanced than, say, physics, because there is no way of measuring the advancement of a science. Everyone else, I think, will agree that the social sciences are, as compared with the natural sciences, deficient. The deficiencies are explained in various ways by various authorities, but we can roughly group them into two general classes: those which allege that the subject itself is especially difficult and those which point to various features of the social environment which make research in the social sciences hard. Since this book is about the social organization of science, I intend to confine myself to a discussion of the second category of difficulties. Nevertheless, candor compels me to say that I am skeptical about the importance of the first group. Having mentioned my skepticism, I am almost required to make a brief digression explaining why I feel that the subject matter of the social sciences is not vastly more difficult than that of the natural sciences.

The view that the social sciences are inherently more difficult sometimes seems to be based on nothing more than ignorance of the natural sciences.[1] From the bare fact that the physicists are obviously making progress, it is deduced that their problems are relatively easy. Even the slightest acquaintance with the history of modern science will rapidly disabuse the student of this illusion. The natural scientists, particularly the physicists, face today, and have faced before, problems of the most appalling difficulty. The difference is that the physicists frequently solve these terrifying problems. If you consider the

1. In "Megaloscience" (*Science,* 148 [June 18, 1965], 1560–64), J. B. Adams points out that much of the research in high energy nuclear physics now is published in multiple author articles with twenty to thirty authors. Given that number of scientists, and about three assistants for each one, he computes a cost of about $3,000,000 per year. "Usually what one gets for this large investment of men and money is just another small piece of a vast jigsaw" (p. 1561). Surely there are few places in the social sciences where it takes this much effort to move even a small step forward.

situation existing in physics in the first few years of this century or the present situation in particle physics, it is hard to believe that more difficult problems are likely to be met in other fields. The general atmosphere in physics, however, is one of hope, not of despair.

Another reason sometimes given for the alleged greater difficulty of the social sciences is the "impossibility of using the methods developed in the natural sciences." It is a little hard to see what is meant by "method" in this case. Scientific method can be thought of as the very general philosophic approach of science or it can be thought of as the series of specific techniques used by individual scientists. In the first definition, the methods of the natural sciences amount to little more than simply making the best possible use of man's mental endowment. Clearly, this is as applicable in the social sciences as in the natural. The specific techniques used by various scientists, on the other hand, are seldom applicable to the social sciences. But while this is true, they are also normally not applicable to other sciences either. A theoretical physicist and an observational biologist have almost nothing in common in terms of specific techniques. This situation exists throughout the natural sciences. The specific methods used in one field are of little use in others. The only general method existing in science is to think hard about the problems and collect data. This can be done in the social sciences.

It is possible that the widespread belief among students of society that the natural scientists have some sort of methodological advantage over them arises quite simply from the fact that English has only one word, "laboratory," for the area where a scientist does whatever he does. Scientists normally do not like to perform their work in the rain or snow. Consequently, they normally work indoors, and the sheltered area in which they work is called, in English, a laboratory. The only thing which laboratories have in common with each other is that they all provide shelter from the elements. Their internal design and equipment and the work done in them vary as much as those of any other type of building. If you visit, successively, the laboratories of a biologist, an organic chemist, and an experimental physicist, the only things that you will normally find in common in the equipment found therein are things you would also find in all sorts of non-scientific surroundings. Tables and chairs will be found in almost all laboratories, and containers made of glass are common in those which deal with liquids. These containers are usually designed for easy washing and this gives them sort of a family resemblance. Careful investigation of what is actually being done in a number of laboratories (and in the studies of a few theorists) will normally convince the student that there is no specific "scientific method" in use by the natural sciences. Scientists are bound together by a common philosophy, described by Karl Popper in *The Logic of Scientific Discovery,*[2] and they are also united by a social organization of a common form. The philosophy is applicable to the social sciences as well as to the natural studies, but, as I will explain later, the social organization of the social sciences is somewhat different from that of the natural sciences.

As a final point, it is sometimes contended that the social sciences deal with human beings, that this presents special problems which are met with nowhere else in the sciences, and, QED, the social sciences are more difficult than the natural. I grant the first two points, but not the QED. Every branch of science deals with some special class of phenomena; that is how we divide the general field of human knowledge into branches. In each case the special phenomena under investigation present special problems which are met with nowhere else. The social studies thus resemble the others in that there are special problems, but there has been less progress in solving these special problems.

So much for my digression. If I have not proved that the social sciences are not more difficult than the natural sciences, I think I have, at least, presented some warrant for my skepticism. We will now turn to the differences between the social organization of the natural and the social sciences. The first of the problems of social organization which I will discuss is that of experimentation. It is often said that we cannot experiment with human beings. This, of course, is quite untrue; such experiments[3] are regularly performed. There are no particular technical difficulties barring experiments on human beings, and the doctors experiment on them all the time. The fact is that there are inhibitions against some sorts of social experiments on human beings. We do not even really like to perform medical experiments on them, and medical researchers take the most extreme precautions when they do so. Nevertheless, the gains which have been made and are being made in medicine are held to justify the very, very careful use of human research animals.

The absence of objection to medical experiments on human beings is, in part, the result of the tremendous progress which medicine has made in recent years. There is a well-merited tendency to assume that such experiments

2. New York: Basic Books, 1959.

3. Lawrence E. Fouraker and Sidney Siegel, *Bargaining Behavior* (New York: McGraw-Hill, 1963).

contribute more to human happiness than their likely cost.[4] Even when a new drug kills someone through a very strong allergy reaction, there is little public commotion. That the medical researchers are very skilful, that they are making very great progress, and that there is necessarily some element of danger in introducing new drugs are all well-known facts. Today an experimenter in the social sciences can hardly hope to have such an "understanding" public. On the other hand, an even more important factor in the lack of objection to medical research of this sort can be used to protect much experimentation in the social sciences. Medical experiments are never performed on human beings without the consent of the subject of the experiment.[5] Obviously, if the man who is to be experimented on has no objection, there is no great reason for anyone else to protest.

Normally the consent of the subjects of medical experiments is obtained by simply giving them something in return. This fact is rather obscured by the fact that the vast majority of subjects of such experiments are sick people who are told that a new treatment, not yet generally available because it has not yet been thoroughly tested, can be used on them. The patient then weighs the risk against the probability of a more rapid recovery, and his decision will be respected by the doctor. Prisoners in penitentiaries frequently volunteer for more dangerous and inconvenient types of medical experiments. The prisoners, who know that the parole board is likely to let people who have volunteered for the experiments out earlier than those who have not, having the trust in modern medicine which is general in the population, sometimes volunteer for quite dangerous experiments.

Direct payment, although not too common in medical research, is not unheard of. When I was in college, some of my classmates were earning pocket money by taking very small doses of various poisons for the medical school. I never heard what the purpose of the experiment was, but the school was very careful to make certain that all of its subjects were actually paid, since the possibility of serious consequences was obvious. Sometimes medical experiments are performed on simple volunteers, people who are willing to permit experiments to be performed on them for essentially humanitarian motives. Usually experiments in which such people are involved are not particularly

4. Lead editorial, "Research with Human Subjects," *Science,* 132 (October 14, 1960), 989.

5. In the case of those not able to give or withhold consent, small children, mental patients, etc., the consent will normally be given by whoever makes the other basic decisions for the patient.

dangerous, but sometimes they are extremely so. The experiments which proved the role of the mosquito in transmitting yellow fever were dangerous in the extreme, and the brave men who volunteered suffered heavy casualties.

It seems likely, therefore, that there would be little objection to the use of experimentation techniques in the social sciences if the human beings used in the experiments gave their consent. In the social sciences, however, many experiments would not be possible if the subjects realized that they were involved in an experiment. We would normally be interested in the behavior of human beings in certain situations, and their behavior may differ greatly if the situation is known to be merely part of an experiment. The fact that the participants know they are being observed, and the further fact that the situation is not "real," may make a very great difference in the behavior of the subjects. The psychologists, confronted with a similar problem, have developed very great abilities in deceiving their experimental subjects.[6]

A subject of psychological research will usually be told that he is participating in a test or an experiment. The experimenter may, however, be extremely mendacious in describing the experiment.[7] The explanation given the subject is frequently simply a "cover" designed to conceal the real experiment from him. Unfortunately, this fact is getting around; experimental subjects may develop a considerable degree of sophistication which will make them systematically distrust the psychological experimenter. But, regardless of the possibility that this type of experimentation may become impossible in the future,[8] it clearly would be possible to utilize the same technique in the social sciences. The experimental subjects could be told that they were being tested for A when the experimenter is actually interested in B.

There are numerous areas where experiments could be run with the full knowledge of the subjects and where considerable knowledge could be obtained. There have recently been many experiments in these fields. It is true that initial results have not been very outstanding. In the natural sciences it was quite a while after investigators seriously turned to experimental meth-

6. A famous experiment involving deception tested individuals for their willingness to inflict torture on others. For a newspaper account of the experiments and the issues involved, see *New York Times,* October 26, 1963, p. 28.

7. Not all experiments in psychology require deception, of course. For an article describing experiments with human beings, see Robert L. Fantz, "The Origin of Form Perception," *Scientific American* (May, 1961), 66–72.

8. Disregarding also possible moral issues.

ods before any really revolutionary results were obtained. The reason is clear. Experiments, necessarily, are set up in terms of hypotheses, theories, and *Weltanschauungen.* If these initial intellectual presuppositions of the experiments are in a primitive condition as they were in the natural sciences several hundred years ago, then the initial experiments are likely to simply indicate difficulties in the theories being tested, but not to lead to any solution of these difficulties. As time goes by, however, new theories which "explain" various experimental results will be developed; these in turn will be tested by experimentation. This will lead to the invention of new theories, and the eventual outcome, we can legitimately hope, will be a much clearer perception of the social reality.

Let us begin our discussion of the use of experimental methods in the social sciences by an example which, in this rapidly developing field, is almost an antique. Lerner and Laswell[9] presented a set of experiments intended to test which of several ways of organizing a five-man group was most "efficient." The method was to set up a series of such groups, give them problems to solve, and then record the performance of each form of organization. These experiments were, in many ways, models of the use of experimental method in the social sciences; nevertheless, they had serious defects. Here I shall talk only about the defects. These all arise from the fact that the experiments were so extremely limited. They were run for only a rather short time, with the result that about all that could be said in practical terms was that the system in which one man gave orders to the other four was the most efficient. They were unable to present much evidence as to the relative efficiency of the other, less efficient, organizations. Further, the confining of the experiment to a group of five greatly limited the usefulness of the results. It should obviously have been tried also with larger and smaller groups. In particular, it should have been tried with groups large enough that the organizational structure would approximate real organizations in having a stage structure.[10]

9. *The Policy Sciences* (Stanford: Stanford University Press, 1951). The most relevant article is "Communication Patterns in Task-Oriented Groups," pp. 193ff., by Alex Bavelas, which discusses research done by still other people. Although these particular experiments are convenient illustrations, compared with some of the recent work, they are rather naïve.

10. I.e., a system under which information and instructions are passed through people as well as to people. For an authoritarian example, consider a structure consisting of one superior who deals with three subordinates who, in turn, each deal with three more inferiors. Would such a system be more or less efficient than some other organization?

We can go on easily. Problems are not all exactly alike. It might be that one type is particularly suitable to a given type of organization, and another type to another organization. Further, the communications system used in setting up the experiments was capable of distinguishing only between completely free communication of ideas, information, and instruction between the subjects in the experiment or no direct communication. Systems under which certain types of communications were channeled according to one net and others through another might well have been much more efficient.

It can be plainly seen that my complaints are in a sense unfair. I do not object to the experiment, but to where it stopped. Clearly, there is no rule that everyone undertaking an experiment must continue to work on it until all corners have been explored. Science has advanced by a process of division of labor under which experiments performed by one man suggest further experiments by another. These investigators surely had a right to stop when they did, but why have the problems raised not yet been solved? There have been very many further experiments in which various methods of organizing groups have been tried, and not only is there no agreement as to the best organization, it cannot even be said that we are any closer to agreement.

The first and obvious reason for this apparent lack of progress is the extremely primitive state of the theories in this area. Most of this research has been done by sociologists and psychologists who have made no real attempt to develop sophisticated theories. This is not to say that they have no theories at all, but only that they are not particularly elaborate. I have on my desk at the moment a study by a professor in a major university on "Political Conflict within Nations" which finds that the principal factors leading to such conflict are "Turmoil, Revolution, and Subversion." This is, of course, an extreme case,[11] but this sort of thing does go by the name of theory in this field. Until complex theories are proposed and tested, little advance can be expected in the field, simply because the experiments will have no real hypothesis to test.

But there is another reason. Experiments using volunteers are likely to be very expensive. Usually the subjects must be paid for their time. Some people are willing to volunteer on a non-compensated basis for such experiments,

11. Also it appears to have little to do with the experiments discussed in the previous paragraph. My excuse for bringing it up in this context is partly the accident that I happened to have received it just before I wrote this page, but more important, the methods and approach are almost identical with those used in many examinations of the organization problem.

but they are by no means a random selection of the population. Further, such people normally cannot be depended on to continue turning up for a long series of experiments unless the experiments are inherently interesting for the subject, unless, that is, they qualify as amusements. This in itself would rule out a large number of possible experiments. Further, such volunteers are not available in large numbers, which again rules out many experiments. Altogether, it would appear that payment is the only way to get an adequate supply of subjects for most experiments.

Suppose, for example, that we decide to run another set of experiments like the one discussed above, except that we are going to test six people. We have ten arrangements which we wish to test, and, in order to make it at least somewhat likely that we are getting a test of the way these arrangements would operate over the long term, we propose to run each group for forty hours on one type of arrangement. This does not, of course, mean that we will have them work a forty-hour week. Such experiments are generally performed as part-time evening activities. The forty hours, then, may well be spread out over a period of months. We can hardly take just one group for each arrangement, however, because that particular group may be in some way abnormal, with the result that our experiment would be biased. Statistical theory would indicate that we should have a very large number of groups trying each arrangement, but we shall compromise by having only ten group trials for each arrangement. This will not permit us to make fine discriminations, but it will be adequate for initial work.

If the subjects are paid $1.50 hourly, this part of our experiment will cost $36,000.[12] But this is not all. We would have to have some supervisory personnel. There would also be the necessity of providing the materials for the problems which are to be solved and the special physical arrangements necessary for the experiments. Fortunately, this experiment does not involve any complicated calculation or statistical work; still, we would be lucky to get off with $50,000. And what would we get with our $50,000? A simple table of times spent by groups solving problems in the various possible arrangements. This table could probably be worked up into a short article, true, but it still seems very little. It is clear that information is most expensive in this field. Only high-energy physics, radio astronomy, and a few other special fields of the natural sciences have to pay this much for each "bit" of new in-

12. $6 \times 10 \times 40 \times 10 \times 1.50 = 36{,}000$.

formation. If we wished really to explore the various possible ways of organizing groups, we would have to perform several hundred such experiments[13] with the total cost running between $5 million and $10 million. At these prices it is not surprising that experimentation started late in the social sciences and is not yet well developed.

Basically it would appear that the problem is analogous to that of starting a new corporation where there is a sizable "entry barrier." There are still relatively few social scientists, or administrators of research funds, who are interested in making such a radical departure from traditional methods. The research would be highly expensive, which makes it hard for eccentric individuals to undertake it. Finally, the first few experiments, like the first few experiments in physics, turned out to be relatively unfruitful. We need to do more experimenting in order to learn to experiment fruitfully. Thus opportunities for very important research are still left unexploited because the first few steps are extremely hard to make. A foundation willing to invest two or three million a year for five years in promoting such experiments might well make a major "breakthrough" in our methods of learning about ourselves. In the absence of such a program, there is a steady and increasing trickle of experiments in this area. Given time, and it may take a great deal of time, this trickle will become a torrent. Needless to say, these experiments will not bring the millennium. They will increase our knowledge, but they will still leave us with innumerable problems.

Even in these areas where experiments are not possible, we are by no means helpless. We have history on our side. There are almost no historical records which are of any help to natural scientists.[14] The social scientist has an almost incredible amount of historical data at his disposal. The formal historical sections of most libraries take up more space than the scientific ones, and collectively they constitute only a small fraction of the historical material in existence. Almost all accounts of human behavior, from balance sheets of obscure groceries to diaries of courtesans, may contain useful data. The quantity of such material available is such that almost no one given library has more than a tiny part of it. The material is either badly indexed or not indexed, but this simply makes the researcher's task difficult, not impossible.

13. It would be desirable to try at least some arrangements with personnel much superior to that which can be hired for $1.50. This would further run up the cost.

14. Among the very few areas where such records are of assistance, only in astronomy can they be counted as of even second-class importance.

The use of historical materials is frequently alleged to be subject to two difficulties which do not dog the natural scientist. These difficulties, both of which arise from the impossibility of arranging the conditions in the way a scientist does in his laboratory, are that many problems which we would like to have answered cannot be treated historically because there simply are no data, and the fact that any historical data will record the simultaneous effects of many causes. Necessarily, there will be many changes in variables other than the one under testing in any historic period. Both of these statements are true. It is frequently not realized, however, that they are also true of experiments in the natural sciences. In both the natural sciences and the social sciences, problems vary in difficulty from the easy to the very difficult, but there is no great gap between the data from the two fields.

The general theory of relativity, for its first twenty years, was hard to test experimentally. There were only a few phenomena available for such tests, and all of them presented great problems of measurement. One of these was the bending of light from stars as it passed near the sun. This effect could, until quite recently, be observed only during an eclipse, when the sun itself is blotted out. Even then it was observed for only a very few stars whose apparent position would be very close to the sun. As a consequence, few observations were available in the early days of the theory. This rather small collection of observations, unfortunately, showed a wide range of variation. None of them was very close to the prediction of Einstein's theory, and some were very far off. Nevertheless, from the first the physicists considered these rather bad data as sufficient to test the theory. They simply thought that there must also be present some other effect of somewhat the same order of magnitude as the predicted one.[15] There is no reason why social scientists should not be willing to accept equivalent data.

Social scientists sometimes seem to think that the natural scientist can simply go into his laboratory and set up a device to test any hypothesis which he cares to. Nothing could be farther from the truth. The state of knowledge at any given time is always such that most of the questions which would occur to a scientist are unanswerable by currently available techniques. Even where, in theory, some experiment can be performed, the physicist, as much as the social scientist, must consider the cost and the available equipment before deciding whether or not to undertake it. Finally, a given experiment may fail. The social scientist who has spent six months in the libraries trying to work

15. This other effect might be inadequacies of the measuring techniques.

out a solution of a problem through the use of historical data only to find that the data are insufficient should have sympathy for the scientist whose experiments just do not come off. Not only has he wasted his time, he may have to explain to his department head why $50,000 has been invested in an elaborate device which simply will not work.[16]

The scientist, guided by his general curiosity, reads the literature and carries out routine investigations until his special curiosity is aroused by some problem which appears to be susceptible to solution by consulting the facts. He then turns to an investigation of the facts and either solves his problem or finds that in the present situation it is insoluble. This description will fit either the social scientist who finds his facts in history or the natural scientist who gets them from the laboratory. In both cases, solutions available from the factual information which can be gathered are only a small fraction of those desired, and, in both cases, the real difference between the great and the mediocre investigator is the ability to guess properly what can be discovered with further research.

The problem of numerous variables which afflicts the student trying to verify some hypothesis in the social sciences is also serious for the experimentalist. It is true that on the whole it is less of a problem for the natural scientist, but in many experiments his problems are just as difficult as those of the social scientist.[17] The problem of detecting the effect of one factor in an environment where many factors are operating is, of course, the reason why statistical method was invented. It works as well in one field as the other. The

16. Another similarity between the social scientist's use of history and the natural scientist's use of experiments lies in "ghost effects." Natural scientists are accustomed to finding unlikely results sometimes in their experiments. These results, presumably the result of some as yet unknown phenomenon, normally eventually fade out in spite of the best efforts of the scientist to keep them alive. The recent discoveries indicating the existence of a four-hundred-year cycle in the appearance of talent in the human race are probably an example in the social sciences. See A. L. Kroeber, "Comments on the Grays' Four Hundred Year Cycle in Human Ability," *Comparative Studies in Society and History,* 1 (March, 1959), 370. For a more expensive example see the "Leading Indicators" developed by the National Bureau of Economic Research. These were statistical series which appeared to "lead" the business cycle. Since they have been regularly published by the Department of Commerce (*Business Cycle Developments*), they have gradually lost their "leading" character.

17. William Farnsworth Loomis, "The Sex Gas of the Hydra," *Scientific American,* 200, No. 34 (April, 1959), pp. 145–46, gives an account of a very ingenious series of experiments in which the experimenter was trying to control seventeen variables at one time, none of which was, as he eventually discovered, relevant.

student of society will search history for cases which are as closely alike in the non-investigated variables as possible and then use statistics to cut out the other variations, which will nevertheless exist. In this he resembles the natural scientist, and he also resembles him in that frequently he is unsuccessful.

This discussion may surprise many students of society who do not realize the similarity between their historical studies and the laboratory work of the natural scientist. It will not, however, suggest much in the way of improvement in their methods. Even a cursory reading of the literature will convince the student that there are investigators whose use of historical materials is every bit as sophisticated as the best experiments of the physicist.

So far I have been discussing those reasons for the backwardness of the social sciences which are commonly advanced but which are, in my opinion, invalid. I should like to turn now to what I believe are the real reasons for this relative retardation. The unfavorable atmosphere for research in the social sciences cannot, I think, be denied. Clearly, the investigator in this field cannot expect that new and radically different ideas which he has discovered will always be granted the type of hearing they would receive in the natural sciences. The field is heavily circumscribed by such problems. Imagine a professor at Yale who makes a set of comparisons between whites and Negroes and finds the whites incontestably superior.[18] In the first place, he would probably be unwilling, personally, to admit that these results are possible. Secondly, if he did complete such work and publish it, he would be subject to the strongest type of pressure from his colleagues.[19] This pressure would normally not take the form of setting up other investigations which might serve to disprove the one criticized, but would be simply an exhibition of moral disapproval.

In a sense this is simply another way of describing scientific backwardness. There was a period when the investigator in the natural sciences was likely to avoid work which might lead him to socially disapproved results. In those days also if he did reach a "wrong" result, he was likely to be subject to con-

18. Or a professor in South Africa who gets the opposite results.

19. Such work is occasionally done, but normally as a result of a sort of accident. A student who has been thoroughly indoctrinated with the current "line," which at Yale is racial equality and in South Africa is racial inequality, might undertake comparative research with the intent of validating it. If the research led to the "wrong" result, it might nevertheless be published, although it would most assuredly be accompanied by an explanation of how the researcher came to undertake the work and some qualifications indicating that he did not really believe his results.

siderable social pressure, which might well include police action. (In a large part of the world, but fortunately not in our own country, the social scientist is still subject to police repression.) Over time this has changed, and the present fortunate state of the natural sciences is, in part, simply the result of such changes. Once the scientists had demonstrated their ability to solve difficult problems, their success led to confidence in them, which, in turn, led them to investigate other problems, which led to more confidence, etc. This process would also have some effect in the social studies if only it could be started. Unfortunately it is both hard to start and unlikely to be as successful as in the natural sciences.

The natural sciences have two special advantages over the social sciences in this regard. In the first place, society is so organized that a minority who have truth on their side in the fields of the natural sciences are frequently able to coerce the erring majority into accepting their views.[20] This process, which will be discussed more thoroughly below, obviously gives a great incentive to the discovery of truth. In the social fields, on the other hand, an erring majority can normally control the correct minority.[21] Since new ideas are always originally held by minorities, this makes the progress of science much easier in the physical fields. Someone who has a new idea in, say, economics must gradually persuade people that he is correct until he has, substantially, majority support before his idea can be utilized. The inventor of something new in applied branches of the sciences, on the other hand, will normally have to persuade only a few people to get his idea into use. Once it is in use, if he is correct, it will usually be impossible for the majority to avoid adopting it. This climate is clearly much more favorable for the acceptance of new and radical ideas.

Another advantage held by the natural scientist is the general obscurity of his field of study. Even if he has new and radical ideas, they are unlikely to

20. In this connection it is not accidental that a number of the early Renaissance scientists were military engineers interested in problems of weapons technology. When Galileo took the chair of "mathematics" at Padua, he was expected to teach military engineering and fortification as well as what we now think of as mathematics. See Giorgio de Santillana, *The Crime of Galileo* (Chicago: University of Chicago Press, 1955), p. 2. The prince who misguidedly opposed "progress" in these fields was likely to be most literally "coerced." Somewhat similar lines of reasoning have led the Soviet Union to keep its ideology out of those branches of science which influence weapons development.

21. Letter by Paul D. Foote, "Majority Opinion: Right or Wrong," *Science*, 142 (October 18, 1963), 341.

arouse much public opposition, simply because they concern subjects on which most people have no ideas at all. Galileo spent a long and useful life revolutionizing whole fields of the natural sciences right under the nose of the pope and got into serious trouble with the Inquisition only once. Suppose he had been a student of society, had begun his investigations with an inquiry into the relative merits of polygamy and monogamy, and then had gone on to consider the political organization of Medici Florence. The shape of the earth is a matter to which few persons devote much thought and one not well calculated to stir strong emotions. Certainly, it has little practical effect on more than a small minority of the human race. The social sciences, on the other hand, have the misfortune to study things which are of immediate concern to practically everyone and about which are clustered strongly felt emotions. It is almost inconceivable that an American social scientist should ever question the superiority of monogamy[22] over polygamy. If he undertook research on this problem and got results contrary to the accepted ethic, he would find himself subject to very strong penalties, not only from nonscientists, but also from his colleagues. They would be, as well-indoctrinated citizens, appalled and, as colleagues, terrified.

The difficulties of research in areas where feelings are strong and where the results of research may outrage the moral ideology of the public, or of the researcher himself, probably account for the rapid development of anthropology in the twentieth century. No one is really offended by the peculiar customs of distant tribes of savages. It is therefore perfectly possible for students to make careful investigations of such matters and even to develop rudimentary theories. The absence of negative social pressure has permitted considerable development in this field, although recent developments seem to imply that the limits have been about reached.

Not only is the climate unfavorable for research in the social sciences, the motives for such research are much weaker than for other types of investigation. This may seem a paradox, since most people would agree that such research is really more important than research in the natural sciences, but remember we are considering individual motives. A man who thinks the social sciences more important may nevertheless be engaged in the natural sciences or in politics or even in business. Individuals are not, in general, led into their lifework by considerations of the general good, but of their own circum-

22. The term "monogamy" in the American context should not be taken as ruling out either changes of spouse or occasional flings.

stances. As it happens, the motives which might lead individuals to engage in research are much weaker in the social than in the natural sciences.

Consider first the motives for applied research. The first thing to note is that there is no patent system for social inventions. If I were to discover, for example, a new sales technique, I would be unable to charge a royalty to others using it. Furthermore, an invention of this sort would be extremely difficult to keep secret, so that even if I did discover it, I probably would not be able to get any gain beyond a sort of head start applying it. If the new idea had, as new ideas frequently do, flaws which would take some time to eliminate, my competitors, who would take over after a little experience had been accumulated, would possibly be better off than I. I might have accidentally alienated my customers in the early stages of applying the idea.

The result is that few people are willing to invest much money in making social inventions. Inventions are made, as they would also be made in the natural sciences without the patent, but they are made only on a small scale. Individuals have ideas which work, entrepreneurs try out different arrangements, and there is the usual accretion of small improvements, but there is little in the line of formal applied research. I once was associated with a major public-opinion-polling organization. It polled the general public for political opinions and also did a lot of contract work for companies interested in the impact of their advertising or the type of product the customer wanted. Although the organization was in the business of selling research, it did little or none of its own.

The chiefs of the organization were highly intelligent men with wide interests and a great competence in their field. As a consequence, they had ideas for improved techniques with fair frequency. Their employees were also frequently highly intelligent and very competent, so they also had new ideas, but there was no formal research staff. This was particularly surprising in view of the fact that a large part of the personnel, both at the highest level and lower down, had started as researchers in universities. The organization, in fact, had been founded to apply new techniques which they had invented. The complete absence of "research-mindedness" can perhaps best be illustrated by their procedure in applying new ideas. They did not normally try out a number of new ideas or variants of the same idea at once. They simply tried to figure out by ordinary reasoning what would work. Sometimes, of course, it did not, but there was no formal technique of trying out a number of ideas with the advance knowledge that only one would be used.

The reasons for this attitude are, of course, clear. Serious research would have amounted to throwing money away. If the company had spent $100,000 developing a new technique, its competitors would have learned about it almost immediately and applied it themselves. The company with which I was associated would then be out its research money and, if it did this very often, out of business. Progress thus came as a sort of by-product of good management. No significant sums were invested in formal research, and the company did not feel that it could "get ahead" of its competitors in methods or techniques except, possibly, for a very short time. Naturally, progress was much slower than it would have been had the research industry been so organized that applied research in its own methodology was profitable.

The unfortunate absence of motives for applied research in the social sciences has undoubtedly been a major factor in the relative slowness of development in this field. The importance of applied work in the early history of the natural sciences is indisputable. Since the social studies are obviously in their early youth, the absence of a large body of empirical knowledge such as that which the natural sciences drew on in their early days is particularly unfortunate. It has often been noted that the developing scientific knowledge of the physicists and chemists had little effect on the average man's life until well on in the nineteenth century.[23] It is not quite so well known that the early scientists were deeply influenced by the "applied research" of practical men in various economic fields. Meetings of the Royal Society might be concerned solely with a description of some mechanical process or productive system in the arts. A great many improvements in the pure field originated from an investigation of what practical men were doing. The famous *Encyclopedia,* in fact, is largely simply a compendium of productive processes. The scientist of that day normally accepted the skilled practitioner of some trade as an authority and tried to work out scientific explanations for his procedures.

To repeat what was said in the first chapter, applied researchers have a role in checking the results of the pure researchers as well as making discoveries themselves. Being interested only in whether things work, they are not likely to be swept along with intellectual fads, and they are uninterested in the intellectual elegance of various theories. Further it is impossible to predict what applications they will make of any given theory. In consequence, they are the strongest possible check on the accuracy of the work of the pure scientists. In the Middle Ages the "theorists" drew maps of the world based on the best

23. The first four volumes of the massive *A History of Technology* (Oxford, 1954–58) are largely devoted to the "prescientific" progress of technology.

current views of cosmography, which had little real relation to the world. The practical navigators also drew maps, but theirs had much more correspondence with reality. A similar interest in only the practical application of theories has characterized the applied researcher to the present day. The absence of a community of such cynical critics in the social studies has undoubtedly greatly hindered their developments.[24]

The second possible motive for scientific inquiry is curiosity. Undoubtedly, most people are more curious about other people than about inanimate nature. This motive, therefore, might lead to more intense research in the social studies than in the natural sciences. Unfortunately, curiosity in this field is likely to be distracted to essentially non-scientific ends. In the first place, there is a strong possibility of artistic distraction. Literature of all kinds is quite frequently based on careful observation of human beings. A large number of brilliant men led by their curiosity to study their fellow men have produced great literature instead of science.

Even among those with no literary talent, curiosity may not lead to much in the way of scientific discovery. Curiosity in the natural sciences is necessarily concerned with generalities. We are simply not much interested in what happens to a single atom or to a given bar of metal. The only things we are curious about are general patterns which cover all atoms or all bars of a certain type of metal. We are therefore normally led by our curiosity to look for general theories. In dealing with our fellow human beings, we will frequently be led to examine unique cases. A man who is very curious about his fellow men may spend his entire life trying to understand various individual men, not in seeking general rules or statements. As a result, he may know certain people or even certain organizations very well, but he will not be in possession of any sort of scientific knowledge.

The same problem is likely to affect historical studies. The historian is largely led by his curiosity to examine some certain period or incident in order to find out what happened. He is, again, interested in particulars and not in generalities. Curiosity in this field, and it is a field of great fascination which has held the interest of many great scholars, usually leads only to particular information, not to general statements. In general the particular dis-

24. It may be that we are witnessing the dawn of applied social research in the fields of industrial management and polling. In both of these fields techniques originally developed by academics are being widely applied by practical men. So far, however, the usefulness of these techniques is very narrow, with the result that they have little effect on most of the social sciences.

coveries of the historians are not aimed at validating or contradicting general hypotheses about human behavior. In fact, of course, because of the complexity of the conditions in which historic events occur, a hypothesis can very seldom be tested by a single historic event. Normally, too many factors will be involved. It takes a sizable population of somewhat similar events to permit conclusions to be drawn by statistical methods, and the historian normally studies unique events, or a series of events connected by some chronological, geographical, or human factor, rather than a series connected by their relation to a hypothesis which it is desired to test.[25] In general, the student of history (or the man who simply studies his fellows) will use vague and untested hypotheses to aid his studies of individual cases, rather than seeking generalizations for their own sake.

In addition to these distractions, the man who is curious about his fellow men is likely to be discouraged by the presently rather dim prospects of really satisfying his curiosity. In the physical sciences there is a long record of successful investigation, and the investigator can feel considerable confidence that his work will lead to concrete results. One of my friends, for example, has just started a project on the characteristics of molten salts which he expects will take him twenty years. He expects to spend his research time for a long period in careful measurement of various constants of molten salts and their solutions. Now, he is certain that he is measuring real quantities and that his measurements, while not exact, are very good. Further, he can feel a fair degree of confidence that when he finally gets a large body of results, they will fall into some pattern which can be used to predict other results. In other words, he has confidence that his curiosity will be satisfied, both as to specific finds and as to general phenomena.

The social investigator could never be sure that he was investigating anything half as real as my friend's "heats of solution" and would know for certain that his results would be subject to large probable errors. Further, he could have little real confidence that his measurements would eventually lead to valid generalization. His situation is thus much less encouraging than that of most physical scientists. It takes a stronger curiosity and greater confidence to undertake investigations in the social sciences. The distractions we have already discussed also reduce the likelihood that curiosity will lead to important discoveries in the social sciences. Altogether, although men are probably

25. A small number of economic historians have recently informally organized the Cliometric Society, which aims at more general testing of hypotheses.

more curious about each other than about the non-human part of nature, curiosity is probably a less strong motive for scientific investigation in this field than in the natural sciences.

The term "induced curiosity" which we have used so far begs important questions. The scheme under which a person's income depends on what he turns out, but under which he is more or less free to look into anything he wishes, will certainly induce some sort of activity. It will, however, induce curiosity only if the rewards are distributed in such a manner as to benefit primarily the man who has actually increased human knowledge. In the natural sciences this is easy. Large numbers of the investigators in those fields are motivated by curiosity, and even larger numbers are interested in applications. To acquire a good reputation with such people, it is necessary to produce things that interest them, and they are interested only in the truth. Since they exercise a dominating control over these fields,[26] this interest is dominant. It is, of course, in general easier to distinguish truth from falsehood in the natural sciences, but this is merely a reflection of their greater development. In this regard, the more developed a science is, the easier it is to develop further.

In the social field, however, things are not so easy. There are almost no applied researchers, and people impelled by curiosity are likely to be distracted from the scientific study of man. As a result the field is dominated by induced participants. Most people in the social sciences undertake investigations largely because that is the way they make their living. This normally leads them to do things they think will have a favorable effect on their future, and thus to a careful consideration of the "climate of opinion." Now, in the physical sciences, composed largely of people who need the truth, either for practical reasons or to satisfy their curiosity, the climate of opinion is dominated by a desire for new knowledge. In the social field, unfortunately, this is only one, albeit a very important one, of the factors involved. Among the other factors which will affect the future of a researcher and which he must keep in mind, there are some which are simply irrational and disturbing from the standpoint of the growth of knowledge.

26. In the early days of science the investigators motivated by curiosity or the desire to make practical applications made up practically the whole body of researchers in the natural sciences. Now they probably are in a minority, but the traditions established in earlier times and the continuing existence of a very large minority of people motivated by curiosity or practical interests make it unlikely that the natural sciences will ever come under the control of "induced" researchers.

We have already discussed the tendency of researchers in the social sciences to avoid dangerous issues, to confine their investigations to "safe" subjects and "safe" conclusions. The bulk of the money available for "inducing" such research comes either from essentially charitable endowments or from government organizations (universities, of course, partake of both) and is likely to become unavailable to a man who annoys people with his discoveries. As a result, the students in this field have a strong tendency to devote large amounts of effort to "confirming" popular opinions. In most fields of science new ideas originate with the investigators and are only subsequently disseminated to the public. In the social sciences there is a strong tendency for the reverse process to take place. New currents of opinion will develop in the "real world," and then investigators will undertake research which "proves" them to be true. The 1930's, for example, witnessed a tremendous change in the economic policies of most Western countries. This was not at all the result of economic research; in fact, the economists largely used theories which condemned the new policies. After it was clear which way the wind was blowing the bulk of the economic profession jumped on the bandwagon, and the economic journals were full of articles which fitted in well with contemporary public opinion.

Why this difference between the social and natural sciences? The answer is, of course, complicated and involves many factors, but one of the most important is the fact that application of new ideas in the social sciences normally is much harder than in the natural sciences. Suppose, for example, that I decide that all automobile mufflers are improperly designed and that a radical change is necessary. If I can convince one of the hundred or so automobile or engine manufacturers in the world that my idea deserves a trial, then my idea will be applied. If I am right, the market process will permit me and my single ally to coerce the overwhelming majority of the manufacturers of such equipment into accepting the new idea. Further, I will be richly rewarded. This impresses a great many people as undemocratic and, in a sense, it is. A minority which happens to have truth on its side coerces the majority. Regardless of the political morality of the situation, this results in a great advantage for truth.[27]

27. In the formalism developed by Arrow the procedure in the natural sciences involves an "imposed" solution, while in the social sciences we try for a "non-imposed," "non-dictatorial" outcome. Kenneth J. Arrow, *Social Choice and Individual Values* (Cowles Foundation monograph; New York: Wiley, 1951, 1963). The 1963 edition is much to be preferred since it contains

The situation in the social sciences is almost exactly opposite. In a democracy a majority must be convinced before the idea can even be tried. Further, it is unlikely that the "inventor" will receive much in the way of reward. In a despotism, only one man must be convinced, but it is a specified man, and it is harder to convince a specified individual than one individual out of a large group. In either case, the new idea must be such as to attract considerable support before it has been tried, or it will never be tried. In the case of a physical invention, support must also be attracted, but only a very tiny amount compared with what must be attained for application for some idea for social change. Further, if some government adopts a proposal for a social change, its prestige is likely to be involved, and it will be reluctant to admit that it was wrong. As a consequence, errors may persist. In the physical sciences the man who guesses wrong also loses prestige if he must admit his error, but he will lose much more if he does not change quickly. The very great difference between the weight held by abstract truth in practical affairs in natural science and in social science is thus a major factor in accelerating the development of the natural sciences and retarding the development of the social sciences.

Another "random" factor in the development of social studies, which results from the relative scarcity of applied or curiosity motives, is the importance which the rather poorly thought out opinions of the people who put up the money assume in directing research. Some time ago I met a most distinguished anthropologist.[28] In the course of our first conversation, he referred to his work and explained that he had spent the morning "correcting" a research paper which one of the men in his department had just sent in from an obscure part of Asia. This activity, which he thought was fundamentally a waste of time, consisted of making some minor changes to bring the paper into complete accord with what he felt were the views of the leading foundation financing the project. He pointed out that the necessity of such "correction" did not arise because of the incompetence of the researcher, who was aware of the views of the foundation at the time he left this country, but who could hardly keep up-to-date on the subject while engaged in studying a tiny village in a backward part of Asia.

Now, of course, the personnel of this particular foundation, whose opin-

---

not only the full text of the earlier monograph but also Arrow's comments on more recent research. See also Duncan Black, *The Theory of Committees and Elections* (Cambridge: Cambridge University Press, 1958).

28. In view of what follows, I should say that the distinction is fully merited.

ions are so carefully studied by leading social scientists, do not wish to produce results which merely confirm their own prejudices. Nevertheless, they must decide who is to get the new grant; this decision will be made largely in terms of past work; and their evaluation of the past work will necessarily reflect their own judgment. They cannot rely on professional opinion because substantially all of the people qualified to have a professional opinion are trying vigorously to please them. Not only is each research project written up in a way thought to be pleasing to the foundation, criticisms of the projects also will be made in the same terms. The result is that the principal effect of much research in certain of the social sciences is simply to "confirm" vague and loosely held prejudices in the minds of the directors of foundations.

A final "irrational" effect arises from the tendency of researchers in the social sciences to "take in each other's washing." If a group of sufficient size, say fifty social scientists, all become interested in a given subject, then they can produce articles and research reports which create each other's reputations by a process of gradually elaborating some fairly simple idea. If the subject they get started with is one of no real importance, this may result in a great waste of effort.

These, then, are "random" factors in the organization of the social sciences which are likely to cause the research to be pointless or misdirected. We will now turn to factors which may lead to quite deliberately false research.[29] The moral and ideological reasons for such fakery have already been adequately discussed. The examples which come most readily to mind in the field of ideology refer to leftist writers in the early part of the century who, it is now being revealed, in such great numbers systematically distorted social data to support various left-wing positions. It should be noted, however, that this phenomenon is by no means limited to the left. While I can think of no single example on the right to put in opposition to the shredding of Beard's histor-

29. This book is not particularly concerned with the subjective state of the consciences of individual researchers, but I suppose I should state my beliefs. In the area to which we are turning, and for that matter the area which we have just left, there are undoubtedly people who quite consciously consider the factors we are discussing and decide on their research results solely in terms of what is in it for them. They are, however, a tiny minority. Another, larger, minority is composed of people who are not very perceptive and who are simply doing things that they have been told are desirable, but who have no idea that they are doing anything other than advancing knowledge in the best of all possible ways. The majority lives in a half-way house between these extremes, with the exact mixture of the two attitudes varying from person to person.

ical work now being carried on by the younger historians, I am sure this merely reflects ignorance on my part.[30]

Whether the distortion of research by conscious effort or subconscious bias of interest groups is as important as the distortion arising from moral and ideological causes, I hesitate to say. Possibly, in the long run, it is more important. Note, however, that the possibility of this type of problem's arising is largely due to the relative absence of people motivated purely to seek the truth in the social sciences. Hobbes once said, "If there were anyone with an interest to argue that 2 and 2 are 5, arithmetic would not be the wonder that it now is."[31] This is something of an oversimplification. There are so many people motivated highly for accuracy in mathematics that no conceivable interest group could overcome this vast interest. Still, if there were such a group, the fundamental and difficult problems involved in the basis of arithmetic would undoubtedly be much better known and much more frequently discussed than they are now.

A friend of mine in physics once said that he could not understand the social sciences. "You're always arguing," he continued. He was, although I do not think he realized it, quite an acute social critic and had neatly placed his hand on one of the major distinctions between the social and natural sciences. The social studies are dominated by arguments, while arguments are much less common in the "exact sciences." Arguments, sometimes bitter and protracted, do occur in the natural sciences, but they occupy much less of the investigator's time. Even a casual inspection of a journal in the natural sciences and one in the social sciences will indicate the great difference in the proportion of space devoted to disputation in the two fields. The social scientist must devote much of his time and considerable energy in "convincing" people, while the natural scientist can give much less energy to this matter. Further, arguments in the natural sciences normally are settled by some further advance in knowledge which makes one point of view or the other (sometimes both) obsolete. This is much less common in the social sciences. The fallacious defenses of tariffs which were invented in the fifteenth and sixteenth centuries still appear with monotonous regularity in the literature.

30. The two principal attacks on Beard's work are Robert E. Brown, *Charles Beard and the Constitution* (Princeton: Princeton University Press, 1956), and Forrest McDonald, *We the People* (Chicago: University of Chicago Press, 1958). There has been a counterattack by the orthodox historians, but in my judgment it has failed.

31. Professor Bruno Leoni of Turin gave me this quotation which I have been unable to verify. If Hobbes did not say it, he should have.

The explanation of this phenomenon is fairly simple. While almost everyone would, in the long run, benefit from the removal of tariffs, and the raising of tariffs is a blow to the welfare of almost everyone, there are, at any given time, minorities which can be hurt by the reduction of specific tariffs and helped by the increase of others. Now the benefits of the repeal of a given tariff are likely to be dispersed over the whole population, while the injury will be concentrated in a small group. Although the benefit will be much greater in total than the injury, it is slight for any individual. The group which suffers concentrated injury, however, is likely to try to convince the majority that really they gain nothing and to hire economists for this purpose. Since there are always some such groups, there will always be economists who have been hired for this purpose.

Not all of the advocates of tariffs, of course, are hired by "the interests." But the existence of people whose living does depend on finding arguments for tariffs and the further existence of another group who think that maybe, sometime in the future, they might need the assistance of either someone who believes in tariffs or an economist who is in this racket makes it possible for them to continue to publish, even in quite respectable journals. Thus a dispute which intellectually was settled over a century ago still continues.

The real difference between the social sciences and the natural sciences, then, is a difference in motivation. Investigators in the natural sciences are motivated by a desire to make practical applications of new knowledge, by curiosity, or by a desire to make money out of research in a field where only research leading to increases in knowledge is profitable. In the social sciences the possibility of practical applications is very limited, and curiosity is likely to be directed at non-scientific ends. As a result, the induced researchers are not subject to the strict controls that cover the activities of those in the natural sciences. Further, there are no significant motives for attempting to obscure or conceal the truth in the natural sciences, while the social fields abound with such motives. The "organization of inquiry" in the natural sciences is a system of voluntary co-operation in which the work of each investigator not only meets his own desires but also helps other investigators. The system works largely because of the similarity of the ends and presuppositions of the scientists. In the social studies, there is less similarity of ends and presuppositions and, consequently, less voluntary co-operation.

CHAPTER VIII

PRACTICAL SUGGESTIONS

It may seem odd to begin a chapter entitled "Practical Suggestions" by recommending that a number of changes not be made, but the first part of this chapter will be devoted to discussing a set of frequently made proposals for reforming science which are in my opinion either impractical or undesirable. The first of these suggestions is that science either be completely stopped or at least drastically slowed down. The proponents of these ideas normally point out that the tremendous improvement in our physical control of the universe has not been accompanied by any conclusive proof of increased happiness of individual human beings. There are, of course, many more men alive than there would be without science (and presumably some of its critics must be counted among those who would not be alive if science were less advanced), but it must be admitted that the evidence of any real increase in individual satisfaction or cultural development from scientific progress is scanty. Elimination of positive pain is all that can be claimed conclusively. Clearly, the improvements in dentistry, for example, have improved human happiness by eliminating certain causes of unhappiness. A man with a persistent toothache is obviously improved in happiness when a dentist cures it. It is possibly for this reason that those who hope to restrict scientific progress normally, but not always, exempt medical research from their ban.

Before turning to my reasons for objecting to this proposed policy, I must record my agreement with some of the "data" upon which it is based. Clearly, very rapid rate of change of the physical environment makes social adjustment hard. Think, for example, of the tremendous effect on that basic social institution, the family, by first the automobile and now by the television set. A child brought up in the pre–World War I period was hardly prepared for the type of family life which prevailed in the twenties and thirties. Similarly, a child brought up then was hardly prepared for the radical changes in family and social patterns inaugurated by the television era. It is frequently said that education should prepare a child for modern life. In fact, it should prepare him for future life, life twenty to thirty years from now, and we do not know what such life will involve. Certainly, in a more slowly changing society, it would be easier to prepare children for their future roles.

Having now briefly stated what I believe to be true in the arguments for stopping scientific progress, I can now address myself to the reasons for not accepting them. In the first place, educating our children for their future roles in society is obviously a desirable goal and, obviously, would be easier in a static society than in a rapidly changing one, but is there any reason to believe that we would be able to do it even in a static society? Our knowledge of what it takes to play a given role in society and how to instill those qualities in individuals is very slight. Improvement of our knowledge of these matters, of course, can come only from further scientific advances. If we examine the more or less static societies which have had elaborate educational systems, traditional China for example, we find that the educational system produced some obvious misfits. Further, there is no particular reason to believe that even those who were not obviously unsuited to their social roles received an optimum education. True, the societies did not immediately collapse, but human societies seem to be quite tough and able to survive a large amount of internal strain. Our present rapidly changing society has also not collapsed.

Even, however, if we did know enough about human society to properly plan an educational and social structure for a static or slowly changing society, this would still not support very strongly a proposal to stop scientific progress. Even in highly advanced countries like the United States, only part of our present scientific knowledge is being utilized. The discontinuance of further research would probably have no effect at all on the rate of technological change for a year or so, and then would be only a gradual leveling off. In less advanced countries, hundreds of years of rapid social change could result simply from applying what we know. Thus the stopping of scientific progress would "benefit" only a small fragment of mankind in the immediate future.

Further, we live in a world of nations. The stopping of scientific research by one nation, even such a major scientific power as the United States, would not stop it everywhere; it is dubious whether it would even seriously reduce the rate of new discoveries. Scientific research, like everything else, is presumably subject to the law of diminishing returns, and elimination of marginal resources will result in a less than proportional reduction in the total output. One thing that the discontinuance of scientific research by one nation would do, however, would be to eliminate that nation rather quickly as a world power unless it took care to adopt rapidly all inventions made abroad. This, of course, would lead to a rapid rate of change, so what could be the gain in abandoning the research?

Lastly, assuming that some sort of world agreement were reached to stop scientific progress, which, let us say, also included an agreement from the less advanced countries to refrain from adopting devices already known in the advanced countries but as yet not applied in their own countries, we would be confronted with a paradox. The problem of when to stop would have to be solved, and no given time would be as desirable as a later time. Suppose it were urged that we stop all research[1] two years from today. It is obvious that stopping two years and six months from now would be better because the discoveries made in the extra six months would then be available to this great static society which we plan to build. It would be just that much better a stasis. Thus, even if we are agreed to the principle that a shift to a more static society were desirable, it would always be desirable to postpone the shift to some future date.

Even if these arguments are unconvincing, however, we simply do not know how to stop the accumulation of new knowledge. There have been societies in the past, and some now exist, in which knowledge accumulates very slowly. We do not, however, know the "secret" of such retardation. The tremendous scientific advances of the seventeenth and eighteenth centuries in Europe were made in a society which looks, in many ways, much like some of today's stagnant societies. Certainly, scientific knowledge will grow rapidly in any politically and economically "open" society, and I doubt if even the most vigorous enemies of such progress would favor a shift to despotic government in order to avoid it. Even, however, if we were willing to make such a shift on a world-wide basis, history indicates that it would not eliminate the growth of knowledge, but merely slow it down. All historical and archaeological investigation shows human societies learning new things. The rate of new discovery may be low, and parts of the world may actually forget things, but some new knowledge is always being picked up.

The radical anti-scientific position which I have been discussing is held by only a few in the present-day world, but watered-down versions are quite commonly believed in, even by scientists. The two most common versions are the belief that scientific progress in the development of weapons should be stopped or slowed down, and the view that research should be shifted from physical to social science. The first is held by many scientists who are naïve outside of their own specialty. In its most widespread and popular version, it consists, more or less, in the wish that the atom bomb had not been invented.

1. Or reduce it to a level which resulted in accumulation of new knowledge at a rate only some fraction of the present rate.

The history of the atom bomb will do as an illustration of the reasons for distrusting this view. The effort to improve our knowledge of the atom was the outstanding field of "pure" science between the wars. While some hoped that atomic energy might eventually be of some practical use, the whole matter was largely one of investigating reality for simple curiosity's sake. No one thought of the accumulation of information as having any military utility, and the scientists of the various nations continued calmly engaging in research (which was not financed by military funds) and publishing their results openly even as World War II approached. When, in 1939, Hahn first discovered the reaction on which the atom bomb was based, he apparently never even thought of its possible military significance, and even the extremely security-conscious German state of that time put no barrier on his publishing it. Even more peculiarly, from the standpoint of hindsight, the pathologically secretive Russians also continued to act openly in this field.

The reason for this lack of caution, of course, is simple: no one realized that this field had any military applications. The most deadly weapon of modern times was developed as the accidental by-product of fundamental research aimed at quite other goals. Thus the proposal that scientists stop inventing atom bombs has the very serious drawback that no one knows in advance when he is inventing one. A biologist studying cancer may tomorrow find an "active principal" which would be easily distributed over an enemy nation artificially; a psychologist may find a method of driving men insane *en masse*. Only stopping all research will stop the invention of new weapons.

A more sophisticated version of this position might, however, be invented. It might be argued that, while the original discovery is essentially unpredictable, it will normally require some development before it is available as a weapon, and the scientist should refrain from taking part in this process. If every single scientist or engineer in the world were united in some general conspiracy to enforce such an "ethical rule," and if arrangements were made to bring into this conspiracy every man who began to teach himself about some field of science or technology, and if none of the members of this conspiracy put his patriotism above his obligation to the conspiracy or was willing to undertake "forbidden" research out of curiosity or hope of large rewards, then this policy might work. Clearly, however, these are impossible conditions. Producing new scientific principles is chancy, and little can be done about planning to produce one in a given area. But once such a principle has been developed, then applying it in a practical device is normally much easier.[2] If we had not invented the atom bomb, someone else would have. True, this invention might have been delayed, possibly for as much as ten years, but there seems no reason to think that this would much advantage the human race.

Further, this position, both in its naïve and its sophisticated versions, holds great danger for the more peaceful nations. Like the pacifist and pro-disarmament position between the wars, it takes effect only in areas where it is not needed. The aggressive and militaristic countries in the 1930's simply prohibited anti-armament propaganda, while the peaceful countries permitted it. The end result of the whole movement, then, was simply that the relative advantage of the potential aggressors over the satisfied powers was increased. The actual practical effect of a refusal of any significant number of scientists to work on weapons in the West would be identical. We may be sure that no such nonsense is tolerated behind the curtain. Surely permitting the Russians to attain a potential killing advantage is no way of promoting peace.

Another mild variant on the theme that we should restrict scientific research holds that we devote too much effort to research in the natural sciences and too little in the social studies. A restriction of one field of research in order to put more resources in the other is not infrequently recommended. That the social studies are in many ways less flourishing than the natural sciences is, of course, clear. Still, in science as elsewhere, resources should be invested where they are most likely to get a good return. We can shift resources to the social studies, but there is no great reason to believe that this would perceptibly improve the situation there. The resources now employed in research in the social fields are already vastly disproportionate to the results being achieved. Most universities maintain large faculties in the various fields of human study, running from history to economics, and these faculties engage in active research. The results, however, are disappointing. It would appear that, if anything, a shift of resources out of the social sciences and into the natural sciences would be wiser than the reverse.

Another widely popular proposal for changing present-day science suggests simply that there be more of it, that we increase the resources devoted to this aspect of our culture. This viewpoint is held most strongly by the scientists themselves, but is held also by many laymen. Like everyone else, the

2. Edward Teller, "Perilous Illusion: Secrecy Means Security," *New York Times Magazine,* November 13, 1960, p. 29.

scientist thinks that his own field tends to be neglected and that it should be given further attention. Most scientists secretly think that their own individual specialties are particularly neglected, and that it would be wise to divert funds from other sciences into those fields, but they normally talk very little about this. After all, they have many friends and associates in the other branches of science, and suggesting that these people have their funds cut is not a good way to get along. The result is a sort of general agreement that the total amount of money put into science should be increased, which will give everyone a share. The analogy with bureaucracies, where proposals for general expansion are always welcomed, but suggestions for economies in one area to permit expansion elsewhere are *de trop,* is close.[3]

There is no particular reason to be disturbed by the fact that scientists share this common human failing, although their almost religious approach to the matter can be irritating at times, but there is also no particular reason to pay any attention to their opinion. They, of course, want more money spent in their fields of interest, but so do sports fans. Any decision on how much should be invested either in science in general or in some specific research project necessarily depends on a guess as to what now-unknown information will be discovered by the investigation. Such guesses are hard to make, and we certainly do not put too much dependence on them. Nevertheless, in other parts of our economy, decisions based on guesses about the future are made.

The usual procedure in a free economy is to permit anyone to make guesses, and then to distribute rewards and penalties according to how well the guesses turn out. This insures that at any given time the people who in the past have been most successful in making such guesses have considerable resources to make further "investments," and those who have failed in the past have few such resources. The patent system, from the standpoint of individual corporations or people, offers just this type of problem. There is no reason to believe that General Motors is any better or worse in making guesses about this matter than about, say, car models. Looked at from our point of view, however, the problem is not so easy. Present laws offer two stimulae to invention, the patent monopoly and certain tax privileges. Our

3. *Basic Research and National Goals* (National Academy of Sciences, 1965) is a collection of statements by prominent scientists which illustrates this attitude. Dr. Harry G. Johnson, an economist, presents a sort of minority report, but even he favors more research in his own field.

question should be whether these stimulae are of the correct strength. Should the patent privilege be strengthened, thus leading businessmen to put more resources in research, or perhaps weakened with the opposite effect? Unfortunately, this is currently an unanswerable question.

When we turn to pure research, the problem is even more difficult. Here, we do not have even the ghost of a theory indicating how much should be "invested." Presumably, such research should be thought of as a consumer good, giving direct satisfaction to various people, but, unlike most consumer goods, its production and consumption both involve the co-operative participation of a large number of people. Further, this co-operation works very well as long as it is largely voluntary, but would work very badly if all pure scientists were integrated in one giant decision-making machine. Under the circumstances, there is simply no way of telling whether any given amount of resources is the correct amount to invest in pure science. The outcome of this discussion, then, is that I do not know how much should be invested in science. This makes it impossible for me to comment on the frequently heard demands for greater diversion of funds into these channels.

But now, having discussed a number of popular proposals for the improvement of science with which I disagree, it is incumbent upon me to justify the title of this chapter by presenting some practical suggestions. These suggestions will, of course, include such trite but sound bits of advice as choosing personnel carefully and not wasting money. But the principal purpose of this chapter is not to repeat the maxims of good management, but to suggest certain specific changes and improvements in our present organization of science. The first of these is that large organizations should confine themselves to cataloguing and indexing knowledge and to providing funds for those very few scientific activities, such as atom-smashing, which require very large amounts of money for a given experiment. The reasons for feeling that large organizations are particularly suitable for such work and unsuitable for encouraging science in general have already been given.

Much scientific work requires relatively little money; the sum total may be large, but individual projects seldom really cost more than $25,000 and may cost only a few hundred.[4] This fact is concealed by the organization of the

4. Jakob Messikomer was one of the important early explorers of the so-called "Swiss lake villages." He supported all of his research from his tiny income as a farm laborer. Alfred Rust, the archaeologist who discovered the Meiendorf and Stellmoor sites, worked as an electrician

giant "wholesaler" foundations which give very large gifts to various agencies for supporting research. In fact, the money is "retailed" by the recipients who break it up into a number of small projects. If such a foundation wishes to dabble in direct support of research, it should first split itself into ten or, better, twenty small foundations, each with completely separate boards of directors. These smaller foundations can then, without the bureaucratic mess which characterizes the giant foundation (or the giant government research agencies), hand out the same total amount of money, but pay it to the individual small projects which are the real recipients of the present grants.

In administering the grants, less attention should be paid to the nature of the specific project proposed for a grant and more to the results achieved by the potential recipient in previous work. The talent for producing a convincing brochure[5] and the talent for actual discoveries are different, and while they may be united in one person, they may also not be so united. Further, the present situation where a great deal of the time and energy of leading investigators is taken up with the preparation of projects for future research is a glaring and obvious waste of talent. There has also been a tendency to develop specialized personnel who are experts at getting grants, having the ability to figure out what will appeal to the foundations and the necessary political abilities to present their projects properly. Under present conditions these people are as valuable to universities and other research institutions as their status would indicate, but clearly their presence and positions of control and prestige represent sheer waste from the standpoint of the scientific community as a whole.

Concern with what has been done rather than with what is proposed for the future would greatly improve this situation. In part, this is already done, although it is disguised. Only a man who is "trusted" by the specific foundation can get a grant, and such "trust" is usually based on previous work. I suggest, however, that this be brought out in the open. Research workers who have had success in the past should simply be given funds to spend on

---

during the winters and did his digging in the summers while living on unemployment relief. The general level of his expenditures on research can be seen from his first expedition, to Syria. He bicycled from Germany and supported himself in Syria by doing electrical repair work. Geoffrey Bibby, *The Testimony of the Spade* (New York: Knopf, 1956).

5. Ernest M. Allen, "Why Are Research Grant Applications Disapproved?" *Science,* 132 (November 25, 1960), 1532–34, gives the administrator's view of the conditions a project must meet.

what they wish, with the understanding that further funds will depend on the results they obtain.[6] This procedure would largely eliminate the present waste of time on preparing projects and would permit scientists to concentrate on their real work.

This program, of course, would make it easier for a man who has already made his name to get funds than it would be for a newcomer. In this respect, however, it would not differ from the present situation. Today, a newly minted scientist has practically no chance of getting a research grant "on his own." He will normally do his early research as the assistant of someone else, or he will receive grants on the recommendation of some more prestigious scientist who knows him. Usually, this means some member of the faculty either at the school where he took his training or at the institution where he is employed. I would suggest that this procedure be formalized. Prominent scientists, in addition to being given grants, could be asked to recommend newcomers for initial grants.[7] If the new men produced good work, then the grants could be renewed, and the senior scientist could be asked to suggest some more. If their work turned out to be inferior, the granting organization would seek advice from some other scientist on its next round. Here again, there would be no need for the institution dispersing the funds to make any attempt to judge the future. All that would be necessary, other than the initial small gamble, would be to judge how good the work done in the past was and to channel funds to people who had done the comparatively best work.

Direct rewards, in the form of prizes, for scientific work would also seem desirable. It is disgraceful that the Nobel prizes and the new Balzan prizes are practically the only substantial ones that a scientist can win. There should be many more prizes, and they should be much larger. There is no reason why a man who has made a really significant contribution to scientific knowledge should not be rewarded by very large sums of money. A system of prizes should be aimed at two objectives: specific discoveries and unspecified developments. The difference between the two may be neatly summarized by two discoveries of considerable importance to astronomy: the chronometer and

6. Scientists, like other people, are subject to temptation. Accounting procedures to make sure that very large grants are spent on research, not on high living, would still be necessary.

7. That this process would not be foolproof is obvious. For a particularly bad example of a misjudgment, see letter by Ralph W. Dexter, "Can One Predict Success in Science?" *Science* (February 15, 1963), 670.

the discovery that the apparent direction of stars shifts slightly according to the direction in which the earth is moving. The first was seen as a need by the British Admiralty, and a prize for the first successful chronometer was offered. Eventually an expert clockmaker succeeded in producing an instrument of the required degree of accuracy and, after some trouble, collected his reward. The second discovery, by Bradley, could not have been specified in advance because no one suspected that it was true. Further, if anyone had suspected it, he could very easily have checked his suspicions. The discovery, although of great importance, could not have been the subject of a specified prize offered in advance. It could, however, have been rewarded by a prize for an "advance in astronomy."

The specified reward is an excellent way of directing research toward some specific end, whether that end is large or small. As an extreme example, surely offering a reward of $1 billion for the first successful ICBM would have resulted in both a large saving of money for the government and much faster production of this weapon. At the other extreme, there are large numbers of minor practical discoveries which would be desirable but which, for one reason or another, are not patentable. Offering rewards for such discoveries would appear to be an effective method of encouraging this type of highly useful science. Much of present-day agricultural research could, for example, be done in this way, and thus the vast bureaucracy which now both carries out and impedes research in this field could be eliminated. Other areas where little or no research is now done could also be fertilized by this method: criminological procedures, for example.

Nor would specified prizes necessarily be confined to applied science. In the pure field, too, innumerable problems are suitable for such awards. But the non-specified award seems on the whole more suitable for the pure field. The patent, of course, is a non-specified reward for research in the applied field, and a most successful method of encouraging research. Non-specified rewards in the present-day world, such as the Nobel prizes, are rare and more valuable for the publicity and prestige than for the money. While I would not decry the value of publicity and prestige, most scientists would, I think, rather have more and larger prizes. But while such prizes are desirable, it would be highly undesirable to have them distributed by the same bodies. The maximum possible dispersion of decision-making powers on the question of who gets a prize is desirable. We discussed previously the advantage that the scientific publication system derives from the fact that there are many journals with diverse editors, so that work rejected by one stands a chance of being accepted by another. The prize-awarding process should be similar. There should be a large number of individuals or boards that could award a scientist a prize, but no one of these should be able to say that he would not get one.

There is little else to say about the organization of these prizes except that diversity is desirable in every way. Not only should there be a number of prizes available in, say, physics, all offered by different bodies, but there should also be some prizes restricted to certain fields of physics, and other prizes for which physicists' discoveries must compete with, say, biologists'. The award-giving process should be so organized that no scientist could greatly benefit his chances for an award by any "politicking." Publication of his work should be all that is needed to make him eligible for an award. The people who decide who gets the award should not require applications, but should simply read the literature and reward the best items they see. Further, since it is sometimes difficult to see the real importance of a discovery immediately, a good many of the awards should be given only some years after a work was originally published. This is particularly important for the largest rewards. Frequently, some line of research which appears important when it is completed is seen four or five years later to be a dead end. The type of premonition which seems to lead some scientists into work which will lead to further great discoveries in the future is a rare and valuable gift, and it can be rewarded only by delaying the granting of rewards.

Some will object to all of this on the grounds that scientists are motivated by other things than a desire for money.[8] In my experience, scientists themselves are particularly likely to make such statements. Their tendency to talk about their lack of interest in monetary rewards is equaled only by their tendency to bemoan their "low" pay. I have divided motives for scientific investigation into three categories: desire to make practical applications, curiosity, and induced curiosity. Clearly, the first is already largely motivated by mate-

8. Practical men have almost always used monetary incentives to "control" scientists. A king of Denmark, confronted with a potential "brain drain" in the form of a proposal of Tycho Brahe to settle down in Basel, wrote the following letter: "We, Frederick the Second, make known to all men, that we of our special favour and grace have conferred and granted in fee . . . to our beloved Tycho de Brahe, Otto's son . . . our land of Hveen, with all our tenants and servants who thereon live, with all rent and duty which comes from that . . . to use, hold, quit and free all the days of his life as long as he lives and likes to follow his studia mathematice." Needless to say, Tycho decided that Denmark was really a much better place to carry on his researches than Basel. I am indebted to J. B. Adams ("Megaloscience," *Science,* 148 [June 18, 1965], 1560–64) for this quotation.

rial considerations. The second would not be greatly affected, but a man who was genuinely interested in some scientific problem might just as genuinely be interested in money. If presented with a choice between investigating the problem that has engaged his interest at a low salary and some other problem at a high salary, he might well choose the latter. If the compensation for his scientific work was the same as for both alternatives, he would probably choose to work on the first. Thus, even for people motivated by curiosity, the amount of money likely to result from scientific or non-scientific activity is relevant.

For the people whose curiosity is "induced," the situation is clear. They will exert themselves in areas where the "inducement" is strongest, and thus provide an exceptionally good area for the application of our suggested methods of rewarding good work. In most real cases, of course, these motives are intertwined, but since in each of the pure cases our system of monetary compensation will be an improvement over the present system, it would also help in these mixed real situations.

The general problem of the level of compensation which a scientist can expect should be briefly discussed. We need pay little attention to the complaints of the present-day scientists about their pay. After all, everyone complains in this way, and everyone is always free to change his occupation. The problem of the type of people who are being attracted into science is, however, a real one. Monetary rewards are certainly not the only motivating factor leading a man into science, but equally certainly, they are one such factor. A college student considering his future career surely will devote at least some thought to likely pay rates, and, in most cases, this will be a highly important factor. Thus, higher compensation should result in some improvement in the intellectual quality of new entries to the field. With a given amount of money for research, of course, higher pay means fewer workers; so the question of whether we would be better off with fewer, but more brilliant, scientists is relevant. I must confess that I cannot answer it. The prize system would permit an implicit compromise, since the duller scientists would obtain a low income from a relatively small number of such awards, while a brilliant man might do very, very well. The rewards themselves would be distributed in terms of contributions, and it seems likely that the amount of research funds invested to obtain a given discovery would be minimized.

In strictly organizational matters, however, two further changes in present conditions are desirable, or, to be more precise, changes in two myths about present-day conditions in order to bring them into closer accord with reality are desirable. These changes involve the present connection between researcher and college teacher and the "tenure" arrangements in most universities. Both of these "institutions" are hangovers from previous historical conditions, and both have been provided with modern rationalizations. In both cases, the present reality is drastically different from the myth.

Let us start with the association of higher education and research. This fairly obviously is the result of the fact that in those fields of knowledge which have little immediate practical application teaching is a possible career. When universities were few, they had their pick of people interested in such areas. They obviously tried to get the best qualified authorities, and these best authorities were likely to be also the men who would produce the best research. Further, at least in England, teaching at a university was far from a full-time job in the early nineteenth century; so there was a great deal of time for research available. The combination of people who were really expert in a given field, intellectual stimulation, and free time led to research. Somewhat similar conditions existed in the Continental universities. The modern expansion of the university system, particularly in the United States, involved a great deal of simple imitation of the great universities at which many of the leading members of the new faculties had gained their training, and thus research as a function of the universities was confirmed in these new organizations.

Although the mating of research and teaching probably does harm in only a few cases, there seems no particular reason why it is necessary. It used to be considered essential to have an exceptional man as a teacher in the universities, but the vast expansion of the university system has resulted in a dilution in the quality of faculties. Many present-day teachers do research only because they are required to do so. The problem arises of whether it might not be better to put those of them who are primarily interested in teaching on teaching full time and those who are best at research on full-time research. It is likely that this would improve both the teaching and the research without in any way increasing the resources devoted to the two activities.

The present scheme is not particularly dangerous to science, but probably greatly reduces the teaching efficiency of our institutions of higher learning. The tendency of faculty members to look down on the students and to put their teaching off on graduate students who are paid but a pittance and of administrations at the better universities simply to ignore teaching ability in hiring faculty, all must greatly reduce the effectiveness of universities as teaching institutions.[9] The possibility of organizing specialized research institutions which do no teaching should be looked into. Today there are a number of such institutions, some under government subsidies and some under private, but, in general, they are organized to deal with applied rather than pure science. Even when, as in some of the Bureau of Standards work, they do pure investigation, their work tends to be routinized projects, with teams of scientists engaging in pre-planned research.

There are a few places where individual scientists, with no non-research responsibilities, are permitted to engage in research in as free a way as in the universities. The system of simply paying the scientist, giving him some expense money for his experiments, and then seeing that what he produces is basic to university status could, I think, be extended to other types of research institutions. After all, our best scientists are very scarce resources, and they would be best employed if they devoted their whole time to research, without "wasting" a lot of it in teaching. Of course, some teaching could be worked in without in any way reducing their research activities if bright students were assigned to them as laboratory assistants. A good deal of the methodology and attitude of science can be transmitted without any formal instruction.

Another field in which the current mythology should be revised is "tenure."[10] This, too, is a survival of the Middle Ages. In the feudal period, most appointments to posts were hereditary, but the faculties of universities were clerics, and they were legally incapable of having children. Consequently, these appointments, instead of being hereditary, were simply for life. European universities retained this custom, and the new universities in America copied them. The tenure system has two advantages. In the short run, it saves the universities money, and it provides some elementary protection for minority opinions. The saving of money in the short run is particularly clear, since the rational faculty member (and we must assume that professors are, at least occasionally, rational) should be willing to accept a

9. There are some devoted and highly intelligent teachers on university faculties who are simply not interested in research. They have a tremendous effect upon the student body, but they are systematically discriminated against by current administrative arrangements.

10. Pyotr L. Kapitsa, in a speech published in the *Journal of the Soviet Academy of Scientists,* attacked the Russian version of tenure on the grounds that it permitted incompetents to remain in their jobs. He apparently thought that we did not have the same problem. *New York Times,* April 25, 1965, p. 18.

somewhat lower wage if he is guaranteed against discharge. Thus the university administrator reduces the year's budget when he offers tenure instead of a higher basic rate to his employees. It is also possible that the political situation, at state universities in particular, may make straightforward wage increases impossible when fringe benefits are feasible. Tenure, of course, is a fringe benefit. The proposal to abolish tenure would be opposed by practically all men who have it, but presumably if the proposal were made in the form of an offer to increase the pay of those who gave up tenure, there would be takers; and the more was offered, the more would take it up.

From the straight monetary standpoint, the proposal to abolish tenure then might appear to be unwise, but in the long run it would probably save money. The gradual erosion of the workload of that part of the faculty which has tenure in modern American academic institutions, in spite of the existence of numerous limitations on it to be discussed below, is a notable disadvantage. Further, some members of the faculty are likely simply to stop their research when they get tenure. Some continue to do research, possibly of improved quality, but some stop, and a great number slow down.[11] Thus it is by no means certain that, in the long run, tenure saves money. In fact, it seems possible that without the numerous "defects" in the present tenure system, it might be a source of tremendous waste and inefficiency.

Proponents of the tenure system, however, hardly ever advocate it as a means of saving money; in fact, they would probably be somewhat annoyed if told that it had this effect, even if only in the short run. Their normal argument is that it provides security, which in turn permits its beneficiaries to take unpopular stands. They can uphold the "truth" even if the "mob" opposes it. There is obviously some truth in the position; society does gain by having some people who are free to take long views and to advocate unpopular courses of action. The only question is whether tenure, as it is currently organized, really serves this purpose.

I am prepared to argue that it does not, or, more exactly, that it does not in most cases. In the first place, tenure in the United States (this is less so in England) applies to the wrong period of life. New and radical ideas are most likely to occur to a man in his youth or at least before thirty. It is true that some people continue having such ideas during their whole lives, but the

11. See also Armen A. Alchian, "Private Property and the Relative Cost of Tenure," in *The Public Stake in Union Power,* ed. Philip D. Bradley (Charlottesville: University of Virginia Press, 1959).

general pattern is clear. This, then, is the period when tenure would be most valuable, but this is precisely the period in which people do not have it. The average scientist who takes up a university career spends this period as a graduate student, instructor, and assistant professor, positions in which he has no security and is subject to the maximum pressure to conform. People with radical and unpopular ideas are likely to be weeded out during this period so that they never even get tenure.

In order to obtain tenure, a young man in an American university must first get good grades throughout his undergraduate days—an achievement which depends on pleasing his professors. Then he must get a fellowship or instructorship for graduate work, normally at another institution. This again puts him under great pressure to please his superiors. He must not only pass; he must get their recommendations to get a job when he finally graduates. Last, but not least, he must please his superiors during his time as an assistant professor so that they will promote him to associate. Even when he achieves tenure, which normally coincides with this promotion, he still had better keep his nose clean until he finally makes full professor if he wants to maximize his income. All through this long period he is unprotected by tenure, and, to repeat, this is the period in which he is most likely to have revolutionary ideas.

Some members of the academic world may, by now, be excited and disturbed by my arguments. The view that tenure protects the academics from the outside world, not from other academics, is widely held and forms part of the personal security system of large numbers of "the profession." They feel that academics (with a few exceptions) are in favor of freedom and against conformity, while the outside world favors conformity. In fact, of course, the academic world is as conformist as any other. It just conforms to a different norm from, let us say, that of garbage collectors. The young instructor in a "good" school who thought that McCarthy was right kept his mouth shut or lost his job in most instances. The tenure system is of some use to a university administration arguing with a legislature or a potential donor about whether some individual should be fired, but its importance in this field is strictly limited. The legislature is not prevented by the tenure system from reducing (or not increasing) its appropriation, and individual and foundation donors are perfectly free to grant or not grant funds as they wish. In fact, most academics, even with tenure, are quite realistic about the necessity of avoiding actions which might seriously affect the financial situations of their institutions. Fortunately, the standards of both legislatures and donors are rather broad in these matters, and they are unlikely to consider the existence of one or two crackpots on a given faculty as much of a disadvantage.

Tenure, however, does prevent department heads from firing senior members of their departments. It also, although this is less important, prevents the president and other administrative officials from doing the same thing. Since administrators normally place few restrictions on who is hired in a given department (they are generally interested only in how many are hired at what cost), it is unlikely that they would be much more interested in who was fired, if firing were possible. The present semi-committee system used in many departments would make it difficult to fire members of the department even in the absence of tenure, of course, but we are now talking about the tenure system. This system, then, protects the man holding tenure status from his fellow academics. He is under less pressure to conform to their views than he would be without it. It does not particularly affect the pressure he is under to conform to the views of the whole community. His protection from the latter type of pressure, insofar as he has any, results simply from the fact that he is a member of a subcommunity which gives no great prominence to the views of the general community. Like the beat generation or artistic communities in general, the academic community offers social support to people who deviate from the average norm, but conform to its own. The existence of such specialized communities which deviate to a greater or lesser degree from the general community is obviously desirable if one believes in a high degree of social "openness," but it has nothing to do with tenure.

Nevertheless, it is an obvious fact that even junior men in the scientific departments of our universities have a good deal of freedom to disagree with their superiors, and even to prove them wrong. The degree of this freedom should not, of course, be exaggerated; a man who wishes to stay in academic research may be well advised to stick to energetic but routine work in the early years of his career,[12] but there is still quite a bit of independent thought even at these levels.

The reasons for this freedom are two, neither of which has anything to do with tenure. In the first place, almost all scientists are really interested in the advancement of knowledge and are therefore likely to consider such an advance, even if it contradicts their own viewpoint, admirable. They are less

12. A friend of mine who has devoted quite a bit of time to advising degree candidates always tells them to write their dissertation on a "trivial" subject and then do serious (and risky) research after they have their union cards.

likely to take umbrage at the brash young man who attacks their position than are people in other fields. They are also, normally, less committed to one position than people in other fields, and the scientific community is tolerant of changes of opinion so that backing down is socially easy. Again, however, we should not exaggerate. A man who disagrees sufficiently with his professors may find himself in difficulty in his future career even though he is consistently right.

Albert Einstein, for example, had not impressed his professors sufficiently favorably to be placed in an academic job when he graduated. He was forced to take a job in the Swiss patent office. Fortunately the Swiss patent office, like most governmental bureaucracies, was so organized that a man who did not care too much about his efficiency rating could spend most of his time each day on matters of interest to him rather than of interest to his superiors. Einstein practiced this type of implicit fraud on the patent office, and the result was the special theory of relativity, his paper on Brownian movement, and much other basic work.

The second factor which gives a junior scientist considerable freedom to disagree with his superior is the scientific community itself. While the individual faculty of some school, even if left to itself, would certainly tolerate a good deal of independence of thought, it is under great pressure from the rest of the scientific community to tolerate even more. The "department" has no control over whether the work of one of its junior members is or is not published by scientific journals, nor any control over the reputation that such a member may develop through publication. Thus an independent young man may well develop considerable assets in the form of outside respect. If he is badly treated by his own department, he can normally easily move elsewhere. Only the less productive scientist need worry about the feelings of his immediate superiors. For the man who really does have independent ideas which work out well, there are innumerable alternative employers. In fact, since every department is interested in keeping its prestige high, his own coworkers have the strongest possible motives to try to keep such a man from shifting somewhere else. Thus the general scientific community protects the junior scientist from possible difficulties with his superiors. Although he has no tenure, he is safe as long as he produces.

In a sense, my opposition to tenure is like kicking a dead horse, since tenure now is only a pale ghost of its former self. Today the "protection" of tenure, even for a full professor, is slight. In the first place, we are in an inflationary era. For the last twenty years—very likely it will continue to do so for the next twenty, too—the value of the dollar has been declining. A guarantee of a fixed dollar income is, therefore, worth less than might be thought. In fact, most men would like to obtain periodic increases; these are distributed according to various rules and may be withheld from anyone. Further, we are in a period of rapidly increasing affluence. The real living standard of every ditch-digger, lawyer, and plumber increases every year (albeit more slowly than his nominal income), and professors would like to share in this growing prosperity. This again requires periodic increases which can be withheld for disciplinary reasons.[13] Altogether, the present-day holder of tenure has real monetary reasons for trying to please his superiors. Again, it is really his reputation in the profession, the product of his research, which gives him his security. The possibility of shifting to another school will be his real reliance against "oppression." In present conditions, it is a full and sufficient assurance.

Another field in which tenure does not protect the profession, but in which reputation does, involves foundation grants. Today most scientists rely on such grants to give them supplementary income during summer vacations and occasional periods when they are relieved from teaching and to provide funds for research assistants and other facilities. Getting a series of such grants is not only necessary for the academic reputation of the average scientist, it usually also provides a substantial part of his income. Here there is no tenure, even in ghostly form. The reputation of the worker, based on his output, is the principal item considered, and a man who has done good work can generally expect to receive such grants regularly.

Can we not, however, think of some institution like tenure which might be of value? I think that we can, but it would require the solution of an extremely difficult problem. The granting of "security" to the vast collection of present-day teachers in our institutions of higher learning, many of whom, alas, are less than distinguished intellectually, is senseless, but a more selective distribution of such "security" might be desirable. Shortly after World War II, it was proposed that special "fellowships" be established. These would give their fortunate possessors a large enough income so that they would not be motivated to try to increase it by economic activities. To this an arrangement for increasing the grant in step with rising national prosperity could be added. It would also be provided that if any of the "fellows" decided to spend part of his income on research, the government would match it on, say, a five-

13. This is not true at Harvard, and it is possible that the Harvard system will spread.

to-one basis.[14] This would provide freedom and security to a selected group of people who would also be given research funds, subject only to their own estimate that the funds were worth making some sacrifice for. The ideal nature of such an arrangement for any given scientist is obvious, and if it were granted to the proper people, its benefit to society would be equally so. The selection of the "fellows," however, would be an extremely difficult task.

The real opportunity for the scientist who, for one reason or another, does not fit into the present professional scheme of things is amateurism. Einstein is an example of a man who could not integrate well enough with the scientific community to get a full-time scientific job. He therefore took an outside job and became the world's greatest scientist in his spare time. In a wealthy economy such as our own, where practically anyone can make a decent living with relatively little work, this course of action is easy. Even in earlier, harder times it was possible. Charles Peach, the private in the "Preventive Service" supporting a wife and nine children on four shillings a day, was yet able to become a great biologist.[15]

The amateur in science has the disadvantage that he can normally devote less time to his field than can the professional, but he also has advantages. In the first place, he is not under any pressure to complete a given piece of work, or, indeed, any work.[16] If he finds a problem which interests him, but which looks sufficiently difficult that nothing is likely to be discovered which can be published in the immediate future, this need not discourage him. He can afford to take risks in the choice of his problem which the professional, with his need to "produce," cannot. At the same time, the amateur, with his marginal contact with the scientific world, is less likely than the professional to be caught up in the fads and currents of opinion which sweep all social bodies. In a sense, the scientific community is an intellectual hothouse, with ideas sprouting and

14. As part of our giant national investment in medical research, "career investigatorships" were established for qualified scholars which closely approximate the suggested scheme. For a plea for an expansion of this system to all of science, see Norman W. Storer, "The Coming Changes in American Science," *Science,* 142 (October 25, 1963), 464–67, especially 467. Unfortunately the program has been curtailed instead of expanded.

15. See the *Encyclopaedia Britannica* for a brief biography of Peach.

16. H. Gerstenkorn, the German high school mathematics teacher who carefully calculated the values for the Darwin theory of the origin of the moon, surely depended upon this. Working without a computer he must have put much more time into the work than any university professor trying to "publish or perish" could have afforded. H. Alfven, "Origin of the Moon," *Science,* 148 (April 23, 1965), 476–77.

spreading at an unnatural rate. In general, this simply accelerates progress, but on occasion it may impede it, and the amateur is less likely to be taken in by a passing fad than is the man who spends his full time in the "profession."

A second advantage which the amateur has is the simple fact that he has some other profession.[17] We have earlier mentioned the desirability of having people in the sciences with unusual combinations of training. The professional hydraulic engineer who has a hobby of marine biology is, necessarily, in possession of such an unusual combination. In his work in marine biology, his background in hydraulic engineering may lead him to certain conclusions that would be rather unlikely for a scientist who did not have this background. In experimental work this is particularly important. All experimental scientists are, in fact, engineers, but they are sometimes not particularly good ones. They learned, while they were learning their science, techniques of assembling apparatus which are traditional in their fields. A man who is fully familiar with another tradition of construction of devices will be likely to perform experiments which would never occur to the professional scientist. This, of course, is not intended to belittle the professional competence of scientists, but merely to point out that they, like everyone, are somewhat specialized. They do not know everything, and an amateur with a different combination of knowledge and ignorance may make discoveries which would be impossible for the professional.

A great many people seem to think that amateurism in science, while possible in the time of Boyle and Hooke, is simply inconceivable today. How anyone can feel this way after the publicity Christophilos received as a result of the "Argus" project, I do not know, but the implication of his work for amateurism seems to have escaped many observers. Nicholas Christophilos was an elevator installer in Athens who became interested in nuclear physics and taught the subject to himself by wide reading during the German occupation of Greece. He then proceeded, in the intervals between installing elevators, to invent the principle of strong focusing for cyclotrons, beating the

17. Alvan G. Foraker, in his letter to *Science* published in the October 4, 1963, issue, pointed out two cases of doctors who did important work in their spare time. Of the first he writes: "An obscure district physician without university or research institute affiliation, he wished to develop original techniques to explore a new field. He worked, not in a laboratory, but in his own house." The second "was a country practitioner, without university or research institute affiliation. He proposed to investigate an old wives' tale. . . . It seems obvious that [they] would have been brushed off quickly by almost any foundation or fund granting agency." Fortunately Robert Koch and Edward Jenner were able to support themselves by practicing their profession.

AEC's professionals to the discovery by more than a year (they had filed his letter without reading it; so the principle had to be rediscovered). As a denouement, he was hired by the AEC,[18] performed the Argus experiment, and is trying to bind the hydrogen reaction for peaceful purposes with a multimillion-dollar laboratory at his disposal. He is still apparently considered a sort of amateur by his colleagues in physics, many of whom do not associate with him socially because he has not had the type of social indoctrination which one normally gets in graduate school and, consequently, does not really fit into academic society.[19]

Another equally prominent amateur scientist is Land of Polaroid. Land began by studying chemistry at Harvard. Long before his graduation, however, he decided he was wasting his time and left to undertake independent research. Later he was entrapped to return for a period by an offer of an unsupervised laboratory, but he never got his degree[20] or completed many courses. Eventually he founded Polaroid, invented the Land camera, and designed the cameras that have so much improved our maps of Russia. I would maintain that at all times he has been an amateur scientist. He devotes more time to managerial tasks, for which he has great talents, than to science, and his scientific activities are highly non-professional. Polaroid, for example, was founded to exploit not chemical phenomena, but physical, i.e., the polarization of light. The Land camera is a preposterous combination of knowledge selected from the most diverse scientific fields, in few of which Land could, by any stretch of the imagination, be considered a professional. Further, Land's attitude is essentially that of the amateur. He obviously gets a good deal of pleasure in simply fooling around in a laboratory. His recent discoveries in light perception were the result of such fiddling. He did not actually doubt the Newtonian theory on the subject; he just liked to play around and, in the course of doing so, accidentally noticed a phenomenon which must have been seen by innumerable predecessors.[21] His contribution was to take the discovery seriously. A wealthy man engaged in pursuing what amounts to a hobby can afford to do things which might lead to his making a public fool of himself while the careful professional man cannot.

18. He installed his elevators so carefully,
That now he's employed by the AEC.

19. *Time,* March 30, 1959, p. 70.

20. Eventually Harvard gave him an honorary doctorate in science.

21. It is actually covered by a series of patents of rather old date.

Christophilos and Land are by no means alone. More than half of all patents are regularly taken out by people who have no technical training. Revolutionary changes in technique or devices are about as likely to be the results of amateur work as professional.[22] The professionals in the applied field are good at elaborating ideas and all types of routine, but major changes may elude them. Professionals, of course, do make basic advances; such advances even come out of "well-planned" and elaborate research programs. But it is at least clear that amateurs suffer no great disadvantage in the field of applied science.

Discoveries by amateurs in the pure field are rarer, however, and we might well spend some time investigating why this is true. In the first place, by definition, pure research pays nothing to its devotees. Working on a practical invention is an economic activity, while pure research is, from the standpoint of the person performing it, consumption. Therefore only people who actively enjoy science are likely to take up pure research as a hobby. Under present circumstances, however, anyone with the brains to be a great scientist and the interest and enjoyment of the field necessary to become a good "hobbyist" can probably get a job doing full-time research. Consequently there is a tendency for people who otherwise might be amateurs to turn professional, as Christophilos has done. This, however, is no barrier to anyone who wishes to take up such a hobby; it only indicates that if he is successful he may be given an opportunity to become a full-time hobbyist.

The absence of part-time hobbyists in the pure field, then, can partly be explained by the opportunities now open to "go professional." In part, however, it also reflects a mythological view, now strongly held, that amateur activity in this field is simply impossible. The view that modern science requires professionals for its work and hence that amateurs cannot contribute seems to many people so obvious they need not explain it. If pressed, they will normally say that modern science requires specialized training, large financial resources for experimental equipment, and superior intellect. The third I do not deny, but I see no reason to believe that there are no superior intellects outside the scientific field. Both of the other two objections are, I believe, false.

The problem of scientific training has already been discussed in Chapter II of this book. My view, and I think that it will not be seriously contested by working scientists, is that most scientific work requires a good deal of "train-

22. John Jewkes, David Sawers, and Richard Stillerman, *The Sources of Invention* (London: St. Martin's Press, 1958).

ing," but that this is largely self-acquired. If one examines the work of any scientist and compares it with his formal education, one will generally find only a minor overlap. Usually only a small part of his formal instruction covered the problems on which he later specialized, and, conversely, most of the information he acquired on his major subjects he obtained by reading and investigating on his own. In fields where progress has been rapid, the scientist of forty may be making no use whatever of his formal education, which would be largely obsolete. Thus the amateur is not so handicapped here as is generally believed. If he simply subscribes to journals, reads articles on a given subject for a few years, and does some additional background reading, he will normally be as well trained in the field of his particular interest as the professional. It is true, of course, that if he can devote only a part of his time to self-education in this field, then he had better choose a fairly narrow specialty. The full-time scientist can keep himself up-to-date over a wider range of subjects than can a man who devotes only part of his time to the matter. Narrow specialties where discoveries can be made abound, however, and the amateur who is interested can easily find one. The biological sciences are particularly rich in such opportunities.

The cost of research is also greatly exaggerated. The reason, I think, is simply that experiments using large, expensive, and complicated equipment get much more publicity than those using small, inexpensive, and simple devices. To read the newspapers, one might get the impression that every laboratory has a set of high-energy accelerators and five or six satellites. Such devices, with costs running in the hundreds of millions of dollars, are obviously out of reach of amateurs, but they are equally obviously out of the reach of all but the most fortunate of professionals. Only a tiny minority of the scientific community uses such equipment, and it is highly doubtful if this privileged minority is really as important as its publicity would indicate. The most important nuclear experiment of the recent period was made, not with a giant accelerator, but with a rather modest device for testing magnetism at low temperatures. Mossbauer got his Nobel Prize for an almost equally important experiment in which an old radio loudspeaker was the largest part of the experimental apparatus.[23] The giant machines extend the range of possible

23. *Time,* in describing the work which got Donald Glasser his Nobel Prize, reports: "Working with almost no funds or encouragement he built his first successful bubble chamber in 1953. It was half an inch in diameter and was filled with ether. 'Ether is cheap,' explains Glasser, 'and I could get it at the chemistry store without any red tape.'" November 14, 1960, p. 89.

experiments, but there is no reason to believe that the experiments performable only with such machines are the most important ones.

If we ignore the glamour of these expensive devices and inquire as to the actual cost of science as a possible hobby, we rapidly realize that it can fit practically any purse, although wealthy men would be able to do things which the poor would not. In the first place, there is theoretical research. This is of the greatest importance and requires little more than a paper and pencil in the way of physical equipment. Surely, financial obstacles will not prevent amateurs from working in this field. A little more active, although still inexpensive, work of a simple observational nature remains to be done in the biological fields.[24] A good deal is still unknown, for example, about the life cycles of the majority of the innumerable known species of insects. Becoming the world's leading authority on the behavior and life of some species of fly may not impress a potential amateur scientist as being very glamorous, but it certainly is a goal he can achieve with little investment in equipment. I should possibly warn that it will involve a sizable investment of time, energy, and intelligence.

For the man who has a normal income and is willing to put as much money into science as he would into any other hobby (including "do-it-yourself" as a hobby), experimental science is also quite possible, although the scale will, of course, be limited by the amount he wishes to spend. For the cost of an outboard cruiser and its motor, an adequate chemical or experimental biology laboratory could be equipped.[25] A respectable program of experiments occupying a hobbyist for, say, eight hours a week could then be run on about what it costs to keep such a boat in fuel and paint. Further it is highly likely that expenditures on a scientific hobby, unlike expenditures on other hobbies, would be tax deductible.

Altogether, cost does not seem to be much of a problem for a man who wishes to engage in science as a hobby. Wealthy men can, of course, carry out projects out of reach of the ordinary worker, but this has always been true.

24. Lionel Sharpes Penrose, "Self Reproducing Machines," *Scientific American,* 200, No. 42 (June, 1959), 105, reports some extremely interesting experiments which surely could have been performed by anyone who had an ordinary home workshop.

25. I do not wish to imply that this sum of money would be useful only in these sciences. The problem is that such sciences as physics use less of what might be called permanent equipment and more special devices constructed for a given experiment than does a laboratory in chemistry or experimental biology. Under the circumstances, physics requires less in the way of initial investment, but more in continuing expenditure than does, say, chemistry.

Boyle's vacuum apparatus seems simple and primitive to us now, but in his day only a man of independent wealth, like Boyle, could have afforded it. Boyle's combination of considerable wealth, a strong interest in the advancement of knowledge, and a most ingenious mind made a great contribution to science. Similar activities by wealthy amateurs could have the same effect today. But I hope I have convinced the reader that wealth, while helpful, is not necessary. Financial problems would not prevent many citizens of the wealthy United States or the somewhat less wealthy Europe from contributing to the advancement of science, if only they wished to do so.

Anyone wishing to take up science as a hobby must have intelligence, but the amount needed can easily be exaggerated. Among scientists themselves are some of our brightest minds, but also, as anyone who knows many scientists can testify, some fairly dull people. The more intelligent, on the average, the more likely that a given man will make major discoveries, of course, but there is a good deal of scientific work which can be done by industrious but not overly intelligent workers. The highly intelligent layman may well be more intelligent than all but the best scientists and, consequently, able to work in the most difficult fields. At the other extreme, routine work can be done by almost anyone.

The advantages of science as a hobby, of course, are the same as the advantages of any other hobby—relaxation and entertainment. If you do not enjoy it, you should not do it, any more than you should fish if you do not like fishing. In science, an additional bonus is provided in the form of a perfectly genuine feeling that the hobbyist is doing something of general significance. He is enjoying himself and, instead of simply consuming resources, actually producing something of great value—knowledge. It is a case where there is both a consumer and social surplus of great size. Nor does there presently appear to be any limit on the amount of work that can be done in the scientific field. The more workers, the faster we learn, although the increase in speed is not proportional to the increase in manpower. Science is a difficult game, but any number can play.

INDEX

References to bibliographic information appear in italics.

The typeface used for the text of this book is Galliard, an old-style face designed by Matthew Carter in 1978, in the spirit of a sixteenth-century French typeface of Robert Granjon.
The display type is Meta Book, a variant of Meta, designed by Erik Spickermann in the 1990s.

This book is printed on paper that is acid-free and meets the requirements of the American National Standard for Permanence of Paper for Printed Library Materials, z39.48-1992. ♾

Book design by Richard Hendel, Chapel Hill, North Carolina
Typography by G&S Typesetters, Inc., Austin, Texas
Printed and bound by Worzalla Publishing Company,
Stevens Point, Wisconsin